Professional Learning for Artist Teachers: Pedagogy, Practice and Partnership in UK Contexts

Professional Learning for Artist Teachers: Pedagogy, Practice and Partnership in UK Contexts

Edited by Rachel Payne
Foreword by Rita L. Irwin

McGraw Hill

Open University Press

Open University Press
McGraw Hill
Unit 4,
Foundation Park
Roxborough Way
Maidenhead
SL6 3UD

email: emea_uk_ireland@mheducation.com
world wide web: www.mheducation.co.uk

Executive Editor: Eleanor Christie
Editorial Assistant: Phoebe Hills
Content Product Manager: Graham Jones

A catalogue record of this book is available from the British Library

ISBN-13: 978-0-3352-5215-2
ISBN-10: 033525215X
eISBN: 978-0-3352-5216-9

Typeset by Transforma Pvt. Ltd., Chennai, India

Praise page

"*This collection of chapters by highly talented authors – amongst the best in their field – serves to both reflect current practice and show ways forward for art in various educational settings. In the context of one of the most difficult times for art and design education that I can remember, Dr Rachel Payne's timely volume gives hope; it provides a valuable and inspirational resource for established and aspiring creative practitioners concerned with meaningful teaching and learning.*"
Richard Hickman, Emeritus Professor of Aesthetic Development and Emeritus Fellow of Homerton College, University of Cambridge, UK and Fellow of National Society for Education in Art and Design, UK

"*This book contains rich and insightful narratives of diverse pedagogy and practice in art education. The powerful benefits of being active as an artist and educator both for the educator and for those that will learn from them, shine through in the accounts of the distinguished contributing authors. The editor, Rachel Payne, has put together an important and timely book principally about the situation in the UK, but it will be of interest to an international audience. Subject-specific professional development is so important; if you are interested in art education or are an artist-teacher, this book deserves a place on your bookshelf.*"
Glen Coutts, Professor of Applied Visual Arts Education, University of Lapland, Finland, and President of the International Society for Education through Art

Contents

List of figures

List of contributors

Professor Jeff Adams is Emeritus Professor in Education at the University of Chester and co-director of the centre for Research into Education, Creativity and the Arts through Practice (RECAP). Jeff developed and managed postgraduate artist teacher programmes at Goldsmiths and Liverpool JMU universities prior to moving to Chester. He is a Fellow of the National Society of Art and Design Education and former Principal Editor of the *International Journal of Art & Design Education*. Jeff has published widely on creativity and arts-based practices and his books include *Documentary Graphic Novels and Social Realism*; *Creativity and Democracy in Education* (with Owens); *Provoking the Field* (with Irwin and Sinner, Eds.); *Beyond Text: Learning through Arts-based Practices* (with Owens, Eds.).

Dionne Freeman has over 20 years of experience working as an arts educator across a broad range of educational and community settings. She is a Fellow of the Higher Education Academy and has worked on the MA in Education: Artist Teacher Practice programme at Oxford Brookes University for the last 12 years. Dionne's art educator practice focuses on working with others, sharing skills, and facilitating projects which support people to express themselves and communicate through the visual arts, specialising in spatial and self-awareness. Dionne likes to use her expressive approaches to explore, experiment, inspire, engage and enthuse others.

Dr Joanna Fursman is an artist, researcher and educator and employs lens-based practice to critically examine contemporary appearances of school. Her practice-led PhD examined young people's reflections on their school environment with digital camera technology. Fursman's research explores how education can be examined through practice-led approaches and how using the camera can make artist-educator identity more complicated. Joanna is the subject leader for PGCE Art and Design at Birmingham City University, has worked in Secondary, Further and Higher Education since 2005 and taught across the Artist Teacher Scheme, BA and MA Art and Education Practices and Primary Initial Teacher Education.

Dr Emese Hall is Senior Lecturer in Art Education and former Director of the Post Graduate Certificate in Education (PGCE) Primary Programme at the University of Exeter, UK. With primary and early years expertise, Emese has worked in teacher education since 2005. She is particularly interested in researching the value of professional learning communities, artist teacher practice, and the potential of art education to address sustainability/environmental issues. Previously, Emese was Vice President of the National Society for Education in Art and Design (NSEAD), Subject Lead for Primary Art, Craft and Design at Oak National Academy, a Member of the National Expert Subject Advisory Group for Art and Design Education, and a South West Regional Network Co-ordinator for the Cambridge Primary Review Trust. Emese is Co-Editor (with Nigel Meager) of the *Pedagogy Volume of the International Encyclopaedia of Art and Design Education* (Wiley-Blackwell, 2019).

Dr Rebecca Heaton is an Assistant Professor in Visual and Performing Arts at the National Institute of Education (NIE), Nanyang Technological University (NTU) in Singapore. She disseminates research internationally concerning cognition, art, technology and education, and in 2019 was awarded the International Society for Education through Art (InSEA) Doctoral Research Award in Art Education. Her recent publications and projects include the co-authored work 'A visual inquiry: Artist teacher perceptions of art education provision in Singapore', published in *Studies in Art Education* (2022), 'Cognition in Art Education' (2021) published in the *British Educational Research Journal* and most recently an (2023) international exhibition and event series exploring The Art of Creative Research: https://www.theartofcreativeresearch.com/exhibition. Rebecca is the programme lead for the MEd in Visual Art Education at NIE, she is an art curriculum advisor for the Ministry of Education in Singapore and has been involved with international art curriculum development through Cambridge Assessment. Rebecca supervises masters and doctoral students in art education and currently delivers modules related to art education pedagogy, creativity and the visual arts and research and issues in art education.

Dr Marike Hoekstra is a Dutch artist-teacher-researcher. In 2018 she graduated as a PhD at the University of Chester with a doctoral thesis titled *Artist Teachers and Democratic Pedagogy*. Marike works as a researcher and teaches at different institutions for higher art education in the Netherlands. As an artist she works with drawing and installation art. Previous research publications concern altermodern art education, artist teachers, young children, professional learning communities and inclusion, and art-based education research. Marike is interested in the way artist teachers and studio spaces can contribute to art education as a site for third space pedagogies. She recently initiated the founding of an informal shared studio space for children and artists in a primary school in Amsterdam where the concept of a democratic artistic community is subject to exploration, development and research (www.stichtingderesident.nl).

Monica Lewis is best known for her works of La Ursa, the dancing Bear from Brazilian carnival culture. Reflecting on her school education under a military dictatorship has inspired her art practice, allowing her to share the realities of the regime through her La Ursa mask. Her illustrations and silent performances of the Bear, a creature that was controlled, silenced and taken advantage of, have allowed her to find her voice and represent that of many women, artists, and other minority groups. She has transformed a beloved carnival character into an activist. Monica was born in Brazil and studied International Human Rights Law both in Brazil and England. Since, she has taught art to a variety of groups, helping many find confidence, success, and their voice in their artistic practice. She truly found her voice, path, and passion through the visual arts.

Tamar MacLellan and **Philippa Wood** are both educators from the creative arts who met when leading further and higher education programmes at Lincoln College of Art and Design in 1994. They began working in partnership in 2006, drawing upon their knowledge of textiles and graphic design to produce artists' books as part of *The Caseroom Press*. Their practice is located within themes of domesticity and examines the way everyday objects lend personal meaning to the spaces we inhabit, and our subsequent relationship with these objects. Tamar and Philippa are interested in exploiting the potential of traditional making processes within a contemporary context and apply systems and cataloguing to inform their responses. This includes the combination of found surfaces, relief and screen-print, letterpress, stitch, and use of the typewriter and copy machine. Books produced have been exhibited and purchased by private and public collections, Libraries, Artists' Book Archives and Special Collections.

Dr Miranda Matthews is an artist educator, writer and researcher. Miranda taught in schools and sixth-form colleges for ten years. She completed her PhD (Goldsmiths, 2012) when teaching in sixth-form education. Doctoral research focused on issues of freedom and autonomy for arts educators in schools and galleries, students and policy makers. Miranda lectures at Goldsmiths University of London, where she is Head of the Centre for Arts and Learning. Miranda is currently researching issues of agency and representation for practitioners in art and design education, and interdisciplinary arts approaches in higher education. Miranda often applies philosophy in practice research.

Dr Diarmuid McAuliffe established Scotland's first Artist Teacher programme over ten years ago at the University of the West of Scotland (UWS) in collaboration with Glasgow Museums. He is the UWS subject lead for art and design education and founder of the *Network of Art Teachers Across Scotland* (NATAS). He has conducted Creative Scotland funded research on the viability of drawing, walking, and extending sites for learning as heuristic tools in curriculum design. His most recent publications are included in the *SAGE Handbook of Critical Pedagogies* (2020) and in *Scottish Education* (5th Ed) (2018) from Edinburgh University Press. His doctoral thesis which he completed in 2021 is titled *Using narrative and arts-based methods to make visible (draw out) learning in secondary art education.*

Dr Rachel Payne works at Oxford Brookes University as a Deputy Head of Education and Student Experience. She was the subject leader of the Secondary Art/Design PGCE from 2004 to 2012, and since 2006 leads the

MA Education: Artist Teacher Practice. Rachel passionately believes that communities of practice can have empowering impact for art and design teachers by elevating professional voices, experiences and status. Research interests focus on emancipatory pedagogies in schools and higher education which lead to transformative artist teacher practices. She champions visual methodologies and arts-based research, both her own and others. As a Past President for the National Society for Education in Art and Design and a member of the All-Party Parliamentary Group for Art, Craft and Design in Education, Rachel lobbies the UK government for high quality accessible art, craft and design education for all.

Vicky Sturrs is Director of Programmes and Collections at The Bowes Museum, Barnard Castle. Before that, she was Head of Learning and Civic Engagement at Baltic Centre for Contemporary Art, Gateshead, leading the strategic vision for learning programmes that valued mutual exchange, playfulness, and hospitality. She led the initiation and delivery of Baltic's play-led exhibitions, extensive online learning assets and civic initiatives that worked across Gateshead and the wider North East. While at Baltic, Vicky managed the gallery's partnership with Northumbria University, Newcastle and resulting relationship with the Baltic x Northumbria University Institute; sharing vision for creative talent development, place-making, public engagement and artistic excellence. Previously, Vicky was Baltic's Schools and Colleges Programmer for four years. Before that she held the Education Officer post at mima, Middlesbrough and completed her Masters in Art Museum and Gallery Education at Newcastle University. Vicky taught on Northumbria University's MA Fine Art and Education for five years, is a Fellow of the RSA and trustee of Lawnmowers Independent Theatre Company.

Dr Judy Thomas is Head of Department, School of Arts and Creative Industries, Teesside University; working with creative practitioners, teachers, professionals from the cultural sector and students from schools and universities, her pedagogical research explores collaborative practice within the context of artist-led learning programmes. Recent activities focus on the *Create Aspire Transform* programme with the Maltings (Berwick) Trust. As Senior Lecturer and Director of Education, Judy teaches across the Foundation and BA Fine Art undergraduate and postgraduate programmes. She is a Senior Fellow of the Higher Education Academy and North East Representative for Engage, the lead advocacy and training network for gallery education. Her previous roles include Learning Manager at Creativity, Culture and Education and Programme Manager (Learning and Inclusion) for Liverpool Biennial. She has also worked at Tyneside Cinema, Waygood and Baltic Centre for Contemporary Art, Gateshead.

Dr Carol Wild has worked across all phases of education as an artist, teacher, mentor, and researcher. She has led postgraduate programmes in education for many years, designing creative CPD for busy teachers and supporting individuals and groups in developing creative research projects in their school communities. She is a passionate advocate for the arts in education and for the role of the subject specialist in Primary and Secondary school contexts. She currently leads the PGCE Art and Design at the Institute of Education, UCL. Carol's research interests include the classroom as an aesthetic phenomenon, speculative and arts-based research methods in education, the histories of the arts and education, neoliberalism and art education and feminist models for creative pedagogy.

Melanie Woodhead is an artist, educator and PhD researcher who has taught in Further and Higher Education and delivered visual art projects in schools, museums, and art galleries for over 20 years. In 2015 she participated in the Artist Teacher Scheme exploring her shifting artist teacher identity through photographic practices. Subsequently, practice-led research on the MA Arts and Education Practices at Birmingham City University investigated how the conditions for creativity and learning flourish in the space between familiar and unfamiliar territory. Current PhD research experiments with digital and alternative photographic practices to examine transitional urban and green spaces, co-creating with their bordering human and nonhuman communities.

Sarah Yearsley has worked in the museum and gallery sector in England and Scotland for over 25 years, most recently leading the programme for Engage, the leading charity for promoting engagement and participation in the visual arts, in Scotland between 2006 and 2022. She has a particular interest in how people engage with contemporary visual art and the methods that galleries and artists use to facilitate access to and enjoyment of the visual arts. Sarah has managed several visual arts education and engagement projects and commissioned a research project with Queen Margaret University to map engagement with art and design education in Scottish schools.

Foreword

One thing I can say about a long career is that it gives a person a perspective that can only be achieved from experience. I remember entering my career as an arts educator full of enthusiasm, energy, ambition, dedication and an abiding love for all things art related. Having grown up in a very rural area of Canada, with little art education at school, I was lucky enough to be raised by a mother who loved art and was always exploring new techniques and media. I learned about artistic processes from her, and I remain ever grateful to her for the many remarkable experiences and projects we shared. I knew the impact of what living a life full of art had meant to me and I wanted to bring that to my work as an arts education specialist in schools. Thus began my own experiences in public education as an art and music specialist. I loved the work, yet needed more and began my graduate journey bringing together curriculum studies and art education. In time, higher education called, and I brought the same enthusiasm and commitment to working with emerging and practising arts educators as a professor. In looking back, I am proud of particular achievements, and yet, I am also saddened, even disheartened, with the direction education has taken. I mention this because many of these positive and not-so-positive reflections are echoed in this extraordinary book.

Taking up the notion of teacher-as-artist in schools and graduate programmes in the UK has been an incredible experiment that has sparked a wide array of artistic forms of enquiry for children, youth and adults alike. It is quite remarkable to see so many projects described and interpreted creatively and critically in this historically significant volume. After more than a decade of the Artist Teacher Scheme across the UK, the authors in this volume point out the unique contributions that artist teacher pedagogies, practices and partnerships bring to vibrant teaching and learning environments. They also remind us of the importance of regional differences and the context of our work. Place makes a difference. The individuals in each place make a difference. It behoves us to remember this. They also highlight partnerships with cultural institutions and the importance of noticing and taking up contemporary art and its practices in these locations.

For me personally, I was pleasantly surprised to see several chapters take up a/r/tography as an artistic practice, as a form of enquiry, and as a learning/teaching encounter. As someone committed to these practices, it was encouraging to see arts educators recognise the potential of this practice-based approach to enquiry not only for themselves as artist-educator-inquirers, but perhaps more importantly, for their students. Some of the most exciting inquiries here is when teachers and students come to see themselves at this nexus. I can feel my enthusiasm swell knowing the potential in these chapters, but also in chapters where a/r/tography isn't mentioned yet the practices are so similar. It gives me hope for the future. This book really is full of hope for what is possible and where we can go and make our educational systems even more impactful.

Yet, this also brings me to the sobering aspects explored by many authors in this book. We need to understand the challenges facing all artist teachers. Indeed, in the UK, government interference with education has pushed many arts educators into marginalised positions, de-professionalising most educators through constant assessment of students and auditing of teachers' practices, all of which must adhere to a centralised curriculum. The result is an incessant delegitimisation of teachers' authority over their own content knowledge and professional experiential knowledge. Governments imagine teaching and learning as standardised and homogenised. Indeed, teaching is increasingly policed by administrators. Such a rationalised, reductive, instrumentalist approach may seek a form of accountability, but it loses all that comes to life in an environment that invites curiosity, experimentation, creativity, and imagination. The latter may indeed yield some missteps, but these are surely important to learning itself.

Despite the challenges surrounding artist teachers and their professional practices, this book serves as a site for inspiration. Whether it is a proposal for democratic pedagogy, student-centred pedagogy or a pedagogy focused on bringing art and activism together, or many other foci for experimental work, this book brings forward a series of case studies and essays that are compelling, convincing and constructive. Those of us in the arts who need reassurance that our work matters, that our work remains essential to a holistic education for children, youth and adults, and that artist teachers can reclaim, recover and reimagine their professional practices in the midst of governmental controls – this is our book.

I began my career in arts education hoping to inspire more creative and critical enquiries into all learning encounters. I have witnessed many remarkable projects over the years and also many challenging circumstances. As this book demonstrates, it is within the capacity of each arts educator to keep pushing the conversation further and deeper into territories that only artist teachers can manage. Whether in our own classrooms, local communities, or countries, we have the knowledge and experience to inspire new ways of learning, new ways of relating to one another, and new ways of being human that offers hope for our futures. I remain committed to this vision. I know the authors in this book are as well. I want to congratulate editor Rachel Payne, and all of the authors for compiling this powerful book. It makes a huge contribution to the field of arts education. May we all hold strong to our commitments to envision and enact an education full of the arts, creativity, and a hopeful future.

Rita L. Irwin, Ed.D.
Distinguished University Scholar
Professor, Art Education
The University of British Columbia
Vancouver, Canada

Preface

Rachel Payne

United Kingdom (UK) artist teacher practices were formalised through the development of continuing professional development (CPD) opportunities clustered together under the banner of the Artist Teacher Scheme (ATS), which supported partnership work between higher education institutions and galleries and museums (Page et al. 2011). Developed in 1999 by National Society for Education in Art and Design (NSEAD) and part-funded by Arts Council England, the scheme was specifically designed for art and design educators. Despite the removal of national funding in 2010, which led to the demise of over half the ATS programmes across England and Scotland, there remain diverse and dynamic practices operating across higher education postgraduate programmes and cultural organisations. However, these have been shaped by political forces. For example, in England, art educators working in schools have limited access to subject specific CPD, experiencing professional isolation and a lack of status in their settings as a result (NSEAD 2016). This has emerged out of an education system which has inflicted systemic marginalisation on our subject (Payne and Hall 2018). The education system is experienced as something that is done to educators, not something we are invited to shape (Ball and Olmedo 2012). In contrast, postgraduate study facilitates artist teachers' agency through approaches which encourage participation in authentic professional practices. Applying for a Masters or Doctorate becomes an act of resistance, an opportunity to 'take responsibility for the care of their selves' (Ball and Olmedo 2012: 85).

I have run an artist teacher Masters programme since 2006, working with hundreds of students and alumni to support their developing artist teacher practices and profiles. In June 2017 I facilitated an exhibition of students' and alumni artworks celebrating 10 years of the MA programme. During this event I conducted research into participants' experiences of the transformative nature of the programme, and have been researching the social situation of the course ever since. Data highlight the fragile yet extraordinary spaces that artist teachers inhabit, championing voices and practices that are so often subjugated. This research project led me to a national artist teacher conference in 2018, which I co-organised for NSEAD working in partnership with Pitt Rivers Museum, University of Oxford. Fuelled by my research findings and discussions with fellow academics and researchers, the conference examined how artist teacher pedagogies have changed since the scheme's inception. There was a consensus that with a decline in external funding, the ATS was no longer considered a national 'scheme', more a body of professional practices and regional communities. The conference provided a platform for many of the authors represented in this book to disseminate their different perspectives, lived experiences and professional practices as artist-teacher-makers, researchers and academics.

Professional Learning for Artist Teachers: Pedagogy, Practice and Partnership in UK Contexts is the first book of its kind in the UK. It is a celebration of our rich community relaying diverse pedagogies and practices, which result in increased resilience and wellbeing. It acts as a beacon to artist teachers, art and gallery educators, and artists globally, advocating excellence in art and design education, and exposing comparisons within the UK context and in international settings. There are six aims for the book: 1) to champion the UK approach by reflecting the unique contribution that artist teacher pedagogies, practices and partnerships bring to professional lives and landscapes; 2) celebrating regional nuance in artist teacher approaches; 3) recognising how the artist teacher narrative applies to an international context; 4) examining the role of cultural partnerships within artist teacher practices and pedagogies; 5) examining how artist teacher practices move art practices forward, and 6) how contemporary art practices emerge as a result. To achieve this, the book is comprised of 13 chapters divided into four sections: Political Landscape; Pedagogies; Practices; and Partnerships. Each section builds connections between socio-political environments and the professional and personal contexts that artist teachers operate in. Political Landscape outlines the context that artist teachers manoeuvre and how these influence behaviours, decisions and experiences. Pedagogies and Practices represent two halves of the artist teacher duality, teaching and making: what we do, where, with whom, why and how. Often these identities and practices are fluid; where they locate in one domain, they may emerge unexpectedly in the other. As the book progresses, a deeper understanding of what it means to be an artist teacher in the twenty-first century – our identities, practices, performances and lived experiences – are revealed. These situate sites of sociality, embodied connection and dissonance, a liminal space that can facilitate transformative learning (Matthews 2020). The final section, Partnerships, considers a core feature of the artist teacher experience, where we locate pedagogies and practices within exciting cultural sites for learning. Partnerships open up possibilities to think about the self and artist teacher practices differently (Ball and Olmedo 2012). Political Landscape and Partnerships serve to bookend the content, providing environmental context to bear on Pedagogies and Practices enacted within. The resultant book can be read as a testament to artist teacher embodiment.

References

Ball, S. J. and Olmedo, A. (2012) Care of the self, resistance and subjectivity under neoliberal governmentalities, *Critical Studies in Education*, 54(1): 85–96.

Matthews, M. (2020) Editorial: discomfort zones, *International Journal of Art and Design Education*, 39(4): 708–711.

NSEAD (2016) *The National Society for Education in Art and Design Survey Report 2015–16* (online). Available at: https://www.nsead.org/news/newsroom/nsead-survey-report-2015-16/ (accessed 14 November 2023).

Page, T., Adams, J. and Hyde, W. (2011) Emerging: The impact of the artist teacher scheme MA on students' pedagogical and artistic practices, *European Journal of Teacher Education*, 34(3): 277–295.

Payne, R. and Hall, E. (2018) The NSEAD survey report 2015–16: Political reflections from two art and design educators, *International Journal of Art & Design Education*, 37(2): 167–176.

Acknowledgements

This is an important book for me as it represents the impetus underpinning my professional career. I am fortunate that many of my co-authors are colleagues and former students I have worked with throughout my career, and am grateful that this book has introduced me to new colleagues too. To provide space to amplify their experiences, practices and research is a privilege. The book would not have come together without their dedication and professionalism. Special thanks goes to Rita Irwin who has written the perfect foreword, which is warm and insightful in equal measure. She aptly demonstrates how artist teacher practices transcend diverse spaces – geographical, metaphorical, experiential and social, themes reiterated throughout the chapters in this book. For example, authors reference collaborating with research participants, students, fellow artist teachers and even family members. A core feature of being an artist teacher is working with others, and here I thank all those who have stimulated us to think deeply about and continue to refine our artist teacher selves. In turn we hope this book challenges you too.

Rachel Payne

Part 1

Political Landscape

1 The rise and fall of artist teacher professional development programmes

Jeff Adams

This chapter discusses my experience of co-creating and managing artist teacher Masters programmes in higher education in the UK – courses that were prompted by the wave of enthusiasm that enveloped the arts and creativity in teachers' professional development around the turn of this century. I developed these courses in two well-established universities where I worked as an art education lecturer – one in the north of England and one in London – with each programme running for several years. My experience of writing and leading the first fed directly into the second, resulting in both having similar structures but each modified and adapted to accommodate their different cultural contexts.

The historical and political context of the period and the theoretical principles at play underpinned the form and character of the programmes, which had a liberating effect upon teachers' personal and classroom artistic practices despite the practical limitations and strictures that education procedures and environments imposed upon them. The dominant neoliberal culture of the recent decade has resulted in the devaluing of creative pedagogies and a demise of funding and support has ensued, which has contributed to the closure of many courses and maintenance structures that formerly enriched art teaching and learning. The incorporation of arts-based practices into mainstream education research has to some extent ameliorated these losses, and in combination with the artist teacher model offers hope for a return to a more progressive model of education.

In my experience, the appetite for artist teacher programmes, as a form of continuing professional development (CPD) for art teachers, was, and probably remains, overwhelming. The National Society for Education through Art and Design (NSEAD) and the UK Arts Councils identified these demands, which had been growing for many years, and rationalised them into the Artist Teacher Scheme (ATS) and supported it with some state funding (Galloway et al. 2006).

It flourished, occurring in many types of institutions and organisations and took a variety of forms, such as day schools, summer schools or fully-fledged part-time Masters programmes for serving teachers over a period of years (NSEAD 2001; Adams 2003). This suited the mood of the time, where there was a groundswell of demand from art teachers for the opportunity and funding to practise their own art. This was justified as a means of developing their subject knowledge practically as well as keeping them well informed about the arts beyond education, particularly contemporary art, by creating and formalising networks of artists and art galleries.

There was a plethora of precedents for the ATS phenomena, and it had a long and slow gestation. Many CPD art courses had previously operated in the UK, some of which I had attended myself as a school art teacher: I had learned to throw pots at evening classes, taken specialist courses in screen printing and etching, and attended seminars and conferences on art history. The funding and local authority support for such courses had waxed and waned according to the political complexion of the state, but overall they remained a feature of support for teachers up until the financial crash of 2008, after which support for the arts in education was greatly diminished, in England especially. Concurrent with that decline was a diminution of the value of the arts in schools, along with any hope of significant funding for art teachers' subject-based CPD. It is, therefore, unsurprising that the ATS courses followed this trajectory in the UK, blossoming in the early years of the century with a steep decline thereafter. The advent of state austerity, whereby successive neoliberal governments imposed a strategy of cutting and then privatising public services, served to acceler-ate the devaluing of the arts in education and with it the corresponding CPD. Nonetheless, internationally the artist teacher movement has flourished with considerable widespread synergy and remains a potent idea, likely to flourish again in the UK when conditions are more conducive.

Artist teacher programmes

Reflecting on the ATS in its heyday, several important principles governed its success, although these were not without some paradoxical effects. The ethos of the ATS could be encapsulated within a deceptively simple idea: that finding ways for art teachers to continue to practise their art while simultaneously being exposed to new forms is the most effective way to maintain and improve their understanding of the subject that they teach. Reviewing early drafts of the potential structure of the programmes that we were developing I now real-ise they closely matched the prevailing discourse in art education at the time. Modules like 'Emerging Technologies', a staple of both ATS programmes that I directed, reflected the fascination with the rapidly-developing phone and video technologies that were to become the dominant modes of communication in the subsequent decade. Although the technology was still rather clunky in the early 2000s, they nevertheless excited the imagination with the seemingly infinite potential for rapid and prolific image-making, both as resource and medium.

The enthusiasm for utilising these new media was matched by the frustration of finding sufficient resources and expert tuition to fulfil the demand, often resulting in wasted hours of wrestling with antiquated machines and software. Nonetheless, the module produced inspired and novel work for many of the ATS participants and opened creative portals that were to be permanently incorporated into their practice, and, as resources allowed, into their pedagogy. One of the first videos I saw created by a student using makeshift digital equipment was a simple film edited to amplify the subtle reflection of raindrops on a shiny car bonnet. The rapid digital reincarnation of a familiar art subject into wide screen film projection was as fascinating as it was surprising to us at that time.

There can be little doubt about the liberating effects of the ATS programmes upon teachers' creative thinking and practice. Evidence for this is provided in numerous autobiographical accounts by participants (Hyde 2007) as well as evaluative and academic accounts (Pringle 2001; Galloway et al. 2006; Daichendt 2010; Page et al. 2011). My own experience confirmed this (Adams 2003): the sheer energy and productivity of the ATS participants throughout my time managing two university masters programmes was testimony enough. The boundary between theoretical and practical knowledge is delightfully uncertain in arts practice, as Pringle (2009: 42) discovered: 'the artists I interviewed saw their practice as a process of conceptual enquiry and of meaning making'. This was equally true of artist learners working alongside artist teachers in a creative shared space.

Another significant aspect of the programme, which was embedded in the zeitgeist of the era, was a focus on contemporary art in the gallery, usually manifested in the programmes by a partnership between a university and a contemporary art gallery. This coincided with the advent of mainstream popular interest in contemporary art in state-funded galleries in the UK, such as Tate. The exponential increase in the gallery-going public in the 1980s and 1990s generated a momentum for art teachers to reflect this new-found fascination in their curriculum for young people. The black British art movement spearheaded by the likes of Yinka Shonibare, Sonia Boyce, Paul Dash and Steve McQueen was well underway at this time, and the success of Young British Artists like Tracy Emin, Sarah Lucas and Damien Hurst imposed themselves and their art upon the popular consciousness of the UK, which spilled over into art education and, importantly, into the practice of ATS participants.

Pedagogical transformations

With their reinvigorated personal artwork and exposure to contemporary practice came a criticality that shaped the thinking of ATS students. The idea of revisiting practice began to take on a new direction for some participants, and issues such as feminism, colonialism and racism came to dominate their work, even where previously they had worked with more traditional image-making themes. In parallel with this, and heavily influenced by the classes held at Tate and other contemporary galleries, their work assumed modes determined by forms that they had newly encountered, such as installation, film and performance.

While the effects upon art practice were clear enough, as researchers our attention was turned to the question of how all this might shape professional teaching practice and pedagogy. Working at its best, the programme participants were not only given free rein to pursue their practice outside of the classroom, but also to find ways to incorporate their practice into pedagogy. As one participant, Helen Jones, explained:

> I have made new discoveries about myself as an artist, for example that my art practice not only influences the way I teach but is simultaneously influenced by my students: the influence is symbiotic. Furthermore, I have identified that this relationship does not need to be made explicit (for example, asking students to view my work or make a transcription of it) as my artistic practice is naturally embedded within my pedagogy through process and philosophy (2018: 11-12).

Hyde (2007) reporting on ATS participants, found changes of emphasis in their work in schools during and after attending courses, such as:

> a shift from skills-based practice to conceptual ways of working; from traditional art to contemporary art in references and sources; openly discussing gender positioning; a transference of emphasis from an observational and skills-based practice towards a more conceptual mode of working; an increase in the use of digital media and other non-traditional modes of working (42).

With these features in mind, and in collaboration with the programme tutors at my London university, we constructed a research programme with Tate looking at how teachers managed dealing with contemporary issues and art practices in school institutional settings (Adams et al. 2008). The findings revealed that a configuration of favourable conditions was necessary for teachers to have both the time and the wherewithal to engage in work with their students that might pass as contemporary in both content and form. These included a receptive and progressive school management, sufficient time and available resources, and teachers confident and experienced in their own updated art practice. The latter was the most significant contribution of the ATS programmes, and perhaps the most important of all the possible conditions required. This is because capable and well-informed teachers have the confidence to petition for the establishment of a modified curriculum conducive to these practices and be confident of their ability to realise it in the classroom, even where the school management had misgivings and the resources were scarce. However, in many cases this proved impossible, especially where there existed a more traditional art curriculum that was well established, and, crucially, paying off in terms of examination results.

Therein lay one of the paradoxes of the ATS as it played out at the juncture of professional and personal practice: often participants found themselves modifying their personal art to accommodate a more critical and contemporary dimension, while maintaining a more conservative approach in the classroom in order to meet the performance demands of their schools' students and parents, who were accustomed to the safer and more familiar territory of naturalistic and skill-based painting, printing, graphics and sculpture. The professional rewards that these well-known and established art educational practices yielded frequently deterred teachers from venturing too far into experimental territory. The prevailing attitude of many teachers was, understandably, to avoid jeopardising proven and recognised approaches: 'Why fix it if it's not broken?' one said.

Role and identity issues

For some ATS participants the revival of their practice, supported by the programmes and the partnered gallery, created a new life world that was entirely incompatible with that of their school. In some extreme cases, they became like undercover agents operating in two mutually exclusive worlds, generating distinct identities and modes of operation for each, and scrupulously concealing their activities in one from the other (Adams 2010, 2011). In schools they were performing the role of professional teacher, responding to management and parental pressures for a narrow and instrumentalised skill-based art curriculum designed to maximise pupils' performance for high level results, while their alter ego as an avant-garde artist might be engaged in highly experimental multimedia work tackling political issues of social justice.

For these ATS participants the gulf between their professional and artistic lives was unbridgeable, often because of the rampant managerialism and performativity that had begun to permeate educational institutions. The increased criticality that accompanies a more rigorous scrutiny of art and its role in an education system can lead to disillusionment and frustration with the limitations and impositions of that system. Hence the irony that sometimes proficient practitioners participating in ATS programmes went on to leave the profession, either partially or completely, to pursue their own practice independently.

Any analysis of the artist teacher movement in the context of neoliberal culture makes for grim reading. Wild (2022) contends that the movement offers a resistance, at least on a personal level, to the corrosive effects of neoliberalism as imposed by school and government policies. She rightly recognises how artist teacher pedagogies are inevitably shaped by institutional politics, but that the teacher's aesthetic life is at least maintained as a presence in their professional as well as personal practice. My own experience bears this out, especially in countries where education institutions are rather less colonised and hollowed out by neoliberal strictures than the UK. Elsewhere in Europe I have witnessed the foregrounding of teachers' practice in the everyday schedule of teaching, where at times the pedagogical practice resembles that of an artist interacting with fellow artists. A power imbalance still exists, with the authority of the teacher maintained as elsewhere, but the voice and agency of the learners is more in evidence. This collaborative and collegiate way of working is the antithesis of neoliberal prescriptions, which demand conformity and homogeneity through obedience and compliance, with an insistence upon a fixed hierarchical epistemology and standardised knowledge maintained by continuous auditing and testing (Adams and Owens 2016).

The artist teacher programmes I helped to create also encountered conceptual challenges that became manifest practically. One of these was the long-standing issue of the problematic relationship between artist and teacher (Day 1986), whereby the cultural authority of the artist, with its inherently high status, occludes that of the teacher. There is a long history to the intellectual fabric of this positioning (Cohen 1967), which has threads woven from European cultural colonialism and the patriarchal male gendering of the artist. Conversely, the teacher has been positioned subordinately, their authority perceived as primarily behavioural rather than intellectual. Although much work has been done to overturn and correct this inequality, the prejudice lives on covertly, sometimes surfacing in the assumptions underpinning curriculum and policy choices (Hargreaves and Flutter 2019). Even in highly successful pedagogical configurations like the Room 13 primary school project, where artists and teachers developed a highly sophisticated and dynamic pedagogy of production integrated into school practices and curriculum, the leaders still repudiated the label of teacher or educationalist (Adams and Owens 2016).

Art teachers in schools occasionally colluded in this deceit, determined to keep separate their identity as an artist from their identity as a teacher (Efland 2002; Eisner 2002). Nowhere was this more apparent than when teachers collaborated in the design of ATS courses: they prioritised a revival of their artistic practices and the acquisition of new art skills over educational learning that may have influenced their pedagogy. This created one of the challenges facing designers of ATS courses: how to distinguish these new programmes from fine art courses and thereby prevent the hosting institutions dismissing ATS courses as duplicates of existing provision.

ABR

The turn to arts-based research (ABR) and knowledge co-creation as dominant themes in art, museum and education discourses in recent years has transformed the artist teacher discourse by establishing the concept of the artist teacher as a researcher. The international popularity of a/r/tography, with its focus on the visual arts, cemented ABR in educational thinking and shifted the axis of the artist teacher conceptual framework (Irwin 2013; Irwin and Springgay 2008). Rather than the notion of the teacher as the practising artist in the classroom, there is the idea of the teacher as the practising researcher.

ABR facilitates ways of exploring deeply subjective learning processes that remain opaque to conventional social science methods. Delving into the poetic domain to generate participant narratives has proved fruitful, as Natalie

LeBlanc (2018) and Fadel Alsawayfa (2019) have demonstrated, the former though visual poetry and the latter through performance. LeBlanc researched personal histories of school through her photographic dissertation project: *In/Visibility of the Abandoned School: Beyond Representations of School Closure*. Her description of one image, *Contents Erased*, illustrates the way that ABR can engage the viewer and help them to articulate responses based on their own experiences:

> Instead of presenting the viewer with a narrative, it captures the static temperament of an abandoned school through a deadpan aesthetic; creating the conditions necessary for a dynamic encounter to occur. It is an invitation for the viewer to enter the image and to ponder the memories, the stories, the myths, and the meanings that an abandoned place provokes (LeBlanc 2018: 16).

Her work is prompted by the broader (Canadian) state education policy of school closures, but is primarily concerned with how such a policy impinges upon personal histories and the emotional responses that visualising its material effects provokes.

As Owens and I point out in our own work on ABR (Adams and Owens 2021), the present moment can be a vital determinant. In ABR practices 'we accept the flow of things as they are in that specific moment and place: the moment can be very important in arts-based practices' (10). This facet of ABR lends itself to teachers, used to the intensity, pace and multiple interactions of the workplace. In the case of active practitioners, the teacher-as-artist-as-researcher makes sense, given the premise that art practice itself can be synonymous with research practice. An example of this occurred when artist teacher Jones (2018) was researching the self-efficacy and creative thinking of the students in her class of secondary school pupils. To accomplish this, she reversed the traditional roles and asked the group to collaboratively decide how she should construct and resolve her painting, based on a series of sketches she had made available to the group. In doing so she gave complete control for all the decision-making to her students, while she became the technician assembling the work under their auspices. The resulting piece was created alongside the students' own work, and her arts-based action research methodology helped reveal the imaginative thought processes of her students in real time, while maintaining a degree of integration with her pedagogical practice.

Artist teachers practising ABR in education settings can have ontological implications (Atkinson 2018): Wild (2022) has done much work on the integration of practices in the classroom, and analyses the fundamental relationship between pedagogy and the teacher-as-artist:

> the choreography of the art and design classroom is not only rhythmic, repetitive and ongoing, but that it is directional, intending towards particular ways-of-being, that objects, in compliance with its dominant flows, help to steer (57).

The ways-of-being in these circumstances have the advantage that they are infinitely malleable, suited to the prerogatives of the learner-artist. Predetermining the pedagogy here is futile and at odds with the potential dispositions of the participants; instead, the pedagogy emerges. This sounds tricky to manage – and it is – but its manifestations in practice are surprisingly ordinary, at least in the context of school art rooms. For example, a joint experiment, a kind of practical 'conversation' between student and teacher, about how to deal with the technical limitations of translating a colour drawing into a colour print may involve a conceptual shift upon the part of the learner about collaborative practice that may have profound consequences for the ways in which they learn as well as for the immediate practical problem.

Although this is an example of integrated practice, many of the effects that the ATS combined with ABR has had upon pedagogy and learning remain difficult to establish in terms of conventional research findings (Page et al. 2006). This may in part be due to the emphasis upon idiosyncratic contemporary art practices. For instance, the researching of an idea about a contentious social justice topic could open many avenues of discourse, some drawn from the learner's own experience. Bennett's (2020) research on art classroom discourse reveals how personal investment in a topic, such as gender identity, shapes not only the art produced but also the modes of learning and the attendant pedagogical practices. In her examples, the sharing of her own work and methods of production facilitate a creative exploration of the ideas, and displace issues of exposure and vulnerability away from the students and into the artworks.

Conclusion

Reflecting on my earlier essay on the ATS (Adams 2003), written in its first flush of pilot schemes rolling out across the UK, I was confident that teachers practising their art could translate their well-informed and new-found confidence into their teaching and pedagogic strategies. However, in the intervening decades there has been a marked de-professionalisation of teachers, brought about by the twin scourges of incessant auditing and a centralised curriculum, which combine to delegitimise teachers' authority over either control or delivery of their discipline. Given the emphasis of the ATS programmes on experimentation and exploration, with the inherent risks that these entail for failure and mistakes, it is fundamentally unsuitable for the homogenised, intensively policed and regulated curriculum that has since been in the ascendency. Where the principal aim of a reductive, instrumentalised education system is grade accountability, the freedom to experiment and make mistakes must be minimised or even eradicated, since they are inherently risky; such proscriptions are the antithesis of ATS values.

The concept of the teacher-as-artist working alongside fellow students-as-artists, cooperating on aesthetic and conceptual adventures together in an ordinary state school classroom, which so appealed to me back then, seems to belong to a universe from which we were evicted long ago. My hope for the future is that the ATS may revive as the value of creativity and imagination in general education is rediscovered once again, as it has been revived before. If this does come to pass, then it is likely that it will acquire new forms commensurate with the age into which it is reborn. From the perspective of the present day, the most promising direction seems to lie with ABR, as demonstrated through the widespread adoption of a/r/tographic methods internationally. Whichever way it unfolds, the concept of the artist teacher in the UK remains strong and proven in practice, ready to flourish again.

References

Adams, J. (2003) The Artist-Teacher Scheme as postgraduate professional development in higher education, *International Journal of Art and Design Education* 22(2): 183–194.

Adams, J. (2010) Risky choices: The dilemmas of introducing contemporary art practices into schools, *British Journal of Sociology of Education*, 31(6): 683–701.

Adams, J. (2011) The degradation of the arts in education, *International Journal of Art and Design Education*, 30(2): 156–160.

Adams, J. and Owens, A. (2016) *Creativity and Democracy in Education: Practices and politics of learning through the arts*. London and New York: Routledge.

Adams, J. and Owens, A. (eds.) (2021) *Beyond Text: Learning through arts-based research*. Bristol: Intellect.

Adams, J., Worwood, K., Atkinson, et al. (2008) *Teaching Through Contemporary Art: A report on innovative practices in the classroom*. London: Tate Publishing.

Alsawayfa, F. (2019) *Travelling to the Top of the Mountain: The use of found poetry to explore Palestinian and Arab teachers' perceptions and experience of their participation in a drama in education summer school* (online). Available at: https://chesterrep.openrepository.com/handle/10034/623550 (accessed 3rd November 2022).

Atkinson D. (2018) *Art, Disobedience and Ethics, the Adventure of Pedagogy*. London: Palgrave MacMillan.

Bennett, L. H. (2020) *Making and Relational Creativity: An exploration of relationships that arise through creative practices in informal making spaces*. Oxford: Routledge.

Cohen E. G. (1967) Status of teachers, *Review of Educational Research*, 37(3), Teacher Personnel (Jun., 1967), pp. 280–295.

Daichendt, G. J. (2010) *Artist Teacher: A philosophy for creating and teaching*. Bristol: Intellect.

Day, M. J. (1986) Artist-teacher: A problematic model for art education, *The Journal of Aesthetic Education*, 20(4): 38–42.

Efland, A. D. (2002) *Art and Cognition: Integrating the visual arts in the curriculum*. New York: Teachers College Columbia University, and Reston, Virginia, National Art Education Association.

Eisner, E. (2002) *The Arts and the Creation of Mind*. London: Yale University Press.

Galloway, S., Stanley, J., and Strand, S. (2006) *Artist Teacher Scheme Evaluation 2005–6: Final report*. NSEAD/University of Warwick (online). Available at: https://www.nsead.org/files/a162324a5f2b5087cf1ca6b93ca65c20.pdf (accessed 14 November 2023).

Hargreaves, L., and Flutter, J. (2019) *The Status of Teachers*, Oxford Research Encyclopedia of Education. Available at: https://oxfordre.com/education/view/10.1093/acrefore/9780190264093.001.0001/acrefore-9780190264093-e-288 (accessed 19 May. 2023).

Hyde, W. (2007) A stitch in time: Gender issues explored through contemporary textiles practice in a sixth form college, *International Journal of Art and Design Education* 26(3): 296–307.

Jones, H. (2018) An autoethnographic exploration of creative self-efficacy (CSE) (online). Available at: https://chesterrep.openrepository.com/handle/10034/621406 (accessed 4 November 2022).

Irwin, R. (2013) Becoming a/r/tography, *Studies in Art Education*, 54(3): 198–211.

Irwin, R. and Springgay, S. (2008) A/r/tography as practice-based research, in M. Cahnmann-Taylor and R. Siegesmund (eds.) *Arts-based Research in Education: Foundations for practice*. New York: Routledge, 103–124.

LeBlanc, N. (2018) 'Abandoned schools', in *From mittens to Barbies*, Tate Exchange Liverpool Catalogue: University of Chester Press: 16. See also: Abandoned Schools (online). Available at: https://www.natalieleblanc.com/portfolio/the-abandoned-school.html (accessed 3 November 2022).

NSEAD (2001) *Artist-teacher scheme statement April 10th, 2001*, 2nd Draft. National Society of Education through Art and Design: archive.

Page, T., Adams, J. and Hyde, W. (2011) Emerging identities: The impact of the artist teacher MA on students' pedagogical and artistic practices, *European Journal of Teacher Education*, 34(3): 277–295.

Page, T., Herne, S., Charman, H. et al. (2006) Art now with the living: A dialogue with teachers investigating contemporary art practices, *International Journal of Art and Design Education*, 25(2): 146–155.

Pringle, E. (2001) *Artist teacher summer scheme: Evaluation report.* NSEAD, ACE and Tate galleries: Tate and NSEAD archives.

Pringle, E. (2009) *The artist as educator: Examining relationships between art practice and pedagogy in the gallery context*, Tate Papers No.11 (online). Available at: https://www.tate.org.uk/research/tate-papers/11/artist-as-educator-examining-relationships-between-art-practice-and-pedagogy-in-gallery-context (accessed 20 October 2022).

Wild, C. (2022) *Artist-Teacher Practice and the Expectation of an Aesthetic Life: Creative being in the neoliberal classroom*. Oxford: Routledge.

2 On not being diminished – being more than is recognised through artist teacher practice

Carol Wild

This chapter discusses the specific context for artist teacher practice in England over the last 25 years, with a particular focus on the impact of neoliberal education policy on those seeking to practise as artist teachers in the secondary school specifically. I begin by describing neoliberal education policy and provide a framework for approaching its impact in the art and design classroom. I then outline the move from seeing artist teacher practice as something that might transform the art and design classroom to something that might resist its powerful flows, and from that to something that might enable the teacher of art and design to escape or survive the neoliberal classroom which diminishes them. I end by proposing that what the last twenty years of artist teacher practice has shown is that artist teacher practice is a way to extend the flows of the classroom beyond the limitations that government policy sets in motion.

Neoliberalism

The implementation of government education policy since the late 1970s has arguably undermined the perceived agency of teachers in England (Skinner et al. 2019; Skerrit 2020). The dominant political and economic force behind the apparent weakening of teachers' self-determination over this period has been a neoliberal drive towards the marketisation of education, accompanied by a new managerialism and performativity (Ball 2003). A neoliberal ideology considers the free market to provide the most fertile system for ensuring economic profitability and individual emancipation (Harvey 2007; Robertson 2008). Bridges and Jonathan (2003: 127) summarise conditions required for the marketisation of education as, 'on the supply side of the educational economy, the creation of diversity and choice and, on the demand side, the placing of information and purchasing power in the hands of "consumers"'.

Neoliberal education policy ensures that schools are amenable to the needs of the self-regulating market through the withdrawal of state control (Robertson 2008). What this means in practice is that schools are placed in competition with each other, as seen in the move of English schools away from local government control through academisation, modelled on U.S. Charter Schools (Goodman and Burton 2012; West and Bailey 2015). These semi-privatised academies can control their own admissions, budgets and staffing and are not required to follow the National Curriculum. However, as fast as education has been marketised, and freed from local government management, it has also been made subject to accountability measures that have exerted ever more control of teachers. This limits their autonomy, in order to guarantee their compliant performance (Craft and Jeffrey 2008; Hill 2012), ensuring that there is apparently very little difference between schools in terms of ethos, curriculum design and pedagogy. As Ball (2003: 216) describes, this creates a 'devolved environment' where the 'freedom' of the market is limited by the overall framework set by the government, within which a culture of performativity plays out in the classroom. Performativity is 'a mode of regulation that employs judgements, comparisons and displays as means of incentive, control, attrition and change based on rewards and sanctions (both material and symbolic)' (p. 216).

The agency of the art and design classroom

A simplistic way of understanding the art and design classroom is as the stage upon which autonomous actors perform the actions of art and design education. The educational space is conceived as a passive background upon which easily detachable people, objects, policy, curriculum and pedagogy can be rehearsed, arranged and rearranged (Wild 2022). Classrooms, however, are more active, complex and entangled than this. Thompson and Cook (2014) describe the components of classrooms as competing and oscillating, close-by and far-away flows, which ensure that although every lesson is different, each also repeats predictable returns of the same. This repetitive movement and intra-action, is referred to by Youdell and Armstrong (2011) as a kind of choreography that ensures that every human and non-human body within the school knows their place and way-of-being. These fluid, entangled relations form what Ingold (2017: 10) would refer to as a meshwork through which 'giving and receiving, wherein lives are rendered answerable to one another, is the very impulsion that keeps it flowing'.

Understanding the classroom as movement requires a reimagining of the concept of agency 'to think outside of the binary, which requires that either we are the master of our actions or someone else is' (Wild 2022: 73; Ingold 2017). It is a binary that only makes sense if individuals are able to pre-exist experience, and as Ingold (2017) emphasises, be applied to the world as if it were a stage, or a background, rather than symbiotically coming into being through moving along and intra-acting with it. Agency is therefore 'not something that people can *have* – as a property, capacity or competence – but something that people do *with* their environment' (Biesta et al. 2015: 626). It makes more sense, therefore, to speak of agency, or the power to act, as being shared across an ensemble of relations-in-movement. The agency of the classroom ensemble is shaped by powerful flows that can 'limit potentialities, directions and movements' (Ellsworth, 2005: 130).

Education policy creates powerful flows within the classroom that the art and design teacher must answer to. Webb and Gulson (2015) speak of it disseminated by the educational assemblage intuitively, provoking distributed affects that can often be anticipatory. They refer to this anticipatory response as policy prolepsis, prolepsis being a kind of premonition or 'flash forward', the opposite of a 'flashback'. As Stephen Ball (2016: 10) states, policy 'cannot not be treated simply as an object, a product or an outcome but, rather, it is a process, ongoing, interactional and unstable'. Thompson and Cook (2014) discuss how teachers must hold in flux the far-away flows of policy with the close-by flows of student needs, this to-and-fro between the far-away and close-by demands being the rhythm that propels the life of the classroom forward.

Transforming the flows of the classroom – The Creativity Agenda

Adams' (2003) paper reporting on the first Artist Teacher Scheme (ATS) cohort at Liverpool John Moores University, notes that,

> helping to shape the context in which ATS would flourish was the renewed government initiative on creativity in education, culminating in the 1999 National Advisory Committee on Creative and Cultural Education's All Our Futures document (p.185).

This document, commissioned by the recently elected New Labour government set out a vision for schooling that apparently had creativity and culture at its heart. This was the policy climate within which the ATS was launched, with the aim of shaping the curriculum and pedagogy of the art and design classroom through shaping the person of the art and design teacher.

All Our Futures stated that the best conditions for promoting creative and cultural development requires a school culture in which there is 'a constant raising of new possibilities', and 'opportunities for reflective time, mental play and self-development for teachers' (NACCCE 1999: 102). It outlined five aims that teaching for creativity encourages: autonomy, authenticity, openness, respect and fulfilment (pp.91–92). Though keen to point out that creativity is not the sole possession of the arts, there was a strong thread running through it that cultural organisations and artists were central to achieving the report's aims. The fruition of this was the launch of Creative Partnerships in 2000 that sought to 'provide enhanced and enriched opportunities for young people to develop skills, knowledge, and critical appreciation of the arts, culture and creativity', to 'provide opportunities for teachers to enhance their creative teaching skills' and 'to build the capacity for the cultural and creative sectors to be able to work effectively with schools in developing creativity in the process of learning' (Sharp et al. 2006: 4). It would seem, from all of the above, that the shared agency of the art and design classroom would be extended through such a policy environment.

Hall's 2010 review of Creative Partnerships describes a policy model which sought expert creative outside agencies to solve problems in schools. She explains how 'many of these agents took a deficit view of teachers' creative capacities, and despite questionable qualifications and experience to fulfil the role, saw their job as advising on curriculum development and creative pedagogies' (Hall 2010: 487). The teacher in school was framed as being outdated in approach, in need of instruction from the authentic, contemporary pedagogical approaches of the creative experts. The ATS arguably followed a similar model, with the art and design teacher understood to be reproducing outdated, inauthentic 'School Art' (Atkinson 2006) practice, and the outside 'experts' of cultural institutions and universities seen as providing a creative solution (Galloway et al. 2006: 6).

The solution to the problem of 'School Art' that the ATS presented was for teachers to become like 'real' artists through the steering of benevolent creative experts, the academics, gallery educators and artists involved. Pringle (2002), and Hall and Thomson (2017) summarise a pedagogical approach unique to artists, which, unlike the pedagogy of the art teacher, models 'authentic' art experiences. Artists, they suggest, like to challenge boundaries, encourage critical dialogue, defend student autonomy and value the process over the end product. Many of these qualities directly mirror the best conditions for promoting creative development as laid out in All Our Futures (NACCCE 1999). These also, as I summarise (Wild 2022), frequently appear in published first-hand accounts of artist teacher practice (Horn 2006; Hyde 2007; Stanhope 2011; Ward 2014; Cusack cited in Vella 2016). These reports of the impact of artist teacher practice are rarely transformative of whole classroom relations, curriculum or pedagogy, however. They are serendipitous interactions between the artist teacher, their arts practice and an individual, or temporary interruptions to the habitual choreography of the classroom.

During the early 2000s, when the ATS was established, the connection of school-based art and design education to authentic arts practice through contemporary arts practice, was central to research into English art and design classrooms (Downing and Watson 2004; Addison and Burgess 2007; Adams at al. 2008). A significant aspect of working with contemporary arts practice was a parallel contemporisation of classroom pedagogy in which not only did the teacher operate as an artist but the student did too (Adams et al. 2008: 6). The art and design classroom was recast as a collaborative site of critical thinking, and creative production shared between the artist, artist teacher and artist-learner.

Resisting the flows of the classroom – problematising the creativity agenda within neoliberal education policy

All Our Futures (1999) defined creativity as 'Imaginative activity fashioned to promote outcomes that are both original and of value' (NACCCE 1999: 29). This echoes international definitions which frame the value of creativity as innovation that promotes economic growth, over alternative understandings (O'Connor 2007; Gormley 2018; Kalin 2018). Jagodzinski (2012) offers a Deleuzian critique of the international neoliberal 'take over' of creativity conceiving it as transcendental (the source of it being outside oneself filling a void or need) or immanent (the source of it being from within oneself, bubbling up and spilling out). Jagodzinski (2012) maintains that the creativity of international neoliberal education policy is transcendental in nature, creativity applied from outside, as a far-away, rather than close-by flow; the classroom as a static background, rather than an influx entanglement of 'potentialities, directions and movements' (Ellsworth 2005: 130).

O'Connor's (2007) review of the 60-year policy journey toward the notion of creativity as a 'cultural resource' from 'the Culture Industry', to the 'creative industries', explores the evolution of the 'enterprising self' and 'self-exploitation' as a key characteristic of the New Labour years (p.52). As both Kalin (2018) and jagodzinski (2012) explore, this self-actualising creativity is something that we are all required to produce within neoliberal, capitalist society, and is a process that is never complete. The neoliberal economy profiteers from the continual self-augmentation of neoliberal citizens. The exploitation of the self is encouraged in neoliberal education contexts via performance incentives through which, as Ball (2003: 218) describes, 'There is 'the possibility of a triumphant self' of becoming a new kind of professional or of entry into the ever expanding ranks of the executors of quality'. It must be acknowledged that the concept of the artist teacher might also be an 'ideal' that stands alongside that of the outstanding teacher as yet another 'performance' required by the art and design teacher. The artist teacher being defined in the English context as not only an 'artist-first' as Daichendt's (2010) theorising explored, but an 'artist-continually'; someone who must forever demonstrate their worth through creatively filling the deficit in themselves that they are 'only' an art teacher.

Ball (2003: 220) describes the 'ontological insecurity' that self-exploitative performativity engenders,

> being constantly judged in different ways, by different means, according to different criteria, through different agents and agencies [...] We become [...] unsure whether we are doing enough, doing the right thing, doing as much as others, or as well as others, constantly looking to improve, to be better, to be excellent.

This appears to be the very opposite to the conditions for creative development outlined by All Our Futures in which autonomy, authenticity, openness, respect and fulfilment are encouraged (NACCCE 1999: 91-92). The culture of performativity in schools under New Labour, as Burnard and White (2008) and Nicholl and McLellan (2008) outline, undermined the rhetoric of creative teaching and limited the 'potentialities, directions and movements' (Ellsworth 2005: 130) of the art and design classroom. When I researched the experiences of art and design teachers in schools in my area in 2006/7 I found, in corroboration of Downing and Watson (2004), that the curriculum and pedagogy was far from the contemporary, creative, democratic, collaborative practice promoted by the ATS. Although there were pockets of notable artist teacher practice that did appear to transform classroom flows and relations, such as Sheri Horn and Gill Jopia's performances and installations (Horn 2006, 2008, 2009), these instances were rare and represented temporary disturbances of otherwise compliantly performative art and design classrooms. These disruptive 'pedagogies against the state' (Atkinson 2013: 138) were theorised as acts of resistance to the performance of School Art orthodoxies that created moments of 'real' learning (Horn 2006, 2008, 2009; Wild 2011).

Surviving and escaping the art and design classroom – Michael Gove and the Knowledge Rich Curriculum

In 2010 a new centre-right Coalition government was formed. In response to the world-wide financial crisis of 2008, they implemented a raft of 'austerity' policies, for example, abruptly halting the Building Schools for the Future programme. Conservative MP Michael Gove was appointed Secretary of State for Education and began to wage a war on those he named 'enemies of promise': academics working in university-based teacher training, teacher unions, and anyone supporting 'progressive' education (Gove 2012). Gone was the rhetoric of creative teaching and learning; instead Gove wanted to return traditional knowledge and direct instruction to the curriculum.

If 'creativity' had been the buzzword under New Labour, it was 'knowledge' that Michael Gove and his supporters favoured (Gove 2013; Gibb 2017). In this he was inspired by the work of E.D. Hirsch, whose intentionalist stance sees knowledge as objectively stable and unchanging (Lavender 1997). In regards to the work of art, the intentionalist would argue that the meaning of the work is constant. What matters is what the artist intended the work to be; for a good discussion of intentionalism see Lavender (1997) and Belluigi (2017). Hirsch's views on the enduring nature of knowledge inform his promotion of a curriculum that provides an unchanging core of knowledge as a route to social mobility and cohesion (Buras 1999; Yandell 2017). In such a policy environment, the idea of the artist teacher creating new ways of knowing through engaging in their own arts practice appeared to be out of sync with the political zeitgeist.

Whatever the merits or not of the knowledge-rich approach, Gove's promotion of knowledge was not equally spread across the curriculum. He promoted some forms of knowledge over others through the English Baccalaureate (Mathematics, English, Science, Modern Foreign Languages and History and Geography). Although this has never been an actual qualification, since 2016 it has been embedded in schools through accountability measures, which measure school effectiveness through the 'progress' students make between their end-of-Key-Stage-3 SAT tests at age 11 and their GCSEs at age 16 (Goodacre 2023). As Webb and Gulson's (2015) theorising of 'policy prolepsis' explores, such policy change is assimilated across the education assemblage in ways that are anticipatory, causing material, spacial and temporal *affects*. These are felt in the way that human and non-human resources are '(re)allocated, (re)organised, (re)purposed or (re)moved' (Wild 2022: 139). The intuitive assimilation of Gove's reforms in schools led to changes to curriculum time and examination options that negatively impacted the reach of art and design. A 2016 survey by NSEAD found curriculum time for the subject had reduced in 44 percent of schools in the previous five years (NSEAD 2016). The Cultural Learning Alliance (2021) reported an eight percent drop in the number of art and design teachers employed in schools 2010 and 2020. The immediate, intuitive, felt impact of Gove's reforms was one of vulnerability across the whole ensemble of art and design education, with advocacy groups such as NSEAD, the Cultural Learning Alliance, and artists such as Bob and Roberta Smith devoting huge amounts of time and resources to defending the subject. Amidst this climate of austerity, reform and vulnerability, Arts Council England's funding for the ATS was ended, leading to the closure of several artist teacher courses nationally. In 2006, Galloway et al. listed 12 ATS centres in England. In 2023, there are only four MA courses still running.

Alongside the vulnerability of art and design within the Coalition and Conservative governments' education policies, the 'terrors' of performativity, outlined by Ball in 2003 also increased, enabled by technological advances that made it possible to collect and report on ever more data (Bradbury 2019; Manolev et al. 2019). As Thorpe and Kinsella (2021: 543) report, one outcome of this is that 'Teacher's discourse is dominated by notions of 'playing the game' of assessment and 'tick box' exercises that have little meaning for knowledge development'. The effect on the art and design classroom is one of 'cultural attrition' (Matthews 2019: 855) and as Adams (2013) makes clear, creativity becomes muted, replaced by less risky, more measurable activities, suggesting that 'This does not necessarily require the removal of arts or creative-designated subjects from the curriculum, rather it entails the extraction of their critical, relational and subjective features, so that what remains is a husk largely devoid of actual creativity' (pp.242–243).

Thompson and Cook (2014, p.283) discuss how the ongoing advance of data collection has covered over the requirement to 'care' for individual students with the 'desire to be responsive to the data generated'. They draw on Deleuze's notion of the control society within which, as Deleuze (1995: 180) stated 'individuals have become "dividuals"... data' and that,

> The continuous collection of data on teaching, such as through high-stakes testing, value-added measures and continual re-accreditation, exemplify this dividuation. Teachers must understand and practise teaching in the context of auditable outputs assembled anonymously and at a distance from the classroom (p. 284).

This, they suggest, interrupts the oscillation of the classroom between far-away and close-by flows. The increased performativity required by the production of data which operates at a distance makes it harder for teachers to *care* close-by for their students and their subject, and prevents them from feeling cared for themselves; they are 'no longer facilitated, energised and resourced at the same levels in a classroom coming to manifest the logic of the corporation' (Thompson and Cook 2014: 289). This leads, as Ball (2003) also observed, to an ontological crisis and the question of 'What am I doing teaching?'. The only viable response for some is to leave teaching altogether.

In 2016, when beginning PhD study into the impact of artist teacher practice in the classroom, I set out to recruit teacher-graduates of artist teacher courses to participate. I found several recommended to me had left the profession, or were planning to, due to the personal confliction involved in their jobs. For more than one of them, it was participation in an ATS course that had prompted these feelings. As artist Elena Thomas stated,

> the prescribing of the curriculum makes you sort of keep your head under the parapet and kind of have this tunnel vision [...] but then you do step out of that, (describing doing the Artist Teacher Scheme) and open that Pandora's Box to something else.

It was certainly the case that much of the artist teacher practice that I encountered during my study, which has been reported in *Artist-Teacher Practice and the Expectation of an Aesthetic Life* (Wild 2022), folded in neoliberal classroom flows somehow, allowing a playful way for the artist teachers to engage with the oscillating flows of their classroom experience: Joanna Fursman's photographic documentation of her classroom being repurposed as an ICT suite; Elena Thomas's exploration of the risk-adverse primary school classroom; Clare Stanhope's (2011) reflections on the censorship of her students' work by senior leaders in her school after an inspiring sharing of her own practice with them; Henry Ward's (2014) account of constructing a cardboard maze in his classroom on the week the school inspectors were visiting, which disrupted their ability to observe the students without entering the maze themselves; Sarah Hughes *A Snail's Pace* involved her feeding discarded sheets of classroom data to snails who ingested the ink and excreted it in their slimy trails (Wild 2022). And finally, eventual participant in my study, Molly's *Doodling*, which she hesitated to share with me, saying 'It's not much really [...] I wasn't sure whether to share them'. Her doodlings were, her words acknowledged, vulnerable – unlikely to stand up to critique, with no robust theoretical position to defend them, and no extended material investigation that might lead to them being considered refined. Over time I noted that it was common for the participants in my study to introduce their work-in-progress with a similar reluctance to claiming it as 'Art', by using the prefix *'It's just…'*, or *'It's only…'*, always indicating that it fell short of being 'real' arts practice. The vulnerability of their classroom agency was represented in the work that they were able to make in the little time they had spare.

The vulnerability of the art teacher within the art and design classroom is explored by ATS alumni, Elinor Brass and Susan Coles. They discuss the motivations of artist teacher participants in the national sketchbook circle that Elinor facilitates, suggesting that it creates a safe space for those who have stopped making their own work, having been 'overpowered by measurability' (Brass and Coles 2014: 372). Referencing Gielen et al.'s (2012) *Teaching Art in the Neoliberal Realm*, they speculate that neoliberal performativity compromises the safe pedagogic space of the classroom for many art and design teachers.

Though Gove, and the eight consecutive Secretaries of State for Education that have filled the role between 2014 to 2023, have claimed to promote teacher autonomy, the lack of curriculum time and resources, a superficial focus on 'knowledge' and increased performativity in schools have collectively diminished the agency felt within the art and design education classroom and as a result limit the potentialities, directions and movements it makes possible. Within this context, it appears that far from transforming the art and design classroom, as the ATS was originally conceived, artist teacher practice perhaps more commonly provides a therapeutic way to survive its diminishing flows.

Expanding the reach of the classroom through artist teacher practice

There is another way to consider artist teacher continuing professional development and the neoliberal art and design classroom, however, as I explore in *Artist-Teacher Practice and the Expectation of an Aesthetic Life* (Wild 2022). If the classroom is made by repeating and oscillating flows, then artist teacher practice can both introduce new flows of close-by attention to materials, processes, and people, and also provide an alternative way of moving with those flows, as artist, rather than teacher; the artist's way of being seeing everything as potentially and equally important (Kaye 2013: 53). These alternative flows and ways of being can counter the compliant performativity and instrumentalisation of the classroom. These new flows need not be disruptive or event-like (Atkinson 2013) although they may be; but, as first-hand accounts of artist teacher practice in the classroom show (Hyde 2007; Stanhope 2011; Ward 2014) they are as likely to be quiet, apparently insignificant sharings of practice and responsive connection with individual students and small groups. Thomson et al. (2019) call this brokerage, and in their study of 'arts-rich' schools (those schools that continued to promote the arts despite government policy in recent

years) they discovered it was a significant characteristic of art teachers' pedagogy in those environments. Brokerage might involve the sharing of techniques
from one's own practice, and linking students with personal networks or local
arts communities. It might also involve the sharing of work-in-progress, engendering conversations that trouble the boundaries of normal classroom relations
to provide a space in which issues such as divorce, parenthood, loss and grief
can be safely encountered (Horn 2006, 2008, 2009; Hyde 2007; Stanhope 2011;
Wild 2022). In this way artist teacher practice holds open spaces where oscilla-
tions of care for rather than exploitation of the self can recur, through 'giving
and receiving' and answering to one another (Ingold 2017: 10). In sharing their
practice with students, however undeveloped, the art and design teacher
demonstrates that there are other ways of being with the ensemble of art and
design other than compliant, performative relations. For art and design teachers
conflicted by teaching in neoliberal contexts, artist teacher practice not only
provides a way to escape or survive the flows that diminish the shared agency
of their classroom, it also provides a way to replenish and extend that agency,
enabling new 'potentialities, directions and movements' (Ellsworth 2005: 130).

References

Adams, J. (2003) The artist-teacher scheme as postgraduate professional development
in higher education, *The International Journal of Art and Design Education*, 22(2):
183–194.

Adams, J. (2013) The Artful Dodger: Creative resistance to neoliberalism in *education,
Review of Education, Pedagogy, and Cultural Studies*, 35(4): 242–255.

Adams, J. Woodward, K., Atkinson D., Dash, P., Page T. (2008) *Teaching through Contemporary Art*. London: Tate Publishing.

Addison, N. and Burgess, L. (2007) Conditions for learning: Partnerships for engaging
secondary learners with contemporary art, *International Journal of Art and Design
Education* 26(2): 185–198.

Atkinson, D. (2006) School art education: Mourning the past and opening a future, *International Journal of Art and Design Education*, 25(1): 16–27.

Atkinson, D. (2013) 'Pedagogy of the not known', in, E. Fisher and R. Fortnum (eds.) *On
Not Knowing: How Artists Think*. London: Black Dog Publishing, 136–145.

Ball, S.J. (2003) The teacher's soul and the terrors of performativity, *Journal of Education Policy*, 18(2): 215–228.

Ball, S.J. (2016) Neoliberal education? Confronting the slouching beast, *Policy Futures
in Education*, 14(8): 1046–1059.

Belluigi, D.Z. (2017) A framework to map approaches to interpretation, *Journal of Aesthetic Education*, 51(3): 91–110.

Biesta, G., Mark P., & Robinson, S. (2015) The role of beliefs in teacher agency, *Teachers
and Teaching*, 21(6): 624–640.

Bradbury, A. (2019) Datafied at four: The role of data in the 'schoolification' of early
childhood education in England, *Learning, Media and Technology*, 44(1): 7–21.

Brass, E. and Coles, S. (2014) Artist teachers exchange: Reflections on a collaborative
sketchbook project for secondary school art teachers, *International Journal of Art
and Design Education*, 33(3): 365–374.

Bridges, D. and Jonathan, R. (2003) Education and the Market, in D. Bridges, R. Jonathan and N. Blake (eds.) *The Blackwell Guide to the Philosophy of Education*, Oxford: Blackwell.

Buras, K. (1999) Questioning core assumptions: A critical reading of and response to E.D. Hirsch's the schools we need and why we don't have them, *Harvard Educational Review*, 69(1): 67–93.

Burnard, P., and White, J. (2008) Creativity and performativity: Counterpoints in British and Australian education, *British Educational Research Journal*, 34(5): 667–682.

Craft, A. and Jeffrey, B. (2008) Creativity and performativity in teaching and learning: Tensions, dilemmas, constraints, accommodations and synthesis, *British Educational Research Journal*, 34: 577–584.

Cultural Learning Alliance (2021) Hours of arts teaching and number of arts teachers in England's secondary schools continue stable after years of decline (online). Available at: https://www.culturallearningalliance.org.uk/hours-of-arts-teaching-and-number-of-arts-teachers-in-englands-secondary-schools-continue-stable-after-years-of-decline/ (accessed 2 February 2023).

Daichendt, G.J. (2010) *Artist-Teacher: A philosophy for creating and teaching*. Intellect Books.

Deleuze G. (1995) Postscript on Control Societies, in G. Deleuze (Ed.) *Negotiations, 1972–1990*, trans. Martin Joughin, New York: Columbia University Press, 177–182.

Downing, D. and Watson, R. (2004) *School Art: What's in it?: Exploring visual arts in secondary schools*, London: National Foundation for Educational Research.

Ellsworth, E. (2005) *Places of learning: Media, architecture, pedagogy*. New York: RoutledgeFalmer.

Galloway, S., Stanley, J. and Strand, S. (2006) The University of Warwick Artist Teacher Scheme evaluation 2005–2006, final report. Prepared for the Artist Teacher Scheme Management Group. CEDAR (Centre for Educational Development, Appraisal and Research).

Gibb, N. (2017) The importance of knowledge-based education. Speech script (online). Available at: https://www.gov.uk/government/speeches/nick-gibb-the-importance-of-knowledge-based-education (accessed 2 February 2023).

Gielen, P., De Bruyne, P., and Bruyne, D. (Eds.) (2012) *Teaching Art in the Neoliberal Realm: Realism versus cynicism*. Antennae Amsterdam: Valiz.

Goodacre, L. (2023) The myth of student progress: Deconstructing attainment measures of secondary English, *Changing English*, 1–10.

Goodman, R. and Burton, D. (2012) The Academies Programme: An education revolution, *Educational Futures*, 4(3): 58–78.

Gormley, K. (2018) Neoliberalism and the discursive construction of 'creativity', *Critical Studies in Education*, 61(3): 313–328.

Gove, M. (2012) Michael Gove speech on academies (online). Available at: https://www.gov.uk/government/speeches/michael-gove-speech-on-academies (accessed 2 February 2023).

Gove, M. (2013) The Importance of Teaching speech (online). Available at: https://www.gov.uk/government/speeches/michael-gove-speaks-about-the-importance-of-teaching#:~:text=Teachers%20are%20the%20critical%20guardians,the%20unacknowledged%20legislators%20of%20mankind (accessed 2 February 2023).

Hall, C. (2010) Creativity in recent educational discourse in England, *World Englishes*, 29(4): 481–492.

Hall, C. and Thomson, P. (2017) Creativity in teaching: What can teachers learn from artists? *Research Papers in Education*, 32(1): 106–120.

Harvey, D. (2007) *A Brief History of Neoliberalism*. Oxford: Oxford University Press.

Hill, D. (2012) Immiseration capitalism, activism and education: Resistance, revolt and revenge, *Journal for Critical Education Policy Studies*, 10(2) (online). Available at: www.jceps.com/?pageID=article&articleID=259 (accessed 10 June 2013).

Horn, S. (2006) Inspiration into installation: An exploration of contemporary experience through art, *International Journal of Art and Design Education*, 25(2): 134–146.

Horn, S. (2008) The contemporary art of collaboration, *International Journal of Art and Design Education*, 27(2): 144–157.

Horn, S. (2009) Performance art at secondary level, *International Journal of Art and Design Education*, 28(2): 160–173.

Hyde, W. (2007) A stitch in time: Gender issues explored through contemporary textiles practice in a sixth form college, *International Journal of Art and Design Education*, 26(3): 296–307.

Ingold, T. (2017) On human correspondence, *Journal of the Royal Anthropological Institute*, 23(1): 9–27.

jagodzinski, j. (2012) The hijacking of creativity: The dilemma of contemporary art education, in N. Addison and L. Burgess (eds.) *Debates in Art and Design Education*. London: Routledge, 34–45.

Kalin, N.M. (2018) *The Neoliberalization of Creativity Education: Democratizing, destructing and decreating*. Palgrave MacMillan.

Kaye, N. (2013) *Site-specific Art: Performance, place and documentation*. London: Routledge.

Lavender, L. (1997) Intentionalism, anti-intentionalism, and aesthetic inquiry: Implications for the teaching of choreography, *Dance Research Journal*, 29(1): 23–42.

Manolev, J., Sullivan, A. and Slee, R. (2019) The datafication of discipline: ClassDojo, surveillance and a performative classroom culture, *Learning, Media and Technology*, 44(1): 36–51.

Matthews, M. (2019) Ethos of ambiguity: Artist teachers and the transparency exclusion paradox, *The International Journal of Art and Design Education*, 38(4): 853–866.

National Advisory Committee on Creative, Cultural Education (NACCCE) (1999) *All our Futures: Creativity, culture & education*. Department for Education, Employment, Great Britain; Department for Culture, Media and Sport.

Nicholl, B. and McLellan, R. (2008) 'We're all in this game whether we like it or not to get a number of As to Cs.' Design and technology teachers' struggles to implement creativity and performativity policies, *British Educational Research Journal*, 34(5): 585–600.

NSEAD (2016) *The National Society for Education in Art and Design Survey Report 2015–16* (online). Available at: https://www.nsead.org/news/newsroom/nsead-survey-report-2015-16/ (accessed 14 November 2023).

O'Connor, J. (2007) *The cultural and creative industries: A review of the literature*. Arts Council England.

Pringle, E. (2002) *'We did stir things up': the role of artists in sites for learning*. Arts Council of England.

Robertson, S.L. (2008) 'Remaking the World' Neoliberalism and the Transformation of Education and Teachers Labour, in M. Compton and L. Weiner (eds.) *The Global Assault on Teaching, Teachers, and their Unions: Stories for Resistance*. New York: Palgrave Macmillan, 11–27.

Sharp, C., Pye, D., Blackmore, J. et al. (2006) *National Evaluation of Creative Partnerships Final Report*. National Foundation for Educational Research (NFER).

Skerritt, C. (2020) School autonomy and the surveillance of teachers, *International Journal of Leadership in Education*, DOI: 10.1080/13603124.2020.1823486

Skinner, B., Leavey, G., and Rothi, D. (2019) Managerialism and teacher professional identity: impact on well-being among teachers, *UK Educational Review*, 73(1): 1–16.

Stanhope, C. (2011) The artist-teacher in the classroom and changes in the teacher–student relationship, with reference to the issue of censorship, *International Journal of Art and Design Education*, 30(3): 389–397.

Thomson, P., Hall, C., Earl, L., and Geppert, C. (2019) The pedagogical logics of arts-rich schools: A Bourdieusian analysis, *British Journal of Sociology of Education*, 40(2): 239–253, DOI: 10.1080/01425692.2018.1554474

Thompson, G. and Cook, I. (2014) The eternal return of teaching in the time of the corporation, *Deleuze Studies*, 8(2): 280–298.

Thorpe, V. and Kinsella, V. (2021) Secondary school arts teachers' practice autonomy perceptions in New Zealand and England, *Journal of Curriculum Studies*, 53(4): 531–545.

Vella, R. (2016) *Artist-Teachers in Context: International dialogues*. Rotterdam: Birkhäuser Boston.

Ward, H. (2014) *Teaching as an artistic practice*. Doctorate by Public Works (online). Available at: https://eprints.mdx.ac.uk/14479/ (accessed 2 February 2023).

Webb, P.T. and Gulson, K.N. (2015) *Policy, Geophilosophy and Education*. Springer.

West A. and Bailey, E. (2013) The development of the academies programme: 'privatising' school-based education in England 1986–2013, *British Journal of Educational Studies*, 61(2): 137–159.

Wild, C. (2011) Making creative spaces: The art and design classroom as a site of performativity, *International Journal of Art and Design Education*, 30(3): 423–432.

Wild, C. (2022) *Artist-Teacher Practice and the Expectation of an Aesthetic Life: Creative being in the neoliberal classroom* [Online]. Abingdon, Oxon: Routledge.

Yandell, J. (2017) Culture, knowledge and power: What the conservatives have learnt from ED Hirsch, *Changing English*, 24(3): 246–252.

Youdell, D. and Armstrong, F. (2011) A politics beyond subjects: The affective choreographies and smooth spaces of schooling, *Emotion, Space and Society*, 4(3): 144–150.

3 Conditions for artist teacher transformations

Rachel Payne

The Artist Teacher Scheme's (ATS) existence has always been shaped by political agendas. For example, the ATS was part-funded by Arts Council England (ACE) (Page et al. 2011) who paid for up to two-thirds of a Postgraduate Certificate qualification. In 2010, the incoming Coalition government removed ACE funding resulting in the demise of over half the ATS programmes in England (Payne 2020). Conclusively, in the United Kingdom (UK) today the ATS is perceived less as a 'scheme' and more as discrete pockets of professional practice delivered through a small number of Masters programmes and postgraduate research degrees.

Despite its diminished presence across UK higher education, it would be careless to dismiss the worth of artist teacher study, which generates safe spaces for professionals experiencing marginalisation (Heaton and Kuan 2022; Payne 2020). By fostering experts' resilience to political disenfranchisement, artist teachers are able to resituate themselves with agency in complex environments. In schools, the arts are relegated in favour of core subjects (Caldwell et al. 2021; Payne and Hall 2018) and in universities 'high-cost subjects' (Williamson 2021: 2) – which excludes culture and media-based degrees, and the arts – are prioritised for government funding. Despite the significant value of these disciplines to individuals and societies, over the last decade artist teachers have experienced the reduction of resources, expertise and status (NSEAD 2016, Thomson and Maloy 2022), department closures and job insecurity (Grady 2022). On a micro-scale, artist teachers often manage their learners' mental and emotional wellbeing as a by-product of art education, and in the process rarely afford the same levels of care to themselves (Bourgault and Rosamond 2023). Those working in the creative industries, museums and galleries have managed substantial impact to their professions as a result of COVID-19 (Gilmore et al. 2021; Walmsley et al. 2022) and the UK's exit from the European Union (Cusimano and Rowe 2022). This political landscape is the backdrop to artist teachers' lived experiences, shaping their motivations to make, educate and research.

This ethno-case study examines the lived experiences of artist teachers studying on an MA Education: Artist Teacher programme in an English university. While findings from the study are extensive, here I examine conditions that facilitate MA study and how participants' motives and experiences are shaped by internal and external forces. How this implicates transformative learning is subsequently discussed.

MA Education: Artist Teacher

Aligning with the ATS vision that by situating teachers in museums and galleries they are exposed to a wider variety of culture and visual arts (Page et al. 2011), the Masters I deliver is run in partnership with a high-profile museum on a three year, part-time basis. Cohorts comprise teachers working across educational phases from early years (0–5 years) to further education (16+ years), teaching assistants (professionals who support teachers and learners in the classroom), artists and educators working in informal settings, and creative freelancers. Regardless of students' backgrounds, participating in pedagogies of uncertainty (Shulman 2005) is fundamental to the course. At the centre of these pedagogies is recognition of the unique way in which artist teachers engage in learning, teaching and research, and the belief that making art generates new meanings and understandings (Payne 2018). In response, students enquire into artist teacher identities, practices and pedagogies by examining tensions that emerge when juggling education and making art. They embrace complexities by making sense of liminal or third spaces (Irwin 2004), which facilitate an examination of 'being an artist teacher' (Payne 2020: 727).

Transformative learning

To celebrate the first 10 years of the MA course in 2017, 27 students and alumni curated a month long exhibition called *Beyond Surface*. Concurrently I was invited to present how the MA supports artist teachers to address neoliberalism at a contemporary gallery. In an attempt to locate the MA for an external audience, I asked *Beyond Surface* exhibitors to write impact statements and was surprised that their testimonials corroborated anecdotal evidence that the programme transformed their professional practices. It was this that piqued my research interest.

Transformative learning can be misrepresented; the urge to focus on success stories rather than messy realities is ever tempting (Wild 2022). To better understand transformative learning, I consider Threshold Concept Framework (TCF), a portal that opens up previously inaccessible thinking (Land and Meyer 2003) and a salient theoretical lens to better understand art related processes and environments (Ravenstahl and Rattay 2020). When considered in relation to education, a student moves across a threshold from one state of knowing to another and so is changed by the process. This transition indicates learning at work. There are four characteristics of a threshold concept (Land and Meyer 2003): 1) it generates a significant shift in the perception of a subject or a concept; 2) it exposes the previously hidden inter-relatedness of something, so the student begins to understand it from more than one perspective; and 3) new learning is unlikely to be forgotten or unlearned, only through considerable effort. Transformation indicates a complete shift in thinking and being as our identities adjust to new knowledge, understandings and perceptions. Finally, 4) it is frequently troublesome. Perkins (1999) refers to the need for troublesome knowledge if the learning experience is to be transformative, what he describes as knowledge that is counter-intuitive, absurd, ritualised or alien. It is destabilising (Ravenstahl and Rattay 2020). Students must be unsettled if they are going to make a transition in their learning where unfamiliar knowledge becomes emotionally and intellectually difficult because it challenges existing learnings, beliefs and values.

A threshold concept may lead to troublesome knowledge or vice versa (Land and Meyer 2003). This ambiguity is abundant on the MA as pedagogies encourage students to explore the intersection between theory and practice and resituate values placed on visual research (Adams 2003). Artistic ways of knowing provide abundant opportunities for transformative learning to occur (Blackburn Miller 2020), redressing academic hierarchies that position the written word as dominant. Here the visual is equally valid, correlating with North American a/r/tography which 'creates an imaginative turn by theorising or explaining phenomena through aesthetic experiences that integrate knowing, doing and making: experiences that value complexity and difference within a third space' (Irwin 2004: 31). In both a/r/tography and artist teacher pedagogies, students are challenged to take responsibility for themselves as learners, examining multiple parts of the self (Blackburn Miller 2020) and operating meaningfully in artist teacher communities. In this context, transformative learning is more than the acquisition of new knowledge as it engenders qualitative changes in learners' capacities, beliefs and/or behaviours (Illeris 2014; Ravenstahl and Rattay 2020), fostering imaginative play through arts-based research (Hoggan et al. 2009). Here 'liminality is the subject and method of art' (Ross, in draft /due 2024:1). This challenging experience results in 'a transformation of personal identity, a reconstruction of subjectivity' (Land and Meyer 2003: 4), which positions affective and cognitive domains centrally (Ravenstahl and Rattay 2020). Troublesome knowledge underpins my desire to locate the genesis of transformations (Illeris 2014); in this chapter I discuss the conditions – or troublesome knowledge – that initiate transformative learning in MA students.

Ethno-case study

An ethno-case study fuses ethnography, or a way of representing the culture of a group or community through writing, and case study which is an empirical investigation of a real-life phenomenon aiming to better understand the phenomenon's relationship to its context (Parker-Jenkins 2018). Where the two overlap, methodological considerations are situated within clear research boundaries that acknowledge the richness of a wider cultural context. Both support enquiry with a group of people using ethnographic techniques where the researcher immerses themselves within the research context and data (Walford 2009). Ethnographically, 'the field of study reflects the interpretations of meanings in the lives of communities [...] capturing lived experiences and respondent insights' (Parker-Jenkins 2018: 19). Subsequently, an examination of learning environments involves interpreting social groupings, processes and pedagogies, and how values, traditions and rituals underpin community practices at work (Illeris 2017). With this in mind, 16 students and alumni exhibiting in *Beyond Surface* gave written consent to participate in the study. All names have been changed to ensure confidentiality.

Ethnography aims to capture the experiences of participants and researchers to generate a cultural depiction where the researcher interprets the unfamiliar through multiple perspectives (Parker-Jenkins 2018). Participants completed semi-structured questionnaires and wrote impact statements in a bid to unearth how artist teacher transformations occur. Via questionnaires, participants communicated the impact of exhibiting on their artist teacher identities and how the MA influenced their professional practices. Eight of the participants consented to a further interview conducted by two alumni research associates (RA) who questioned them about the role of artist teacher communities, relationships between artist teacher curriculum and pedagogy, and the resulting impact on their practices in professional settings. All interviewees worked in secondary and further education settings. If ethnographers are to understand how people behave within their cultural contexts, Parker-Jenkins (2018) warns of the dangers of relying primarily on interview data. Despite this, commentary here focuses on interview findings only to maintain concision. Interviews are crucial if researchers are to capture what participants have to say about their experiences and facilitate participants to co-construct through dialogue a narrative of self (Shreeve 2009).

Data were collected over a 12-month period, enabling the examination of artist teachers' experiences without committing to a longitudinal study or compromising ethnographic principles. Timeframes in ethno-case studies are more contained than in traditional ethnography, an extended process ensuring trends are identified and theory generated from data (Hammersley 2006). This enables the researcher to assimilate into the community, building trust while simultaneously maintaining distance from the data through reflexivity (Parker-Jenkins 2018). While it is not uncommon for the ethnographic researcher to become or already belong to the group being studied, I found sustaining distance particularly challenging. I am the MA subject coordinator; at the time of research I was also the exhibition lead and I identify as an artist teacher, an educator who makes and researches through and with art. While I have led the MA programme since 2006, it was not until conducting this research that I recognised it as a reflection of my lived experience:

> They [interviewer and respondent] are discussing how artist teachers have to stand up and challenge their colleagues' perceptions of our subject. And suddenly the initial talk of professional isolation resonates. I am also them [...] I have made a programme that builds on values and practices that are important to me (my analytical note, 31 January 2019).

In this context I am implicated by my ongoing experience of the research field, which raises issues of legitimacy and power. I played a significant part in generating the narratives presented by participants (Wild 2022). Where ethnography exposes hidden structures and hegemony, the researcher may use data to act on their own agenda (Parker-Jenkins 2018), especially when already situating a position of privilege. Collaborating with alumni RAs helped limit my bias as their interviews facilitated conversations I could not and enabled my distance from the research. The RAs understood the context for research differently to me; they embody artist teacher students' lived experiences, providing opportunities to link 'perceptions and interpretations arising from their social worlds' (Milstein 2010: 2). There is a familiarity that positions artist teacher students and alumni differently to me, fostering a unique perspective on the research focus.

Data analysis

Utilising grounded theory, where theory emerges from inductive analysis of data, our immersion into interview transcripts was reinforced through keeping reflexive notes to identify rudimentary categories (Hammersley and Atkinson 2007). Memo comments were assigned to each transcript acting as a bridge between initial sense-making of data and reflections. They enabled consistency when identifying codes by supporting cross-referencing at different stages of data organisation and analysis (Angrosino 2007). We coded each interview transcript individually, systematically making notes for comparison during online meetings, and in this way honoured our differing interpretations. We mapped evidence of transformations and environmental influences against pedagogic and curricular structures, focusing on questionnaire findings: community; how pedagogy is structured, and how values embodied within the programme influence professional status. Findings indicate relationships between motivations, professional practices and environments, emotion, validation and tensions developed through community participation. Participants explained the importance of feeling valued on the MA, which facilitated their voices and agency.

In the following ethno-reflexive account, I problematise findings in an attempt to elucidate the genesis for artist teacher transformations. By narrowing down analysis, I indicate how motivations, identity and community collide, signifying troublesome knowledge and threshold concepts at work.

Motivation

Motivation is ever present when examining transformative learning (Illeris 2014) and unsurprisingly it underpins initiation of MA study for the artist teacher interviewees. This specifies troublesome knowledge in the form of intellectual, emotional and environmental gateways (Land and Meyer 2003; Ravenstahl and Rattay 2020). Participants indicate their motivations to enrol on the programme originate in a number of complex desires and conditions. These include negative experiences at work, lack of subject-specific continuing professional development (CPD), low confidence, and professional isolation, responses reiterated more widely by UK art educators (NSEAD 2016; Payne and Hall 2018; Thomson and Maloy 2022). Most interviewees joined the programme to seek out a community of like-minded colleagues and gain subject-specific input to alleviate their frustrations:

> So before taking part in the artist teacher scheme, I found apart from immediate colleagues, I felt quite isolated from other art teachers (Evelyn).

> I think that was a big motivation to join, to meet like-minded people [...] because I was quite removed, I'm at the centre here. I'm a key holder, so I don't meet that many other professionals (Cate).

Barriers act as an impetus for Evelyn and Cate with the 'transition to understanding [their experiences] proving troublesome' (Land and Meyer 2003: 1). On the one hand, participants recognise the impact of external constraints over which they have no control (Ball and Olmedo 2012). Formal education operates as a system where the value of teaching and learning is reduced to data-driven transactions (Payne and Hall 2018). Auge (1995) calls the neoliberal classroom a non-space, risk-adverse and de-humanising, generated around the need to measure and compare performance rather than focus on human experience. Wild (2022) expands on this notion of deficiency engendered through the subject's and art educators' vulnerabilities, which are by-products of performativity. Art teachers live with constant surveillance from education stakeholders, yet they are disregarded by those same stakeholders as the subject is relegated. This dichotomy informs teachers' practices, perceptions and motivations and here acts as an environmental gateway or threshold.

Participants articulate internal motivations too – desires, frustrations, interests and convictions to their identities and practices. For example, wanting to learn new things, to learn with and from others, and to fulfill a craving to be challenged and to take risks. As Sam indicates:

> The main aim for me was to re-invigorate my practice [...] So when you meet those people for the first time, who have all had similar types of thoughts as you, about wanting to get involved and looking more closely at their own artist teacher identity, or their own practice, I found it really liberating to have conversations with them.

It is vital to recognise artist teacher agency and intentionality here. While a professional is shaped by the environment they operate within, they can still enact a choice to 'appropriate, transform or ignore the social practices they encounter at work' (Shreeve 2009: 152). This is further borne out by Rebecca:

> My initial expectations [of the MA] was this kind of coming together and learning together and learning from each other and I think that the structure of the artist teacher scheme was very much in line [with] how we teach in the school that I'm in.

Challenging the pervasive artist teacher research narrative that represents the art classroom as inadequate (Wild 2022), Rebecca's motivations for joining the MA programme are thought-provoking. Her account correlates with her peers in that she seeks out a community of practice beyond school, but it also deviates as she perceives the MA as sympathetic to how she already operates in school. Crucially, motivations are self-initiated and defined by the participant, not the programme. Rebecca's motivations reinforce intellectual curiosity rather than seeking out ways to overcome epistemological or ontological barriers.

The relationship between internal and external motivation is complex, determined by how individuals experience professional contexts and their self-perception as artist teachers. Illeris (2014) specifies three conditions for motivation and transformative learning. Motivation or need for transformative learning can arise in anyone at any time, particularly taking into account the ambiguous nature of contemporary life. When motivation does arise it can be experienced as an imposition, a risk, a need or the next logical step, and at its core the student believes they can attend to something within that learning experience. Intellectual and emotional domains are central and as Ravenstahl and Rattay (2020) argue, visual art offers a unique opportunity to enable the student to navigate liminality. Thus, the student reveals that they can address challenges, feel achievement and even empowerment in the face of barriers they have overcome. These challenges indicate troublesome knowledge at work. In an academic sense, a threshold concept is something distinct that enables a student to progress with their studies (Land and Meyer 2003). This is not the case here; instead participants locate a way to change their contexts for living. While this ultimately impacts academic study, at this stage troublesome knowledge initiates subjective transformations because participants' shifts in perception influence their performance of self.

Artist teacher identities

Identity is how humans assemble and reassemble in response to the world (Shreeve 2009), and how we subsequently perform our sense of self. We construct identities through reflexive action, a continual negotiation with our environments and ourselves as subjects. The interaction between personal and professional selves is ever-changing as identity is shaped by multifarious factors, including the expectations of a professional role, the education context and how they are experienced (Beauchamp and Thomas 2009). While identity change tends to be gradual, surprising experiences can trigger profound shifts in core identity (Illeris 2014). For example, art teachers experience identity transformation when they first become teachers, as they move from the world of visual practitioner to beginning art teacher (Adams 2007). This professional modification demands different ways of thinking, working and being; the art teacher changes their view of professional self to align more closely with how others view them (Thornton 2013). Art teachers struggle with performative surveillance (Wild 2022), a lack of recognition from employers for their professional needs (Thornton 2013) and the 'complex questions' (Prentice 2000 cited in Thornton 2013: 50) they ask about compromising artistic integrity. While assimilation into an educational setting enables the teacher to participate in shared professional identity, the individual still needs to imagine themselves within that world (Shreeve 2009). Where this breaks down, threats occur to one's identity:

> You can just do your repetitive day to day tasks and you can be quite comfortable in your teaching, because you've been doing it a long time, you can do it to a certain level and it can all seem on the surface all very equitable and all very straightforward and ticking along, but actually you're bored (Cate).

> I was about to leave teaching, because I'd had enough of the, what felt like very unethical changes to education and a shift in global education towards managerialism (Evelyn).

'Transformative theory builds upon the assumption of the human need to understand and make meaning of our experience and to integrate it with what we know' (Ravenstahl and Rattay 2020: 130). Conclusively, motivations are underpinned by a sense of self, and for many this becomes troublesome when they feel dislocation in their professional identities. To act on motivations is to actively alter personal and professional identities, although what is unknown at this stage is how change will occur. Once artist teachers have an opportunity to explore their changed positions, new troublesome knowledge emerges. For example, data indicate tensions in how participants perform the values of the programme in professional settings:

> I think it's quite difficult, because in some ways you are fighting the tide, the status quo, which is all about conforming and all about don't question anything just go with what is decreed already, the rules and regulations so to speak. So I think that creates [...] a potential conflict of interest, because you've been, it's a bit like you've had your eyes opened to all these potentials, potentiality, but then you go back to your everyday and it's all shut (Cate).

The values Cate performs as a result of engaging with the programme stand in opposition to her colleagues' values, generating cognitive dissonance. Land and Meyer (2003) argue that travelling through a threshold concept leads to a privileged view; the student's landscape has been transformed by generating a greater understanding of the complexities of neoliberal education. Cate's values and attitudes change as a result of making connections between the previously hidden inter-connectedness of things. As she articulates above, insights gained can result in a sense of loss as they are unsettling; one's illusions are removed and the resulting understandings might not be welcome (Land and Meyer 2003). However, Ravenstahl and Rattay (2020) argue that professional dislocation can lead to a repositioning of art education in the curriculum, and Jo indicates below how this might be initiated:

> This links back to a need to question what is going on in the current political and educational reality that is the everyday. The support and understanding from the like-minded cohort [on the MA] is tantamount.

It appears that a salient condition to facilitate transformative learning is community.

Community

There is a danger that the dual position of artist teacher favours the artist. Multiple texts (for example Thornton 2013, Hoesktra 2015, Wild 2022) discuss perceived divisions between art in school and universities, and between the artist's visual practices compared with art teacher pedagogies. Conclusively, the artist is deemed authentic, whereas the teacher lacks legitimacy. This may explain why interviewees desire new communities of practice outside school, rather than inside it and why motivations articulated at the beginning of the interviews are predominantly influenced by the need to identify more with an artist than a teacher. Sam exemplifies this:

> So when you meet those people for the first time, who have all had similar types of thoughts as you, about wanting to get involved and looking more closely at their own artist teacher identity, or their own practice, I found it really liberating and to have conversations with them that were beyond the general drivel of school progress, or bitching, it was really refreshing. So in terms of a community, absolutely.

However, on closer inspection, data indicate that studying on the MA programme enhances cohesion by increasing students' sense of belonging to and being valued by a community, positively altering their experiences of professional settings (Payne 2020). While motivations to join the MA link closely to their experiences of professional communities, these are not limited to the artist teacher's immediate MA cohort. All participants indicate benefits from engaging in professional dialogues within their immediate cohort, across cohort year groups, with alumni, and through opportunities beyond the immediacy of the programme. Enabling spaces that facilitate re/connection with content that matters to the artist teacher enables meaningful dialogues across inner and outer worlds (Bourgault and Rosamond 2023). For example, contradicting assumed divisions between artist and teacher/school and studio, Sam generates CPD opportunities with school colleagues, across her school partnership and on a national platform, while Cate generates new pedagogical relationships with her adult learners, and Evelyn maintained a community with her artist teacher cohort long after she left the MA, motivated by making days she held in school. Each participant formulates their own version of a professional community that involves seeking out dialogue and interaction, actively expanding communities beyond the parameters of the programme, and frequently bringing practices back into educational contexts.

Inert knowledge, or not understanding connections between things learnt in the past and how they relate to the present (Perkins 1999) is a category of troublesome knowledge that is important here. One needs to be aware of inert knowledge, to make connections between contexts, times, experiences and people, before integration is possible (Land and Meyer 2003). I believe that community is important as artist teachers identify gaps in their experiences and identities, and use the MA to actively fill those gaps in a way that makes sense to them. Transformative learning enables deeper connections with community contexts that matter most to participants (Bourgault and Rosamond 2023). This is intuitive initially, but becomes deliberate as the programme develops and is often beset by difficulty. There needs to be a willingness to engage not only with self, but with 'others and otherness' (Lehner 2022: 92). Sam explains her frustration at being rejected from wider artist communities because her artist-self was perceived as inauthentic. Opportunities to exhibit are available through alumni networks but are closed to 'legitimate' artist groups in Sam's location. These barriers originate from values that participants perceive as underpinning the programme, values that they embodied themselves and by extension want to perform with others yet are not recognized by those operating in artist communities. Thus, troublesome knowledge emerges after the MA, signifying that the context for transformative learning is rarely complete. There is no final definitive transformation, but a series of small transformations with each new layer of understanding leading to a new gateway, to more troublesome knowledge. It is a process, not an outcome (Ravenstahl and Rattay 2020). Much like art production and visual research, this helps artist teachers reclaim professional autonomy.

Concluding comments

The aim of this chapter is to locate conditions that facilitate MA study and subsequent transformative learning; I recognise these as thresholds, gateways and/or troublesome knowledge. To better understand this context I consider how artist teacher motivations and experiences are shaped by internal and external forces. The study's findings indicate the beginning of fundamental shifts in the students' performance of self, constructed in response to political landscape, professional environment, personal desires and intellectual curiosity. Conclusively, data demonstrate that the emotional, cognitive and social are situated at the heart of transformative learning (Illeris 2014). Motivations are underpinned by a sense of self which becomes troublesome when participants no longer envision themselves within specific contexts, when they no longer fit in. To act on motivations begins a chain reaction that changes their subjective selves. With new insights comes struggle, a coming to terms with change and loss.

Transformative learning is complex and rarely complete. Troublesome knowledge is hopeful as engaging with the liminal results in infinite starting and ending points (Ravenstahl and Rattay 2020), positioning artist teachers in a constant state of becoming (Ball and Olmedo 2012), of transforming (Payne 2020). While the individual is transformed, what initiates and sustains transformation is how the MA fosters alternative perspectives through an interweaving of individual and community voices, practice, research, agency and determination to counter symbolic violence enacted in neoliberal environments.

References

Adams, J. (2003) The artist-teacher scheme as postgraduate development in higher education, *Journal of Art and Design Education*, 22(2): 183–194.

Adams, J. (2007) Artists becoming teachers: Expressions of identity transformation in a virtual forum, *International Journal of Art and Design Education*, 26(3): 264–273.

Angrosino, M. (2007) *Doing Ethnography and Observational Research*. London: SAGE Publications Ltd.

Auge, M. (1995) *Non-places: Introduction to an anthropology of super modernity*. London and New York: Verso.

Ball, S. J. and Olmedo, A. (2012) Care of the self, resistance and subjectivity under neoliberal governmentalities, *Critical Studies in Education*, 54(1): 85–96.

Beauchamp, C. and Thomas, L. (2009) Understanding teacher identity: An overview of issues in the literature and implications for teacher education, *Cambridge Journal of Education*, 39(2): 175–189.

Blackburn Miller, J. (2020) transformative learning and the arts: A literature review, *Journal of Transformative Education*, 18(4): 338–355.

Bourgault, R. and Rosamond, C. (2023) Artistic research, healing, and transformation: Shared stories of resilience, *Journal of Transformative Education*. Available at: https://doi-org.oxfordbrookes.idm.oclc.org/10.1177/15413446231154892 (accessed 12 May 2023).

Caldwell, H., Whewell, E., Bracey, P., Heaton, R., Crawford, H., and Shelley, C. (2021) Teaching on insecure foundations? Pre-service teachers in England's perceptions of the wider curriculum subjects in primary schools, *Cambridge Journal of Education*, 51(2): 231–246.

Cusimano, A. and Rowe, J. (2022) *International Connections: The Impact of UK's Departure from the European Union on the Visual Arts Sector Final Report*, a-n ,The

Artists Information. Available at: https://uk.icom.museum/international-connections-the-impact-of-the-uk-departure-from-the-european-union-on-the-visual-arts-sector/ (accessed 28 June 2022).

Gilmore, A., Dunn, B., Barker, V., et al. (2021) When policy meets place: 'Levelling Up' and the culture and creative industries, *Creative Industries Policy & Evidence Centre* blog post, NESTA. Available at: https://pec.ac.uk/blog/when-policy-meets-place (accessed 28 June 2022).

Grady, J. (2022) UCU letter to Nadhim Zahawi, Secretary of State for Education, 1 June 2022. Available at: https://www.ucu.org.uk/media/12875/Nadhim-ZahawiJune2022/pdf/Nadhi-ZahawiJune2022.pdf (accessed 27 June 2022).

Hammersley, M. (2006) Ethnography: Problems and prospects, *Ethnography and Education*, 1(1): 3–14.

Hammersley, M. and Atkinson, P. (2007) *Ethnography: Principles in Practice*. London: Routledge.

Heaton, R. and Kuan, S.C.L. (2022) A visual inquiry: Artist-teacher perceptions of art education provision in Singapore, *Studies in Art Education*, 63(2): 115–133.

Hoekstra, M. (2015) The problematic nature of the artist teacher concept and implications for pedagogical practice, *International Journal of Art and Design Education*, 34(3): 349–357.

Hoggan, C., Simpson, S., & Stuckey, H. (2009). *Creative Expression in Transformative Learning: Tools and techniques for educators of adults*. Krieger Publishing Company.

Illeris, K. (2014) *Transformative Learning and Identity*. Abingdon: Routledge.

Illeris, K. (ed.) (2017) *How We Learn: Learning and Non-Learning in School and Beyond*, 2nd ed. Abingdon: Routledge.

Irwin, R. (2004) A/r/tography, A Metonymic Métissage, in R. Irwin and A. de Cosson (eds.) *A/r/tography: Rendering self through arts-based living inquiry*, Vancouver: Pacific Educational Press.

Land, R. and Meyer, J.H.F. (2003) *Threshold Concepts and Troublesome Knowledge: linkages to ways of thinking and practising within the disciplines: occasional report 4*, ETL Project, Universities of Edinburgh, Coventry and Durham.

Lehner, D. (2022) The heroine's/hero's journey—a call for transformation? Transformative learning, archetypal patterns, and embodied knowing/learning, *Journal of Transformative Education*, 20(2): 88–104.

Milstein, D. (2010) Children as co-researchers in anthropological narratives in education, *Ethnography and Education*, 5(1): 1–15.

NSEAD (2016) *The National Society for Education in Art and Design Survey Report 2015–16* (online). Available at: https://www.nsead.org/news/newsroom/nsead-survey-report-2015-16/ (accessed 14 November 2023)

Page, T., Adams, J., and Hyde, W. (2011) Emerging: The impact of the artist teacher scheme MA on students' pedagogical and artistic practices, *European Journal of Teacher Education*, 34(3): 277–295.

Parker-Jenkins, M. (2018) Problematising ethnography and case-study: Reflections on using ethnographic techniques and researcher positioning, *Ethnography and Education*, 13(1): 18–33.

Payne, R. (2018) 11.30am on a Sunday morning: Making meanings with Mary, *International Journal of Art and Design Education*, 27(4): 560–573.

Payne, R. (2020) Shock of the new, *International Journal of Art and Design Education*, 39(4): 724–738.

Payne, R. and Hall, E. (2018) The NSEAD Survey Report 2015–16: Political reflections from two art and design educators, *International Journal of Art and Design Education*, 37(2): 167–176.

Perkins, D. (1999) The many faces of constructivism, *Educational Leadership,* 57 (3): 6–11.

Ravenstahl, M. J. and Rattay, J. (2020) Bringing the Apple and Holding up the Mirror: Liminal Space and Transformation in Visual Art Making, in J.A. Timmermans and R. Land (eds.) (2020) *Threshold Concepts on the Edge.* Leiden; Boston: Brill Sense.

Ross, C. (in draft/due 2024) Liminal space: Non-place and spatio-temporal knowing, in G. K. Erk, N. Theo and J. Jordaan, *THE SPACE OF IMAGE: Architectural Experience through Media.* Intellect Books.

Shreeve, A. (2009) 'I'd rather be seen as a practitioner, come in to teach my subject': Identity work in part-time art and design tutors, *Journal of Art and Design Education* 28(2): 151–159.

Shulman, L. (2005) Pedagogies of uncertainty, *Liberal Education,* 91(2): 18–25.

Thomson, P. and Maloy, L. (2022) *The Benefits of Art, Craft and Design Education in Schools: A Rapid Evidence Review,* The University of Nottingham.

Thornton, A. (2013) *Artist, Researcher, Teacher: A Study of Professional Identity in Art and Education.* Bristol, UK/Chicago, USA: Intellect.

Walford, G. (2009) For ethnography, *Ethnography and Education,* 4(3): 271–282.

Walmsley, B., Gilmore, A., O'Brien, D., and Torreggiani, A. (2022) *Culture in Crisis: Impacts of Covid-19 on the UK cultural sector and where we go from here.* Leeds: Centre for Cultural Value, © Centre for Cultural Value 2022.

Wild, C. (2022) *Artist-teacher Practice and the Expectation of an Aesthetic Life: Creative being in the neoliberal classroom.* London and New York: Routledge.

Williamson, G. (2021) *Guidance to the Office for Students — Allocation of the Higher Education Teaching Grant funding in the 2021 -22 Financial Year,* Department for Education letter. Available at: https://www.officeforstudents.org.uk/media/a3814453-4c28-404a-bf76-490183867d9a/rt-hon-gavin-williamson-cbe-mp-t-grant-ofs-chair-smb.pdf (accessed 27 June 2022).

Part 2

Pedagogies

4 Crafting and cultivating an international repertoire of artist teacher pedagogies

Rebecca Heaton

Several factors like locality, awareness and willingness influence how an artist teacher crafts, cultivates, and nurtures their understanding and use of pedagogy. This chapter voices how artist teacher pedagogies need crafting, cultivating, and nurturing in response to personal, social and institutional expectations and changes in art education. The chapter also connects pedagogic theory and artist teacher experiences to show how, why and where pedagogy has importance for the artist teacher. International experiences with artist teacher pedagogy help demonstrate multiplicity in the ways pedagogy can be approached by artist teachers, and intersections between different disciplines, contexts and partners help illuminate how the artist teacher pedagogic skill set is unique. This chapter contributes artist teacher and pedagogically-orientated insights into artist teacher pursuits that position artist teachers as an asset to the development of learning provision in different contexts.

Crafting and cultivating pedagogies: An introduction

Pedagogy, 'the art and science of teaching, as professional practice and academic study' (UNESCO 2022: 1), is a vast, complex, and widely deliberated concept and act in education. Manifestations of pedagogy are extensive. For example, researchers have enquired into spatial pedagogies to map meanings in educational contexts (Lim, O'Halloran and Podlasov 2012), pedagogies of silence which consider conscious reasons educators may abstain from interventions (Ollin 2008) and critical pedagogies that can destabilise notions of power concerning race, gender, class, or identity (Talukder and Samuel 2018). Pedagogies can be considered in relation to different sites like schools, universities, the home, museums, galleries and in communities and they can be connected to teachers' and researchers' identities, interests, and contexts

(Meager and Hall 2019). Scholars have proposed that educational change is needed to support educators to be proactive and open possibilities for learning about and using pedagogy that takes account of conceptual progress and uses knowledge to stimulate critical and creative reasoning (Hoadley et al. 2019). Therefore, as educators become inclusive in their use of pedagogy (Veck 2014), they should also consider how they can be creative with it, for what purpose, and its effects and affects on the people, policies, practices and communities connected to it. For example, Symeonidou (2022) discusses how engaging with disability art narratives can educate for inclusion, anti-oppressive pedagogy and curricular development. To consider pedagogy in this interconnected way is not easy, but it is necessary if pedagogy is to engage with educational complexities, with diverse student groups and with change – in knowledge(s), culture(s), time(s) and space(s).

Scholarly work concerning pedagogy in art education is vast and intersected. In the recent three-volume *International Encyclopaedia of Art and Design Education* (Hickman et al. 2019), Volume III is dedicated to exploring pedagogy. Art education pedagogy is approached from international perspectives, it is considered with different art forms, alongside curriculums and policies, in varied contexts and from methodological stances. These scholarly pedagogic intersections demonstrate how pedagogies have unique and malleable qualities, how pedagogy can be interpreted in a shared and individual manner and evolve in relation to thoughts, experiences and knowledge. This consideration is important when thinking about how pedagogies can be crafted and cultivated in art education, the aim of this chapter. This is because when artist teachers problematise pedagogy they approach it from different starting points: with diversity in their questions and desires, and with different experiences and exposure to pedagogy in their teaching, research and art practice. Artist teachers unite art and education pedagogically in multiple contexts – psychological, historical and contextual, for example. It is also likely that as artist teachers' lives and careers progress, their understanding, use and critique of pedagogy will alter. Therefore, in this chapter I share insights into factors that may influence the craft and cultivation of artist teacher pedagogies. I share stories, conversations and experiences that have influenced the pedagogic crafting of the 'self' and 'other.' I propose the idea that pedagogic cultivation is an important conscious, cognitive, and connective competency for artist teachers to learn, to be at ease with the complexities and changes that affect pedagogy in multifaceted domains.

Insights into artist teacher pedagogy

I define and position the artist teacher, like Hoekstra (2015), Daichendt (2009) and Scott (2014), as individuals who are creative, authentic and reflexive while teaching and making art. They perform, use, engage and sometimes discover pedagogy to generate knowledge and experiences which facilitate learning.

Artist teacher pedagogies distinctly afford authentic learning because they unite teaching and contemporary art while engendering criticality (Hoekstra 2015). Artist teacher pedagogies are also art forms and spaces where 'teacher' and 'artist' knowledges and practices can complement one another and intersect (Selkrig 2017). In this section, I consequently share insights into personal engagements with artist teacher pedagogies to demonstrate their complexity, individuality, influence and possibility to develop learning.

I am an academic artist teacher who has worked in art education for almost 20 years, nationally and internationally; at present I am based in Singapore. Through my career I have worked in and with early arts, primary, secondary and higher education institutions. I have also worked in and partnered with museums and galleries, charities, industry organizations and artists. Through these artist teacher experiences (Kenny and Morrisey 2021), the way that I have interpreted, used, critiqued and researched pedagogy has evolved, and this continues. From experience, I have gained awareness that artist teachers encounter and engage with pedagogies in several ways. For example, they may use pedagogies that are often associated with specific subjects like drawing pedagogy in art (Riley 2021) or socio-constructivist pedagogies in education (Dias 2019: 5). These are explored in universal and creative ways, often in ways that the academic authors intend but society sometimes challenges. The capability the artist teacher frequently affords is their expertise, as an artist and educator, to merge multiple domains due to their ability, openness and willingness to disrupt and apply pedagogy differently (Hoekstra 2015). This action engenders variety and forges space for new and engaging learning possibilities across contexts.

Another insight I can share where artist teachers engage with pedagogic concerns is in school curricular and training. In Singapore, the primary and secondary art education curriculum (Ministry of Education (MOE) 2018a: 20; MOE 2018b: 19) is designed around a model of pedagogic practices which focus on generating a positive classroom culture, effective lesson preparation, enactment, assessment and feedback, application and reflection. These are pedagogic practices which artist teachers (working in formal and informal settings, like schools, galleries, prison service, enrichment centres, etc.) could use to underpin and design learning opportunities. They are universal pedagogic practices that in the curriculum model are intended to support art educators and artist teachers to implement pedagogy with some degree of continuity across learning experiences. These pedagogic practices are advantageous in some respects; they show awareness of pedagogic underpinning to elicit quality learning and progression, they help reduce disparity in experience and provision, and provide a scaffold for lesson design. Their implementation could also be seen to reduce individuality and creativity in lesson design or experience. However, in Singapore all school-based art teachers are trained through an artist teacher model, where they learn and practise as an artist as well as an educator, at the same institution. This training provision ensures that all schools have artist teacher expertise, and artist teachers with knowledge of a range of pedagogies and pedagogical practices. Schools can also en~

artists, vendors and other forms of artist teachers to enhance and support their art offering. An implication of such an in-house training model could be that artist teachers may only be knowledgeable of the pedagogic discourses and narratives that they encounter, so if these are not regularly updated, internationalised or considerate of diverse communities, then pedagogic development could be affected. However, artist teachers trained outside of Singapore can work in local Ministry educational settings if their qualifications meet certain criteria.

The engagements with and insights into pedagogy that I have as an artist teacher challenge my own identity, ideas and outputs. If you are pursuing an artist teacher journey, now may be a good time to consider what pedagogy means to you. What role does it play in your being or practice? And how open are you to crafting and cultivating pedagogy alongside your changing self, circumstances and time? Asking questions about your connection to pedagogy can help you become more confident in your understanding and use of it.

Artist teachers and art educators can sometimes feel vulnerable in their encounters with pedagogy. They may feel vulnerable that they are not using or applying the 'latest' pedagogies in their practice, or in the right way. Confusion can also exist about multiple pedagogies emerging in one experience, lesson or scheme of work and artist teachers may not know which to prioritise or give credit to. Artist teachers may also be pressured to implement a pedagogic strategy because policy, leadership, research or another colleague has reported its effectiveness. In contrast, having insight into one's artist teacher use of pedagogy can afford confidence in the pedagogical decisions made. It can help artist teachers to see how their pedagogic understandings and use evolve, and it may assist them to identify space for change.

When artist teachers learn about pedagogy and its influence, they can gain some clarity about its relationship with personal artist teacher identities and experiences or their individual life worlds (Barritt 2021). Life worlds are a means to develop one's self-becoming with the world through consideration of person–environment relations. Such understanding and exploration can be advantageous for the artist teacher because they can enter and invite learners to enter a dialogue with the world, a key feature of art education's purpose (Biesta 2017). Through considering the pedagogy of, and in, their life worlds an artist teacher can perhaps also make more informed judgements about pedagogies of relevance to artistic and educational provision. This entity is needed when there is increasing documentation suggesting that the content, extent and quality of art education provision is disconnected or not appropriate to learners' lived experiences (Payne and Hall 2018; Heaton and Chan 2022; Thomson and Maloy 2022: 3).

Artist teachers are also experiencing a time where multiple pedagogies exist in art education: queer pedagogy (Millet 2019), loving pedagogy (Grimmer 2021), relational pedagogy (Irwin and O'Donoghue 2012), creative pedagogy (Lin 2011; Selkrig and Keamy 2017), nature pedagogy (Warden 2019), new materialist pedagogy (Bobadilla 2018; Shin and Yang 2021) and student-centred pedagogy (Orr et al. 2014), to name a few. Such diversity and choice can make selecting, using and navigating pedagogy challenging, but equally this breadth presents opportunity for experimentation and change. The challenge for the artist teacher is to explore some of these pedagogies in ways appropriate to their own and others' life worlds and learning pursuits.

Multiple approaches, like the physical and digital (Heaton 2019; Edwards et al. 2021), are being used to enact and explore pedagogies in art education. Academics have proposed approaches like storytelling (Deniston-Trochta 2003), dance (Parrish 2016) and a/r/tography (Barney 2019) can assist pedagogic exploration because they can affect, untangle, express and facilitate life worlds (connections between people, their identities, experiences and environments). These approaches, which may assist pedagogic understanding, are developmental. Often, they embody artistry (Dunn and Stinson 2011), reflexivity, problem-solving or curation to gain knowledge about pedagogy – practices which artist teachers are often competent in (Scott 2014; Hoekstra 2015). If artist teachers explore and reflect on their use of pedagogy, which many may already do, their pedagogic use and understanding would become more purposeful in the learning profession, perhaps creating more diverse and appropriate experiences for learners in art education.

Pedagogy is complex – engage to cultivate it

By engaging the artist teacher practices of risk, vulnerability and reflexivity (Grushka 2005; Kamler and Thomson 2006; Sayers 2016) artist teachers can reveal complexities associated with pedagogy, like its multifaceted role, position and use. Pedagogic engagement can help to delve into its contribution to and development of theory, teaching, artistry and research. Pedagogy can be approached from many perspectives: the artist, teacher or academic, or at different levels, policy, political or school, for example. The pedagogic insights I share in this chapter hopefully show that engagement with artist teacher pedagogy is accessible. As an artist teacher, you will engage with pedagogy, so afford time and space (Kenny and Morrisey 2021) to consider how past, current and future pedagogy is shaping the provision, practice, or research you are involved in. Pedagogy can also be explored by engaging in a reflective sketchbook (Hall 2020), which could take the form of a creative digital or physical space, a patchwork, blog, or website, for example. It acts as a space where the artist teacher can enquire, take risks and reflect about their pedagogic understanding and use through making.

When engaging with pedagogy, the artist teacher needs to consider their understanding of other postmodern pedagogies, like visual and material culture, community-based art education or eco-pedagogies (Bertling and Moore 2021) that intersect with artist teacher pedagogies. These are pedagogies that shift art and education's focus towards moral, ethical, environmental and socially just principles. With such shifts, be they ontological, epistemological, methodological, or pedagogical, in art, education and artist teacher practice (Barritt 2021) there is a need to look at these complexities and their relationships with pedagogic provision to ensure future provision is cultivated critically and purposefully, to enable learners to dialogue with their current and evolving worlds.

Through personal engagements with pedagogy alongside artist teachers in the United Kingdom and Singapore, I have become aware that factors like mindset, locality, sociality, willingness and transition shape pedagogic repertoires. I now share some empirical stories of pedagogy being crafted, engaged with, and cultivated to demonstrate how an openness to pedagogic change can be beneficial to artist teacher and learner growth and development. The first experience I share was encountered with primary art educators in Singapore.

An international perspective

In a conversation about art education pedagogy I had with three experienced artist teachers in May 2022, during a secondment experience at a Ministry primary school in Singapore, pedagogies were likened to trends. Blended learning, design pedagogy, problem-based learning and inquiry-based learning were recognised as pedagogies applicable to art education. They were also seen as principles and practices that required implementation in art education to satisfy institutional and policy-orientated expectations or requirements that were perhaps fostered to pursue educational fashions or indicate pedagogic success. The artist teachers involved in this discussion critically questioned whether being an art educator was about using knowledge of multiple pedagogies, in and beyond their discipline of expertise, autonomously to achieve competency in teaching and learning. They also questioned whether art education was now subject to factory-orientated provision where the teacher implemented pedagogy robotically and systematically as instructed. The artist teachers suggested that the competent educator would professionally select and manipulate pedagogies to suit the art education experience they found themselves in, acknowledging that some pedagogies like Inquiry Based Learning (which is a base for the art education curriculum in Singapore (MOE 2018a, 2018b)) already provide foundations in art education, but that these can be layered with and enhanced by using pedagogies individual teachers are aware of. The artist teachers expressed that it is difficult for educators to claim their pedagogic use because of the fluidity and complexity in how pedagogy is implemented.

What is interesting about this case is recognition of pedagogies as malleable, layered and interconnected entities subject to critique, adaptation and exploitation. Here, artist teachers are often expected to claim use of pedagogies without full consideration of how or why they connect with learning values, experiences and scenarios. Part of engaging, crafting and cultivating pedagogies, therefore, involves voicing responsibility for their use. To support mobilisation, artist teachers may benefit from greater opportunities to enquire and dialogue about pedagogic use to develop competency and confidence regarding art education, an entity this chapter supports. If such provision can occur, and in some settings it already does, then artist teachers will be positioned to challenge rhetoric and implement and manipulate pedagogies in their subject in the best interests of their learners, not just as means to conform.

International case studies

To show how artist teachers engage with and cultivate pedagogy I draw on two cases of primary art provision in Singapore. One celebrates a drawing encounter at a Ministry (local) school and another honours provision at an International school. Both cases involve artist teachers crafting pedagogy differently.

Case A

To share the pedagogy of Case A, I draw on Figure 4.1, which details two children's drawn responses to market encounters which connect to the 1978 artwork *Drying Salted Fish* produced by Singaporean and Nanyang artist Cheong Soo Pieng (https://www.nationalgallery.sg/gallerykids/pdf/explore/Awesome-Art-Drying-Salted-Fish.pdf). The artwork *Drying Salted Fish* is created in Chinese ink and watercolour on cloth and depicts a scene likely encountered at a local fishing village. The artwork is also featured on Singapore's $50 note and its presence is believed to pay homage to the time when Singapore was part of Malaysia.

To arrive at the drawings shown in Figure 4.1, a class of 6–7 year olds in a Ministry school had been guided by their artist teacher through the enquiry-based learning pedagogy, to explore and feedback about Cheong Soo Pieng's artwork. To do so, the children were encouraged to dialogically enquire into the artwork making connections to prior work produced (watercolour paintings of fish), images of real fish, a shared text *The Rainbow Fish* by Marcus Pfister and their own experiences of catching, eating and buying fish. After, the children wrote about these connections in their sketchbooks, using the 'see,

Figure 4.1 May 2022, A4 drawings of market encounters, by Primary 1 children (age 6–7)

think, wonder' thinking routine as a prompt. They were also asked to use their visual voice to draw an expression of the artwork in the present day.

When I observed this lesson, several pedagogic entities struck me. While using Inquiry Based Learning (IBL) as a pedagogic base, the learning experience unfolding also connected to Brent Wilson's (2020) ideas that there are three sites of visual culture for children's art education: 1) the child initiated space – which in Figure 4.1 could be shown by the children's imagination, memories or experiences shopping at supermarkets Shen Siong, Fair Price and at Hawker stalls, or through their interest in a culturally fostered Manga style of drawing; 2) the adult initiated (school) space – which could relate to the IBL pedagogic choice, the artwork selected for study and the way the learning sequence was enacted; and 3) the collaborative space could be seen through the children's interactions with each other, the artworks, stories and through the sociality of people and spaces depicted in the drawings – the markets, families and expressions as possibilities. The artist teacher, knowingly or unknowingly, had engaged pedagogic layering in her teaching. Several competencies associated with artist teachers had been engaged: pedagogic creativity, process driven experiences and connections to artworlds (Hoekstra 2015).

Learners had opportunities to explore and dialogue into and between different visual cultural spaces in the same one-hour lesson. A pedagogy of cognitive curation (Heaton 2021; Heaton and Chan 2023) also appeared because opportunities were provided, through links between artworks, discussion, making and sharing, that facilitated knowledge transfer between cognate, verbal and visual domains. In facilitating links for cognitive curation, the artist teacher demonstrated an ability to craft pedagogy in a way that sees educational and artistic pedagogies as complementary (Selkrig 2017).

What felt important about this artist teacher's lesson was that enacting artist teacher pedagogy brought the cognitive depth of art learning forward. Often cognition is not always seen, valued, or reflected on in art education. Thankfully, I have heard several artist teachers say, 'Please experience my lesson, do not judge the learning on outputs.' Such sentiments are important because I hope, as this case has modelled, artist teacher pedagogies and art education learning are complex and deep. Learning depth can be influenced by our pedagogic engagement and cultivation.

Case B

The pedagogic example shared next involved a group of five trainee artist teachers working with an international school in Singapore for three one-hour sessions integrating art and literary learning. The experience was designed to enable the artist teachers to a) experience pedagogy in an international school and b) to afford freedom to craft a thematic pedagogic experience. In consultation with the school, the artist teachers delivered three lessons to Years 4, 5 and 6 (pupils aged 8–11) informed by thinking of drawing as a contemporary pedagogy, that facilitates the transformation of mental concepts (ideas for artworks based on world experiences) into a visible form for sharing (Riley 2021: 337).

In their literacy lessons, the children involved were studying the texts *Podkin* by Kieran Larwood (Year 4), *Brightstorm* by Vashti Hardy (Year 5) and *Cogheart* by Peter Bunzl (Year 6). The artist teachers used drawing to challenge the children's 'complacency of everyday seeing' in the texts, so their understanding of the text and worldly experiences 'may be construed with flexibility resulting in fresh insights, understanding new knowledge' (Riley 2021: 328). Through the pedagogic enactment that connected art and literacy using drawing, the children produced the responses in Figure 4.2.

I now share how the experience provided new insights, understanding and knowledge for the children and artist teachers by connecting again to Wilson's (2020) three sites of visual cultural learning.

In the child-initiated space, all year groups used drawing to imagine, dialogue about and reimagine characters, objects, scenes and compositions from the texts learnt about. In doing so, they created new life worlds – fabulous resources for narratives, dialogues, stories and artworks to come. The artist teachers had the privilege, through pedagogic enactment, to enter this child-initiated space where they applied a pedagogy of listening (Chung 2022) to access the children's ideas – listening and seeing thinking.

The artist teachers formed adult-initiated spaces through their decisions to use drawing pedagogically to engage with the texts being studied and to collate the drawings as a collaborative cross-year-group set of dioramas. The creation of this pedagogic (adult (artist teacher) initiated) space, developed as a collaborative place for reciprocal learning between the child space and adult space. The artist teachers and children could forge and curate knowledge in this third collaborative space. For example, when compositions were formed (drawn characters, scenes and objects were joined together) and displayed in

Figure 4.2 March 2022, Collaborative dioramas depicting literary texts, by Primary Key Stage 2 Pupils (age 8–11)

a communal school space (physically and online) for community-sharing. In this case, the artist teachers crafted pedagogy authentically uniting the pedagogy of drawing (Riley 2021) in the educational setting (Hoekstra 2015) while engendering partnership (Kenny and Morrisey 2021). Children in and across year groups dialogued about their texts, drawings and art techniques, taking on artist teacher personas themselves. Some children continued drawing at home and further developed the display. A community of pedagogic learning evolved through this experience; the artist teachers, educators, learners, and parents shared a learning dialogue. If artist teachers can cultivate pedagogic experiences with this level of influence, then they certainly have a unique skill-set that learning settings need.

Nurture pedagogy: A conclusion for the artist teacher

In this chapter, I have shared several ways that artist teachers can engage with pedagogy. However, in 2017 Dennis Atkinson, an Emeritus Professor of Art Education, proposed a pedagogy without criteria, a means of experiencing art education where pedagogy can remain unjustified in favour of experiencing the force of art itself. Thus, allowing teachers and learners to use art to become, transform, explore with relevance, and engage in artistic adventures. In a sense, Atkinson's (2017) view counters the need to cultivate pedagogic awareness I have discussed. What Atkinson suggests is that when teachers use pedagogy, perhaps we can constrain learners and overlook the importance of how art matters or affords meaning. In crafting and cultivating pedagogy, maybe there is a need to sometimes negotiate pedagogic spaces without boundaries, to encounter new pedagogic adventures in the pursuit of knowledge. Such pedagogic adventures are necessary because of a need for international, local and glocal (interconnected global and local issues) pedagogic provision to assist student mobility, accessibility, inclusion, co-existence and de-colonisation (Gupta and Tan 2019; Milatovic et al. 2018). Artist teachers need to hear learner voices to ensure provision occurs in ways appropriate and valuable to the learners. Artist teachers also need to reclaim and rediscover the art (of pedagogy) in teaching (Pearse et al. 2011) to ensure quality and thoughtful action while adding excitement and transformation to pedagogic performance.

Teaching in Singapore has raised my awareness that achieving harmonious pedagogic provision is challenging. Teachers sometimes need to satisfy local desires (perhaps from leaders or parents) to provide education with a specific (perhaps culturally conservative) emphasis that is highly productive, while offering provision that uses perceived western (or more global) pedagogic norms, which locate learners holistically and centrally in educational provision. Academics (Bautista et al. 2021; Yang et al. 2021) suggest Singapore operates in a third hybrid space where coexistence of western and Asian pedagogic theories occur to enable glocalised pedagogic and practice transformation to take place. When embarking on pedagogic adventures in art education, which explore international life worlds, artist teachers need to learn, dialogue about and if necessary, work to implement or disrupt local, global or glocal norms or expectations in the interests of their learners' education. Doing so can make vulnerability surface. One must, therefore, draw on their professionalism, resilience, and knowledge to generate pedagogic ripples that nurture new cultivations of pedagogy.

The need to nurture pedagogy is not a new idea. Hayes (2008) wrote about the need in early childhood and teacher education to integrate spaces between care and education while nurturing interaction to reform teaching. She reminded readers that educator calibre and training are determinants of quality provision (p.437). Tsyrlina-Spady and Renn (2020) also edited a book regarding nurturing, care, respect and trust as transformational educational pedagogy. If artist teachers can nurture their pedagogic pursuits (which they may be starting by reading this book) then professionally they will be contributing to pedagogic advancement. This is because, as Haley (2021) suggests in his article about walking and ecological arts pedagogy, you will not be walking alone. Through dialogues, interactions, making and teaching about, experiencing and reflecting on artist teacher pedagogies, a pedagogic adventure will be encountered (Atkinson 2017). One that will engage you in life worlds (Barritt 2021) to better understand your pedagogic self. You may even become informed about pedagogies of mattering (Gravett et al. 2021), that consider how objects, bodies and spaces interact relationally to create caring and nurturing educational environments. Artist teachers, please craft, cultivate and nurture a pedagogic repertoire that is unique to you, your learners, and the time, space and climate you educate and create in.

References

Atkinson, D. (2017) Without criteria: Art and learning and the adventure of pedagogy, *International Journal of Art and Design Education*, 36(2): 141–152.

Barney, D. (2019) A/r/tography as a pedagogical strategy: Entering somewhere in the middle of becoming artist, *International Journal of Art and Design Education*, 38(3): 618–626.

Barritt, L. (2021) (Re)Considering pedagogy – Entangled ontology in a complex age: Abstraction pedagogy and the critical pedagogical importance of art education for other discipline areas, *International Journal of Art and Design Education*, 40(4): 784–793.

Bautista, A., Bull, R., Ng, E.L., and Lee, K. (2021) 'That's just impossible in my kindergarten.' Advocating for 'glocal' early childhood curriculum frameworks, *Policy Futures in Education*, 19(2): 155–174.

Bertling, J., and Moore, T. (2021) The U.S. K–12 art education curricular landscape: A nationwide survey, *Studies in Art Education*, 62(1): 23–46.

Biesta, G. (2017) *Letting art teach: Art education beyond Joseph Beuys*. Arnhem: ArtEZ Press.

Bobadilla, M.P. (2018) Círculo de investigación artística: New materialist pedagogies of resistance, *International Journal of Education Through Art*, 14(1): 59–78.

Chung, K.D. (2022) A dialogical artmaking space: Cultivating a pedagogy of listening in early childhood art education, *Studies in Art Education*, 63(3): 188–201.

Daichendt, G.J. (2009) Redefining the artist-teacher, *Art Education*, 62(5): 33–38.

Deniston-Trochta, G. M. (2003) The meaning of storytelling as pedagogy, *Visual Arts Research*, 29(57): 103–108.

Dias, I.S. (2019). Socio-constructivist pedagogies: The interaction as the foundation of the child's development and learning, *Contemporary Themes in Early Childhood Education and International Educational Modules*, DOI:10.18690/978-961-286-269-5

Dunn, J., and Stinson, M. (2011) Not without the art!! The importance of teacher artistry when applying drama as pedagogy for additional language learning, research in drama education, *The Journal of Applied Theatre and Performance*, 16(4): 617–633.

Edwards, J., Caldwell, H., and Heaton, R. (2021) *Art in the Primary School: Creating art in the real and digital world*. London: Routledge.

Gravett, K., Taylor, C., and Fairchild, N. (2021) Pedagogies of mattering: Re-conceptualising relational pedagogies in higher education, *Teaching in Higher Education*, DOI: 10.1080/13562517.2021.1989580.

Grimmer, T. (2021) *Developing a loving pedagogy in the early years: How love fits with professional practice*. London: Routledge.

Grushka, K. (2005) Artists as reflective self learners and cultural communicators: An exploration of the qualitative aesthetic dimension of knowing self through reflective practice in artmaking, *Reflective Practice: International and Multidisciplinary Perspectives*, 6(3): 353–366.

Gupta, A. and Tan, G. (2019) Globalisation, human capital development and cultural ecology, in G. Tan, G. Wilgus and A. Gupta (eds.), *Investment in Early Childhood Education in a Globalised World*. New York: Palgrave Macmillan, 3–23.

Haley, D. (2021) A walk on the wild side: Steps towards an ecological arts pedagogy, *International Journal of Education Through Art*, 17: 135–152, DOI: https://doi.org/10.1386/eta_00054_1

Hall, E. (2020) 'Beanz Meanz Professional Learning': Beginning a pedagogical reflective sketchbook, *International Journal of Education Through Art*, 16(3): 372–379.

Hayes, N. (2008) Teaching matters in early educational practice: The case for a nurturing pedagogy, *Early Education and Development*, 19(3): 430–440.

Heaton, R. (2019) Digital art pedagogy in the United Kingdom, in R. Hickman, K. Freedman, E. Hall and N. Meager (eds.), *International Encyclopedia of Art and Design Education*. London: Sage.

Heaton, R. (2021) Art education and cognition, *British Educational Research Journal*, 47(5): 1323–1339.

Heaton, R. and Chan, S. (2022) A visual inquiry: Artist teacher perceptions of art education provision in Singapore, *Studies in Art Education*, 63(2): 115–133.

Heaton, R. and Chan, S. (2023, in review) *Curating cognition in the teaching-research-practice nexus of higher degree art education*.

Hickman, R. Hall, E. and Meager, N. (2019) *International Encyclopaedia of Art and Design Education*. John Wiley and Sons.

Hoadley, U., Sehgal-Cuthbert, A., Barrett, B., and Morgan, J. (2019) After the knowledge turn? Politics and pedagogy, *The Curriculum Journal*, 30(2): 99–104.

Hoekstra, M. (2015) The problematic nature of the artist teacher concept and implications for pedagogical practice. *The International Journal of Art and Design Education*, 34(3): 349–357.

Irwin, R. and O'Donoghue, D. (2012) Encountering pedagogy through relational art practices, *International Journal of Art and Design Education*, 31(3): 221–236.

Kamler, B.A and Thomson, P. (2006) *Helping doctoral students write: Pedagogies for supervision*. London: Routledge.

Kenny, A. and Morrissey, D. (2021) Negotiating teacher-artist identities: 'Disturbance' through partnership, *Arts Education Policy Review*, 122(2): 93–100.

Lim, F.V., O'Halloran, K.L. and Podlasov, A (2012) Spatial pedagogy: Mapping meanings in the use of classroom space, *Cambridge Journal of Education*, 42(2): 235–251.

Lin, Y. S. (2011) Fostering creativity through education – A conceptual framework of creative pedagogy, *Creative Education*, 2, 149–155.

Meager, N., and Hall., E. (2019) Introduction, in R.D Hickman et al. (eds.), *International Encyclopedia of Art and Design Education*, London: Wiley, 1191–1211.

Milatovic, M., Spoto, S., and Wånggren, L. (2018) International education, educational rights and pedagogy: Introduction, *International Education Journal: Comparative Perspectives*, 17(1): 1–6.

Millet, T. (2019) Queering the art classroom: Queering matters, *The International Journal of Art and Design Education*, 38(4): 809–822.

Ministry of Education, Singapore (2018a) Art syllabus: Primary one to six. Student Development Curriculum Division (online). Available at: https://www.moe.gov.sg/-/media/files/primary/2018_primary_art_syllabus (accessed 22 September 2022)

Ministry of Education, Singapore (2018b) Art syllabus: Lower Secondary. Student Development Curriculum Division (online). Available at: https://www.moe.gov.sg/-/media/files/secondary/syllabuses/arts-ed/2018_lowersec_art_syllabus.ashx-?la=en&hash=94062FB0CA596094D082963CB9986A0A5C9CCB95 (accessed 22 September 2022).

Ollin, R. (2008) Silent pedagogy and rethinking classroom practice: Structuring teaching through silence rather than talk, *Cambridge Journal of Education*, 38(2): 265–280.

Orr, S., Yorke, M., and Blair, B. (2014) 'The answer is brought about from within you': A student-centred perspective on pedagogy in art and design, *International Journal of Art and Design Education*, 33(1): 32–45.

Parrish, M. (2016) Toward transformation: Digital tools for online dance pedagogy, *Arts Education Policy Review*, 117(3), 168–182.

Payne, R., and Hall, E. (2018) The NSEAD Survey Report 2015–16: Political reflections from two art and design educators, *International Journal of Art and Design Education*, 37(2): 167–176.

Pearse, H., Snider, A., and Taylor, C. (2011) The lost art of pedagogy, *Canadian Review of Art Education: Research Issue*, 38(1): 5–16.

Riley, H. (2021) A contemporary pedagogy of drawing, *Journal of Visual Art Practice*, 20(4): 323–349.

Sayers, E. (2016) The artist teacher, *Goldsmiths Research Online* (online). Available at: https://research.gold.ac.uk/id/eprint/23709/1/Sayers_TheArtistTeacher.pdf (accessed 22 September 2022).

Scott, L. (2014) 'Digging deep': self-study as a reflexive approach to improving my practice as an artist, researcher, and teacher, *Perspectives in Education*, 32(2): 69–88.

Selkrig, M. (2017) Teachers adopting artists' pedagogies: Is it really that simple? *International Journal of Education Through Art*, 13(3): 333–347.

Selkrig, M., and Keamy, K. (2017) Creative pedagogy: A case for teachers' creative learning being at the centre, *Teaching Education*, 28(3): 317–332.

Shin, R., and Yang, X. (2021) A Daoist pedagogy encountering new materialism in art education, *Studies in Art Education*, 62(3): 236–249.

Symeonidou, S. (2022) Teacher education for inclusion and anti-oppressive curriculum development: Innovative approaches informed by disability arts and narratives, *International Journal of Inclusive Education*, 26(7): 659–673.

Talukder, A. and Samuel, M. (2018) Problematising problematisation: Insights from critical pedagogy in a writing lesson in Bangladesh, *Cambridge Journal of Education*, 48(2): 213–226.

Thomson, P. and Maloy, L. (2022) The benefits of art, craft, and design education in schools: A Rapid Evidence Review (Online). Available at: https://www.nsead.org/files/6f85ab8587bc53ce653702da1cc15690.pdf (accessed 22 September 2022).

Tsyrlina-Spady, T. Renn, P. (2020) *Nurture, care, respect, and trust: Transformative pedagogy inspired by Janusz Korczak*. Myers Education Press.

UNESCO International Bureau of Education (2022) Pedagogy (Online). Available at: http://www.ibe.unesco.org/en/glossary-curriculum-terminology/p/pedagogy (accessed 19 September 2022).

Veck, W. (2014) Inclusive pedagogy: Ideas from the ethical philosophy of Emmanuel Levinas, *Cambridge Journal of Education*, 44(4): 451–464.

Warden, C. (2019) Nature pedagogy: Education for sustainability, *Childhood Education*, 95(6): 6–13.

Wilson, B. (2020) Art classrooms, comic markets, and the digital cosmos: Children's visual worlds as pedagogical spaces, in R.D Hickman et al. (eds.), *International Encyclopedia of Art and Design Education*. London: Wiley.

Yang, W., Li, H. and Ang, L. (2021) Early childhood curriculum policies and practices in Singapore: The case of glocalisation, *Policy Futures in Education*, 19(2): 131–138.

5 Artist teacher practice: Maintaining the role of the facilitator

Dionne Freeman

Introduction

For a number of years, I have worked as a practising artist alongside my various teaching roles. I describe my professional identity as an artist and arts facilitator. I have been very fortunate to work with artist teachers in various capacities including running arts consultancy, continuing professional development (CPD) and creative courses in educational settings. One of my long term roles has been working as a tutor on an Artist Teacher MA course in an English university. This involves delivering academic content in accessible, visual and inspiring ways: challenging artist teachers to spend time with their artist identity, unpicking and discovering the artist self, and examining how the significance of their artist self impacts their profession as a teacher. On the course I share my experiences of managing the tensions between making and teaching. Personal strategies for sustaining my art-making include reflective practice, maintaining a routine, creating an effective studio environment and nurturing an awareness of the complexities of audience. I believe that it is this experience that helps me be an effective facilitator for other artist teachers.

Through this chapter I aim to draw on my personal experience as both a practising artist and a teacher of artist teachers to explore how to maintain a visual practice, something many of my students struggle with initially. As a visual artist I have a need to share how I experience the physical landscapes surrounding me through my painting; it is this same need to share that drives my desire to teach and impart knowledge. I am interested in how artist teachers adopt the wealth of arts tools used within their teaching into their arts practice to ensure continued making and maintain an authentic sense of self. Practical approaches like sustaining a routine, allocating dedicated time to make and having a supportive working community are essential. However, recognising key environmental and personal elements that contribute to artistic practice are also fundamental to understanding how the artist teacher can ensure progression.

I am interested in how as teachers and learners, artist teachers often underestimate existing skills and knowledge. This then inhibits how artist teachers utilise these skills to be able to unlock future learning, attitudes and approaches. During my time teaching on the artist teacher MA I have observed how students, having a renewed sense of connection and ownership of their artist identity in the classroom, can enable making in the studio. Continuing to nurture and respect one's perspective of making can be complicated. Establishing practical elements of an artist teacher's practice alongside reflexivity and awareness of potential barriers inhibiting engagement will enable deeper understanding and ultimately progression of both artist and teacher identities.

In addition to drawing on my lived experience, in this chapter I reflect on the implications of artist pedagogy for artist teachers from the viewpoint of a practising artist. Through this exploration of pedagogical impact I identify the potential barriers artist teachers may face when combining teaching and making, and which factors ensure both individual wellbeing and progression of artistic practice. How can artist teachers use these approaches to achieve and inform an authentic sense of self? Being an artist teacher is hugely complex. To navigate this I focus on how the creative self enables the artist self, which in turn nurtures the teacher self, and vice versa.

Environment and routine

A good starting point for enabling a positive artistic practice is considering how to make. In my practice, where I make and how I approach the making environment is crucial to unlocking a sustainable practice. Creating a setting with an embedded confident attitude influences how I work in the studio and is essential to my artistic practice. And I am not alone. Studio spaces are completely unique to every artist and are linked closely to their professional identity (Bain 2004); as such, they are spaces which enable the artist's unique practice. Addressing and sustaining routine can enable the artist self, which in turn maintains my role of the facilitator. From a practical perspective, environment and routine intertwine; in this sense studio becomes a site for action where I inhabit the space both physically and mentally (Hannon 2014). For example, it is important to recognise potential distractions within my studio to routine and to employ strategies which circumvent them.

Another important element involving environment and routine is artist community and audience (Howells and Zelnik 2009) – how I connect with others in an informal way to enrich the possibilities of my work. Spaces to make need to inspire and enable making to avoid compromising the facilitator's role However, this can become complicated, for example, when I teach artist teachers who inhabit both student and audience identities simultaneously. Building an awareness of my immediate audience and channelling their productive feedback into my practice can generate a more constructive working environment, as Blazwick (2013: 23 in Bickers and Wilson 2013) argues:

> Work might be first shared with peers while still in progress, but secondly it is presented to the art world's gatekeepers. The former might involve other

artists or friends becoming collaborators, contributing expertise or skill. It might require a discussion or simply an opinion as to which is the right ending.

How I separate the instinct to make from the exterior and interior influences that challenge and compromise those instinctive reactions needs examining. The foundations of this lie in maintaining the role of artist, assigning the respect needed for this (Bain 2004), and equipping one's self with the confidence to value and maintain making spaces in order to be productive. Artists such as Grayson Perry are uncompromising in their approach; for example, Perry's (2014: 129) routine involves protection of artist self:

All artists carry within themselves, in their own way, an indistinct glowing ball of creative energy that they have to nurse through the assault course of becoming and growing as an artist. This is a tender cargo many artists, myself included, find it hard to talk about because we move around in the atmosphere of the art world, which is often very caustic – corrosive to such a delicate organism as one's creative drive. I protect my ball of creative energy. I protect it with a shield made of jaded irony, a helmet of mischief and a breastplate of facetiousness. And I wield my carefully crafted blade of cynicism. Because the part of myself that keeps me working year after year is too vulnerable to expose fully to the glare of the world.

Another routine that I implement correlates with Cameron's (2020) recommendation to use basic tools to generate instructions for making, like a daily ritual. Cameron stipulates that definitive time for making art should become an essential routine. This made me reflect on how I allocate time for exercise or make time to fit in an unscheduled meeting and this mindset attaches the same time and importance to making; to label it as a job. This indicates a commitment to the art practice 'as a central life activity and as a publicly proclaimed profession' (Bain 2004: 172). Part of perceiving art as work involves experiencing the art of others as essential for fuelling ones' creativity and being aware of how others approach their creative practice. Drawing on their approaches can stimulate new conceptual enquiry and meaning-making (Pringle 2008). For example, Yinka Shonibare shares reflections on the role their studio plays in their work routine, embracing the possibilities of collaboration and participation:

The studio is productive for me, but not only in relation to the creation of art objects. It is divided into two parts. The top part is where I do my production meetings and my drawings and paintings. But I also have a project space, which I see as an essential part of my practice – it has a more performative element to it that involves a wider constituency and public than just having a studio where you work. I have a proposal box outside. Young artists put proposals there and I select three projects a year. The kind of old- fashioned studio where the artist works. This is a space for the exploration of ideas. It therefore has a broader remit than just my needs (Amirsadeghi et al. 2012: 320).

I often pose the question of what a making space is to my artist teacher students: what it needs to be for them – not what it should look like or what they would like it to look like, but how it will function day to day in order to enable them to create work. A making space can be a sketchbook, a space at a particular time in the classroom, or the kitchen table; the ideal is not important, but embracing the reality of artist teacher lives is. Is it our own preconceptions, our own set of rules which inhibit us from allocating studio time? Mimicking the challenges that Shonibare invites from artists, sometimes in my studio I set myself particular ingredients of media, time and layout which can inhibit my work – a way of placing limitations on my practice to create a personalised environment (Amirsadeghi et al. 2012). Whichever approach is chosen, it is crucial that artists structure their studios in ways completely suited to their needs. As I can attest, this can be an uncomfortable experience but one that cannot be compromised and has to be given respect to be productive.

Community

Networks and support are essential in maintaining a confident mindset to create work in a sustained way. Engaging with audiences and channelling their productive feedback into my practice generates a more constructive working environment (Blazwick 2012 in Amirsadeghi et al. 2012). Community is something that is a key component to the success of the Artist Teacher MA, both receiving and giving support (Payne 2020), which moves beyond the limits of one session. Trust in the community builds over time through ongoing informal and formal conversations in tutorials and through social media posts, which support content and structure of the taught sessions. Informality is key, as Block (2018: 191) argues:

> The new context, the context that restores community, is one of possibility, generosity, and gifts, rather than one of fear, mistakes, and more problem solving. Communities are human systems given form by conversations that build relatedness. The conversations that build relatedness most often occur through associational life, where citizens are unpaid and show up by choice, rather than in large systems where professionals are paid and show up by contractual agreement.

During my 14 years working with artist teachers, I have witnessed creative transformations during studio days and through support networks within year groups and across the whole community. This community is really powerful; there is power in the shared experience. The generosity of sharing ideas, materials, processes and safety engendered within these spaces provide a willingness to take risks, problem-pose and solve together. It has to be a space of support, trust and equality to enable progression.

The Programme Lead and I create the structure of this community. Through carefully planned sessions and consideration of environment we lay the foundations for continued and self-sustaining work through the artist teacher community. This includes visitors to the course, prospective candidates, students and alumni. The individual smaller year groups form close networks and support systems which provide the ethos for larger artist teacher events, and subsequently engenders community:

> Small groups have the most leverage when they meet as part of a larger gathering. At these moments, citizens experience the intimacy of the small circle and are simultaneously aware that they are part of a larger whole that shares their concerns. The small group gains power with certain kinds of conversations. To build community, we seek conversations where people show up by invitation rather than mandate, and experience an intimate and authentic relatedness (Block, 2018: 97).

In January of each year I run a session at a local museum for artist teacher students and alumni. I have observed how that ongoing conversation about one's art within a museum setting facilitates students' progress. The need to make and feel inspired by cultural stimulus like a museum visit often only happens when formalised through a group trip. In this way the MA provides permission for students to engage in culturally challenging activities, stimulating imagination and 'the ability to feel wonder and the desire to respond to what we find startling' (Tempest 2022: 5). The springboard of visiting an exhibition and/or a museum and generating exciting conversations within those spaces involves setting aside making time in response to exhibits; participants make in dialogue with visual culture while feeling inspired together. Feeling connected while being in an inclusive environment that facilitates creativity and focus, 'fully immersed in whatever occupies you, paying close attention to the details of experience' (Tempest 2022: 5), is created on the MA virtually and in person as a result.

Having the opportunity to be fully immersed with one's artwork, being fully present, can be complicated to achieve both inside and outside the structure of the artist teacher community. Artist teachers experience pressure to make artwork, which they sometimes compare to ways of working in the classroom. This complicates making as they experience tensions of being both a maker and a teacher of others who make. Likewise, the prospect of sharing work with peers on the course can also be daunting. However, it is important to recognise these tensions in order to progress. I sympathise, as feeling confident in my practice is an ongoing project, and recognising the role of audiences and the importance of sharing one's practice is another matter. When sharing, we are committing our practice as being worthy for public consumption. For Perry (2014: 10) 'the artist does not need the public to think his work is any good if they are not paying his wages or boosting his self-esteem', but for artist teachers, recognition beyond the classroom is vital. Pringle (2008: 46) asserts that artist pedagogies are underpinned by co-construction, a need to 'question and reorganise knowledge' through dialogue. However, it is the formalised experiences of public exhibition that reinforces artist identities and affirms a sense of authenticity, even if it is fraught with challenge.

> We are often told that art can't really change anything. But I think it can. It shapes our ethical landscapes; it opens us to the interior lives of others. It is a training ground for possibility. It makes plain inequalities, and it offers other ways of living. Don't you want it, to be impregnate with all that light? And what will happen if you are? (Laing 2020: 8).

I love this quote from Laing (2020). It helps me explore the question: how do I enable my own possibilities? It is a responsibility of the artist to share their way of seeing and experiencing the world. The responsibility teachers feel to share knowledge is the same responsibility artists have to share their unique perspective with others. It is a gift artists need to offer up to others even if it is challenging, which leads me to the next section on permission and barriers.

Permission and barriers

My barriers to making art include time pressures and recognising priorities. I address them through maintaining a reflective practice and practical routines. Through teaching I like to share my methods of maintaining self-awareness and practical approaches, to examine and equip artist teachers with what I call *the mindset of making*. I believe that reflective practice and self-awareness are the foundations of maintaining and sustaining the role of facilitator, as well as supporting artist teachers to identify and implement strategies to overcome common barriers they experience. This includes granting themselves permission to enable the mindset of making, which leads to confidence to make. To better understand the mindset of making, it is important to consider barriers in more detail.

I have always seen my art as a battle. First, there is a battle between my need to paint with creating space and time to paint. Then there is the battle with the painting itself. I see these barriers as situating two strands: my interior barriers, the barriers I create, and exterior barriers or those created by others or environments. When identifying their presence, both strands embody the added complication of being emotional and/ or physical. For example, lack of space could be a physical barrier and confidence to locate a suitable physical space could be an emotional or psychological barrier. Hatfield et al. (2006: 42–47) argue that a sense of failure is compounded when artist teachers fight the urge to exhibit with limited 'time and/or courage to create and show artwork'. Exterior barriers and conflict can hang on practical elements like space and carving or negotiating a time within the week to make. Once this time and space is allowed, the artist teacher is then creating a mindset which is predicated on granting oneself permission. I find building an awareness of different artists' strategies helpful and reassuring. For example, Frank Auerbach made similar observations about the ongoing struggle of making:

> I can't talk a great deal about the look of my paintings because they are really on the other side of the footlights. I find it somehow fruitless and it makes me self-conscious. Painting for me is a set of connections, a set of sensations of conflicting movements and experiences, which somehow, one hopes, has congealed or cohered or risen out of the battle into being an image that stands up for itself. I don't spend a lot of time looking at my own painting (Lampert, 2019: 9).

How I approach permission and barriers is underpinned by values I attribute to my creative and artist selves. How do I measure and justify studio time against paid work or other commitments, for example? To prioritise making and assigning more value to studio time over other demanding tasks can be conflicting (Cameron 1994). How artists assign value within the act of making, within the finished work, and then how it is presented to audiences all need to be considered. Assigning value to studio time and my art practice can often mean asserting these values with others as well as myself, whether it is with colleagues, friends or family. This is aided by confidence and self-belief, which are a whole other area of self-development!

Once artist teachers allocate time to make they are often faced with the realisation that they are not sure what their practice looks like. Artist teachers give so much to their learners that it can be difficult to know what it looks or feels like to give back to themselves. Cameron (1994: 11) talks about 'recovering creative process', noting that 'we are victims of our own internalised perfectionist, a nasty internal and eternal critic, the censor'. Sometimes the need to construct meaningful subject matter detracts from meaning already formed or partially understood. To counter this, I project a sense of what something could be rather than what it is right now. Unlocking a sense of freedom within one's working practice is empowering when striving to achieve an authentic voice. As Michael Craig-Martin (2015: 298) argues, 'the more your art reflects you, the more it will speak to other people'.

With my own painting (Figure 5.1), I found I was carrying work with me like old baggage so I started to paint over the surface of old pieces, embracing the time and legacy within the work. I was breathing in fresh perspective and embracing the present. Hodgkin (cited in Cook, 2015: 14) notices:

> To me, a picture is really finished when, in theory at least, it's as far away from me as it would be from anyone else. So that the emotion – is often extremely intense, the subject of the picture, the situation – becomes so completely turned into an object, a thing, in other words a painting, that I look at it as a painting that is being transformed.

Figure 5.1 Dionne Freeman (2022) *Dyke Hills Study*

Giving myself permission to accept that no work ever has to be finished or completed is something I regularly share with students. No piece or body of work has to define the artist.

Understanding and progression

Addressing potential barriers within my practice enables me to move forwards as an artist teacher. This is linked to the drive to make and the desire to teach, which helps me generate and maintain a sustainable practice. For me, approaching an art practice and how to make artworks is a circular process: identify – understand – progress – identify. One driver engendering this process and simultaneously underpinning artist teacher pedagogies I deliver involves recording in different ways and for different purposes. For example, my instinct is to facilitate mine and others' art practices through continued research, which stems from a need to record the visual (through my painting) and to share the experience with others. How to record and understand the visual and impart resulting skills is crucial. I recall how Berger (1972: 55) describes the painter's experience in relation to recording the nude. This helped me reconsider the experiences I record and re-create, and indicates the same drive and intent to share my experiences. Reflective practice is an essential element here; it enables an understanding of my work and myself. Reflective practice takes different forms for different artists. In my work, it takes the form of photography, sketchbooks and note-taking, which enable me to spend time with my thoughts, considering how they align with the artworks generated within my studio. This reiterates Laing's (2020: 171) observation about how portrait painter Chantal Joffe approaches subject matter: 'you can't paint reality: you can only paint your own place in it, the view from your eyes, as manifested by your own hands'.

From my privileged position of observing artist teachers I have noticed that their criteria for making is sometimes self-imposed and can restrict in a negative (rather than purposeful) way, fixing their artistic identity and their path forward. It is important to challenge this and I often ask artist teachers why they set these restrictions on their making and thinking, yet expect flexibility from their own learners. Conclusively, I also reflect on restrictions and purpose within my making: What am I making? Who is it for? Myself? Others? Reflective practice is essential for all artist teachers as these are difficult questions to answer. To support students I often talk through my approach by holding a mirror up to what I am doing and explaining why I am doing it. Likewise, I am conscious that 'the problem with reflection is that before looking in the mirror, we compose ourselves. So what we see is what we hope to see' (Tempest 2022: 13). To counter this, I encourage artist teachers to maintain ongoing conversations with myself and each other, which are essential to unlocking deeper understanding. It is generating an understanding of self through dialogue that helps generate a sustainable reflective practice, and enables artist teachers to respect and contribute to an artist teacher community. In turn, this supportive environment is fundamental in facilitating artist teacher confidence to perform the artist in the classroom. Ultimately, it is the feeling of authenticity and inner peace generated from my art practice that enables me to be a practising artist in the classroom.

Conclusion

Through the process of writing this chapter I reflect on what I would tell my artist teacher self 20 years ago. It would go something like this. I am an artist and I take myself and my practice seriously, with the same professionalism that any other career demands. My starting point then was my studio space. This has taken many different forms over the years, but as Bain (2004) argues, the importance of physical space in whatever form is the starting point to committing to an artistic practice. Beyond that, it is important to recognise potential tensions that surround me and my practice, experimenting with strategies to find out what works, and being realistic about what is possible within my routine and home/working environment. All of this is only possible if I maintain a strong sense of self. Using tools I am drawn to with ingredients like self-reflection, community, and physical and physiological spaces of support enable me to develop and address barriers that impact or inhibit my work.

Making and being able to make requires permission from the artist self, which is facilitated by confidence. Engendering that position involves a mixture of practical and psychological steps. When setting up my studio I made the decision to share part of the space with my daughters (Figures 5.2a and 5.2b). Both under seven years old, I wanted to give them the opportunity to make but to also embrace the freedom of their creative approaches, to celebrate my studio as a space of joy and experimentation, and not limit its

Figures 5.2a and 5.2b Dionne Freeman's Studio (2022)

(a) (b)

identity or what can be made in the space to just the confines of my painting and drawing. The area my girls occupy is full of drawers of materials and shelves and surfaces bursting with artwork they have created. When they make, anything is possible; the media is simply the vehicle for the idea. This energy and openness helps my art because when the making ingredients are disrupted it extends my thinking and I can re-focus on the subject matter and purpose for making differently. This concept of making ingredients is important to recognise as an artist and teacher because it can be easy to label one's practice and then become bonded by the medium worked with, instead of exploring and challenging it. So the ingredients artist teachers supply themselves with can either inhibit or enable.

Building resilience is key to sustaining and challenging an artist teacher's practice. Sustaining agency in the classroom and self-belief as an authentic artist, and feeling and remaining confident with exterior influences ever present requires courage and self-care; to not fear or separate artist and teacher, but operate in a fluid and symbiotic way is the artist teacher goal. Sharing creative processes, maintaining routines and establishing effective making environments helps artist teachers retain flexibility and 'increase[s] the likelihood that they will accomplish original work' (Csikszentmihalyi 1997: 343).

Throughout this chapter I have unpacked how myself and other artist teachers can identify and enable our artist positions. Performing the artist in the classroom helps sustain artist teacher MA students' making practices and generates their authentic artist teacher selves. Maintaining the role of the facilitator requires embracing the hugely complex and complicated roles of teacher and artist, how feeling confident within one's creativity manifests in all areas of self – in teaching and making. Upholding the role of the facilitator is ultimately about practising positive routines, preserving studio space, nurturing drive and opportunities for deep reflection on the interior and exterior factors that impact ones' ability, motivation and confidence to make. This in turn enables certainty, self-awareness and the ability to feel comfortable with one's sense of self and creative output.

References

Amirsadeghi H., Blazwick I., Cork R., and Morton T. (2012) *Sanctuary. Britain's Artists and their Studios*, London: Thames & Hudson.

Bain, A. (2004), Female Artistic Identity in Place: The Studio, *Social & Cultural Geography*, 5 (2): 171–193.

Berger, J. (1972) *Ways of Seeing*. London: Penguin Books.

Blazwick, I. (2013) Introduction, in Bickers, P. and Wilson, A. (eds) *Talking Art: Interviews with Artists Since 1976, Volume1*. Ridinghouse.

Block, P. (2018) *Community: The Structure of Belonging*. Oakland: Berrett-Koehler Publishers, Inc.

Cameron, J. (1994) *The Artist's Way*. London: Souvenir Press.

Cameron, J. (2020) *The Artist's Way: A Spiritual Path to Higher Creativity*. London: Souvenir Press.

Cook, R. (2015) *Face to Face: Interviews with Artists*. London: Tate Publishing.

Craig-Martin, M. (2015) *On Being an Artist*, London: Art/Books.

Csikszentmihalyi, M. (1997) *Creativity: Flow and the Psychology of Discovery and Invention*, New York: Harper Perennial.

Hannon, A. (2014) Fleeting occupations: The 'studio' as an extension of psychological inhabitation, *Journal of Visual Art Practice*, 13 (1): 50–60.

Hatfield C., Montanta V., and Deffenbaugh C., (2006) Artist/art educator: Making sense of identity, *Issues Art Education*, May 2006: 42–47.

Howells, V. and Zelnik, T. (2009) Making art: A qualitative study of personal and group transformation in a community arts studio, *Psychiatric Rehabilitation Journal*, 32 (3): 215–222.

Laing, O. (2020) *Funny Weather. Art in an Emergency*. London: Picador.

Lampert, C. (2019) *Frank Auerbach: Speaking and Painting*. London: Thames & Hudson.

Payne, R. (2020) Shock of the new, *International Journal of Art and Design Education*, 39(4): 724–738.

Perry, G. (2014) *Playing to the Gallery*. London: Penguin Books Ltd.

Pringle, E. (2008) Artists' Perspectives on Art Practices and Pedagogy, Ch. 3 in J. Sefton-Green (Ed.) *Creative Learning*, Arts Council England: Creative Partnerships.

Tempest, K. (2022) *On Connection*. London: Faber & Faber.

6 The value of uncertainty in artist teacher pedagogy

Marike Hoekstra

Introduction

I clearly remember the moment when my enquiry into the implications of being both teacher and artist began. At the time I had started working as a teacher in painting and drawing in a community art centre. In a staff meeting the question was raised why it was relevant that all of the art teachers present were also active artistic practitioners. None of my colleagues doubted the fact that it was important to remain active as an artist, nor did I. Not only did making art fulfil a deeply felt personal need, but it was also something our course participants greatly valued. Despite the practical difficulties of combining different professional careers, everybody agreed that it was worth the effort. Up to that moment I had considered it to be a sign of ambivalence and uncertainty that I could not really decide whether I identified more as artist than as teacher. In the years to come, when I entered other areas of education, I was frequently confronted with the question of how I would describe my profession. I started to notice that more often than not, there seemed to be a rigorous divide between the two professions. Artists in the Netherlands are hired to work in schools in short term extracurricular projects and are expected to bring about something creative and unexpected. They are not considered real teachers (Haanstra 2003; De Backer, Lombaerts, De Mette et al. 2012; Hoekstra 2015, 2018). Art teachers, on the other hand, might well engage actively with any form of art-making only to be considered amateur artists at best, but never professional artists. The opinion held within the community art centre where I worked, where all the teachers were also artists, has to be taken as an exception. Still, many of the artists and art teachers I met over the years combine artistic activities with teaching.

It was only after my interest in teaching artists became the inspiration for doing academic research that I became aware of the inconsistencies between this rigorous divide and the lived reality of teaching artists. In the Netherlands there was not much research to draw upon, and I started to widen my scope internationally to discover the literature on the Artist Teacher Scheme (ATS). Despite the many differences in the training of art teachers in the Netherlands and the UK, making comparative studies difficult, many of the characteristics and considerations of British artist teachers can also be found with their Dutch colleagues (Haanstra, Van Strien and Wagenaar 2008; Hoekstra 2010; Jacometti 2011). Thornton's (2005) research findings on identity issues of artist teachers helped me identify relevant similarities and apply an analytical framework based on literature on UK artist teachers to investigate the practices of Dutch artist teachers. One of the main findings in Thornton's research is the importance of a personal commitment to both professions. In my doctoral study, I implemented questionnaires and interviews among Dutch artist teachers to understand their commitment to artist teacher identities. The findings confirmed me of the fact that an investigation of Dutch practice underpinned by data on the ATS would be valid, regardless of educational national policy and thus become relevant across our nation's borders and educational systems. This would help me understand on a more fundamental level why it is relevant that artists teach and what this dual practice implies for pedagogy.

In this chapter it is explained how the empirical findings of case studies of two Dutch artist teachers – who feature anonymously in this chapter by their pseudonyms Anna and Jill – inform an understanding of a dual professional identity for pedagogical practice. The uncertainty which is caused by the fact that an artist teacher needs to be able to work in two complementary or conflicting domains can be considered a distinguishing feature of artist teacher practice. However, in this chapter I argue that uncertainty does not degrade the artist teacher, but in fact qualifies artist teachers as agents of change.

Conceptual framework

The artist teacher is considered a model of interdisciplinary fusion (Hall 2010), a hybrid professional who takes an individual and sometimes flexible position on the continuum of artist and teacher (Hoekstra 2015). Teaching practice and artistic practice are able to mutually inform each other in the person of the artist teacher. The artist teacher concept allows for both a strong model and a weak model of this hybrid practice. The weak model focuses on the deficiencies in either of the roles. The aforementioned assumption that artists cannot be real teachers, and art teachers are in fact amateur artists, exemplifies the existing distance between art and education. Art is supposedly a liberated domain which is constantly subject to change and critique, whereas education has developed into a structured institution dominated by accountability and regulations. In the weak model, the artist therefore remains an outsider in the school. On the other hand, in the strong model the whole is more than the sum of the parts. The fact that artist teachers are able to work from two different domains is considered a distinguishing quality. The strong model places the artist teacher in the heart of education. The strong model – which is pivotal to the ATS – focuses upon the capability of the artist teacher to bring together two different and sometimes conflicting domains and thus, bring art within the educational system (Adams 2005).

Teachers who maintain active contemporary art practices have distinguishing qualities that stretch from the content of their teaching to modelling risk-taking, experimentation and play. Artist teachers create learning spaces like artist studios as 'hospitable, unstructured opportunities for interactions' (Graham and Zwirn 2010: 230). Artist teachers are considered authentic models for art education who represent contemporary art practice in the classroom (Haanstra 2003) and the embodied knowledge of the artist teacher allows for 'artistry in teaching' (Eisner 2006: 45). Eisner's ideal of a synergy between artistic practice and teaching practice can, however, be hard to accomplish for art teachers, because of the fact that this ideal draws from a mythical understanding of artists. The artist teacher concept of embodied artistic qualities is too fluid for most art teachers to deal with the delicate balance between the two practices (Hickman 2010; MacDonald and Moss 2014). As Eisner (2006) also points out, the similarities between making art and teaching not only involve aesthetic qualities of the teaching process but align foremost with the uncertainties that come with both the teaching and the art making process. Teachers and artists both make decisions based on reflections in-action (Schön 1991) and it is the routines of professional practice that enable both artists and teachers to focus on 'what is emerging' (Eisner 1979: 154). Daichendt (2010) takes this alignment between art making and teaching further by placing the artist teacher in a postmodern framework. A mythical understanding of the artist teacher can be contested when romantic and modernist ideals of universal quality are traded for a shift toward a continuous reinvention of artistic practice. Multimodal contemporary artistic practice implies an embodiment of diversity. Taken from a postmodern perspective which allows for individuality and local practice the artist teacher 'recognizes the unique, rewarding and multifaceted qualities that are present in art-making experiences. The experiences are as diverse as the artists. Thus, the possibilities for teaching art are endless' (Daichendt 2010: 149). Shifting paradigms in art and art education dispute the idea of universal values and make room for local truths to emerge (Atkinson 2011). The change that is proposed, to advance from a mythical embodiment of universal artistic quality to a concept of embodiment of diversity of individual and local strategies, allows for a more democratic understanding of the artist teacher.

A democratic understanding of the artist teacher opens up the possibility to consider the artist teacher an alternative to default pedagogy (Adams 2005; Atkinson 2011). In my doctoral thesis I propose a definition of democratic pedagogy – as opposed to default pedagogy – by identifying the main motives in some of the most prominent democratic movements in pedagogy. Largely, the underlying motives in different theories and practices of progressive pedagogues over the last century can be categorised into three interacting motives (Hoekstra 2018). Firstly, democratic pedagogy concerns the emancipation of children and learners. Secondly, democratic pedagogy is critical of the school as an institution of power. Thirdly, democratic pedagogy is about inclusion. These three motives strive to abolish or at least diminish existing inequalities: inequalities between children and adults, unequal relations between individuals and institutions, and inequalities between different children or groups. Although not all three principles are equally important in every histori-cal initiative to reform education, together they roughly outline the inspiration for what I have summarised as the project of democratic pedagogy: a century of pedagogical reform that starts with Dewey (Adams and Owens 2016; Aubrey and Riley 2016). The consequences of these interacting motives concern both theory and educational practice.

Creating a studio

One of the artist teachers who participated in the research is Jill. Jill is in her late 40s and works as an art teacher in an Amsterdam grammar school. She identifies mostly with the teacher role, because of the fact that she currently does not have a studio and spends most of her working time as an educator. She is quite strict in the way she attributes professional criteria for artists on herself. For example, Jill considers making money with art and having a studio space conditional to be able to identify as artist. On the other hand, she often connects aspects of her teaching with her experiences as an art student and as an artist, which makes her a living and accessible model of artistic practice (Sholette 2016). As an artistic practitioner she is literally not bound to a single discipline, because of the fact that she has a double professional background in music and the visual arts, and is keen to try out a range of other media, for example, creative writing. According to Daichendt (2010), artist teachers teach in ways that are derived from their personal commitment to (contempo-rary) art practice. Jill says she does not experience a strict divide between her teaching role and her work as an artist. On her initiative, I have observed her teaching a class of approximately 20 students aged 17–18, who were preparing for their final exams, which are somewhat similar to A-levels. Over a period of two months I went to observe the weekly lessons in the school's art classroom, where students were engaged in individual projects around the few themes prescribed by an official national examination programme. According to Jill, her artist teacher identity would be most prominent in this context. What Jill aspires to is to create an artistic community with these students where she can cross the boundaries of artist and teacher in order for the students to be able to cross the boundaries between artist and student (Page 2012). In the analy-sis of the way this creation of an artistic community works for her students, I have identified different perspectives which could be attributed to the way artistic or creative strategies in contemporary art practice are modelled in the classroom.

Firstly, there is the aspect of hybridity (Van Winkel 2012). Van Winkel argues that artists more often than not combine their artistic practice with other pro-fessional activities such as, for example, teaching. He identifies several levels in the way the different practices can be integrated in the professional identity of one artistic individual. Artists can combine their practice with other activities without any fusion of their various activities, but the different practices can also become completely integrated, something Van Winkel (2012) identifies as hybrid practice. Jill struggles with the conflicting demands of her pedagogical responsibilities and her identity as an artist, but she says that in both aspects of her practice she is similarly drawn to the uncertainty the work confronts her with. In teaching, like in making art, she has to deal with the unexpected which challenges her to respond to whatever manifests itself to her. Shulman (2005) argues that this aspect of uncertainty is characteristic of a pedagogy that is organized according to the features of the professional practice it educates for, like, for example, hybrid artistic practice.

Secondly, there is the aspect of making meaning from experience (Dewey 1916). Jill employs several techniques in her conversations with students that help them to experience situations of uncertainty in order to be able to connect these with pre-existing knowledge and make meaning of these experiences. Her own positive inclination to uncertainty as an artistic strategy is an aspect of embodied artistic practice and this artistic know-how is stimulated in the students by processes of meaning making that happen when relations are made between experiences (Pringle 2009).

Lastly, there is the aspect of conversational teaching. Jill draws a comparison between having a conversation with a student and having a monologue interieur when making art. In her own hybrid practice she freely transgresses boundaries between artistic disciplines. Transgressing the boundary between making art and teaching relates to developments in contemporary art practice where social interaction becomes an actual part of the artwork (Helguera 2011; Kalin 2014). The dialogue Jill engages in with her students can, therefore, not only be considered an aspect of her teaching but becomes part of the art making process. This blurring of disciplines aligns with a holistic perspective on teacher professionalism. For example, the observed lessons were rather informally organized. Jill does not seem to have a problem with the fact that students might consider her chaotic or personally involved. In my thesis, I argue that a teacher who does not appear to be in control and includes her own private and artistic perspectives aligns with aspects of what bell hooks (1994) describes as engaged pedagogy. Engaged pedagogy, with its strong focus on inclusion, is one of the appearances of the overarching concept of democratic pedagogy I developed as an analytical framework. Although being uncertain might appear a weakness to some, it is in fact a strong incentive for democratic pedagogy and creates equality between teacher and student (Rancière 2004). When a teacher does not claim to have answers to any given situation, and thereby steps away from the authoritarian teacher role, like Jill does in her conversations with students and in her modelling of a somewhat absentminded artist who likes uncertainty, she creates room for the student to share authority over the learning process (hooks 1994). Jill explicitly refrains from advice but describes her feedback as 'thinking with the students' in a creative process where neither of them knows exactly where it will end. She is able to teach what she does not know by investigating different options together with the students. It is then up to the students to decide what they do with her suggestions.

The described case study illustrates the implications of hybridity for the considerations and performances of the artist teacher and how this raises questions and conflicts. This artist teacher has high expectations of uncertainty and disruption which might conflict with her pedagogical responsibilities and it is exactly this tension which opens up the art classroom as a place for discourse and dissensus. The fact that Jill struggles with being both artist and teacher makes her vulnerable and in this way creates another layer of uncertainty which allows for an engaged pedagogy to emerge, where she is not the all-knowing teacher but fully human and able to be involved in a dialogue with her students on a basis of equality.

Drawing alongside

The conflict between giving freedom to learners and intervening to enhance the learning process, which characterises Jill's practice, also plays a part in the case study of the artist teacher I introduced by her pseudonym Anna, but is addressed differently. During my observations, Anna works as a visiting artist in an after-hours project in primary education. Nine children aged 6–9 voluntarily participate in a short series of meetings called *Art Workshop*. The project is funded by local government and, therefore, the admission fee is low for all. This context forces Anna to improvise, firstly because she has never before met the children she will be working with, secondly because the room she has to work in does not have studio qualities and is hardly fit to facilitate any art-making, and thirdly because time is limited to just over an hour for each session. Limited time, however, does not lead to strict planning. In fact, Anna's approach to take time might be one of the key features of her practice. Taking time is essential, Moss (2001) argues, in order to be able to listen to children and create a democratic pedagogy of listening, where the teacher tries to observe and understand the processes at work when children are learning and respond according to what children need in the moment. Moss's concept of pedagogy of listening is inspired by Reggio Emilia pedagogical practice and is another example of the many different approaches included in the concept of democratic pedagogy.

Anna does not plan much in advance, but allows herself to respond flexibly to the needs and interests of the children. She is an artist teacher who is able to recognise how 'a sense of adventure, to try to draw alongside how something matters for a learner in his or her learning' (Atkinson 2017: 149) can become a meaningful learning experience, and she is able to improvise and flexibly handle time management. Unlike Jill, Anna does not explicitly express a preference to work from uncertainty, but she does not seem to be bothered by the fact that most of her work depends on improvisation. It is her conviction that she must follow the children in their initiatives and although she does deliberately introduce different materials and tools, she does not insist that these should be picked up on by the children.

One of the things Anna tries to invoke is cooperation. For her, a collaborative project of two or more children is valuable, because it allows her to join in and work alongside the children. Cooperation with the children is one of her preferred teaching strategies. What she does to stimulate children to start on a collaborative project is providing them with larger-sized materials and increasing the size of the workspace by sitting down on the floor, instead of working on tables. When children pick up on these implicit invitations to start on larger-scaled collaborative projects, the dialogue which develops between the children offers Anna an entrance to participate. In collaborative work, Anna relinquishes her position as a teacher to briefly become one of the community of learners (Lave and Wenger 1991; Adams and Owens 2016) and temporarily assumes a place alongside the children. She does not explicitly tell them to cooperate but she implicitly provides them with the circumstances and the problems that instigate collaborative projects. Anna explains that she does not agree with what she describes as a formal prescript for collaborative work in art education, because it might not align with the preferences of the children. In her opinion, children must also be allowed to work alone when they prefer that.

This kind of flexibility is also expressed in the way Anna handles the spatial circumstances where she works. She believes in the positive effects of a studio environment and advocates access to studio spaces for children, but with regards to the room where I observe her, she is pragmatic. She appears indifferent to environmental factors, but explains that experience has taught her not to be bothered too much by these circumstances. It would take too much of her time to try to improve the given situation and she therefore adapts. It struck me that she does not mention any of this to the children, but models a way of ignoring the poor circumstances. She does make slight alterations in the arrangement of furniture and effectively places materials, but does not explicitly address this. Shulman (2005) argues that in signature pedagogies it is not only important what one does, but equally important what one does not do. What is excluded is as equally important as what is included. Anna does not draw attention to the fact that the room is different from a classroom and leaves it to the children to decide for themselves how to use this room: sitting at tables, lying on the floor or moving around. By not drawing attention to the features that distinguish her practice from the default pedagogy of the school, she in fact critically questions the power structures that underpin our understanding of educational spaces, which creates room for a third space or hybrid space to emerge (Hall and Thomson 2016; Soja 1999; Wilson 2008).

A third aspect of the way Anna welcomes uncertainty in her teaching is her approach to themes. She does not introduce a theme, because she is more interested in the themes the children bring forward. In the first lesson she initiates a group discussion about the title of the workshop series and that brings the conversation to the subject of art. Children express their thoughts and opinions about what art is, and Anna now and then summarises their input. In this way she helps the children to focus on themes and subjects they suggest and uses her experience to listen and recognise rich themes with potential, for example, the idea of collections, something which is proposed by one of the children and immediately picked up by the others. She connects the things the children say to relevant interventions and invites the children to elaborate on the ideas that are mentioned, by experimenting with materials and techniques and finding their own creative solutions. Anna aims her interventions on the increase of focus and on providing challenge for the children. She listens and is not worried by the fact that her interventions are not always immediately picked up. Her interventions are not aimed at production or learning goals but are relational, providing receptive attention (Noddings 2012) that creates room for experiential learning.

It is most important for Anna that the children are able to follow their preferences and initiatives. This requires a pedagogy of listening (Moss 2001) and flexibility in offering support. This also implies that it cannot be predicted what interventions are needed or even what materials. The way she welcomes the uncertainty that comes with responding to children's autonomy is an essential feature of Anna's pedagogy. What I have been able to analyse is how Anna creates a democratic learning environment by allowing uncertainty. She responds to the children by offering materials and tools, improvising work spaces, modelling productive and collaborative behaviour. She facilitates children to experience, make meaning from their experiences by responding affirmatively and allows the children's process to follow along non-linear lines. She is motivated to give children autonomy over their learning process – even if this places her in an uncertain position and forces her to improvise – in a way that aligns with child-centred democratic pedagogy.

Making a thirdspace

Duality is a pivotal feature of the complexity of the artist teacher. The diversity of contemporary artistic practice creates a multimodality of pedagogical practices, which is further complicated by the many personal approaches to integrating complementary or conflicting domains (Adams 2005). I argue that a traditional binary logic, which places the artist in opposition to the teacher, fails to comprise the working of a hybrid practice and pertains the myth of the artist teacher as 'other'. A binary understanding of the world is a simplification with no room for the messiness and uncertainties of a lived reality (Soja 1999). What I have strived to investigate is the working of the many decisions made in action and on action which can be attributed to the fact that artist teachers have to work in this tension between being artist and being teacher, and what this signature pedagogy of the artist teacher (Thomson and Hall 2015) implies for a democratic understanding of pedagogy.

When binary oppositions fail as models to comprehend the lived reality of duality in individual practices, an alternative perspective is required. This alternative perspective aligns with theory on pedagogical thirdspace (hooks 1994; Soja 1999; Wilson 2008). Thirdspace as a theoretical concept originates from radical post-colonial and feminist theory and works from the idea that in the margins between the domains of oppressor and oppressed there is room for negotiation and dialogue. The radicality of what the concept of thirdspace entails is what bell hooks describes happens when the binary between different locations is being transgressed:

> Those of us who live, who "make it", passionately holding on to aspects of that "downhome" life we do not intend to lose while simultaneously seeking new knowledge and experience, invent spaces of radical openness. Without such spaces we would not survive. Our living depends on our ability to conceptualise alternatives, often improvised. Theorising this experience aesthetically, critically is an agenda for radical cultural practice. For me this space of radical openness is a margin - a profound edge. Locating oneself there is difficult yet necessary. It is not a "safe" place. One is always at risk. One needs a community of resistance (hooks 1989: 19).

The conflict which is created by the different modes of being in different locations – locations like contemporary artistic practice and schools – manifests itself in what I have identified as uncertainty in artist teacher practice. As hooks (1989: 20) explains, marginality in this respect is not a site of deprivation but of radical possibility because it counters hegemonic discourses and becomes a place to stay in, because of the fact that 'it offers to one the possibility of radical perspective from which to see and create, to imagine alternatives, new worlds'. From a pedagogical point of view, thirdspace can be the location where the hierarchies that divide adults from children can be redistributed and where everybody's voice is heard. Children or students are no longer othered (Lahman 2008) and are not silenced (hooks 1989; Ranciere 2004). A pedagogical thirdspace creates a children's public sphere (Negt and Kluge 1990) for engaged pedagogy (hooks 1994): a democratic and critical educational model. The need for artist teachers to create new spaces where they hold on to the world of artistic practice – the studio, the art school, the creative collective – while striving to perform professionally in the world of educational institutions, allows for uncertainty because these spaces are not fixed and require flexibility and improvisation.

Figure 6.1 Marike Hoekstra, *A Third Pedagogical Space 1*

Figure 6.2 Marike Hoekstra, *A Third Pedagogical Space 2*

Figure 6.3 Marike Hoekstra, *A Third Pedagogical Space 3*

Figure 6.4 Marike Hoekstra, *A Third Pedagogical Space 4*

Figure 6.5 Marike Hoekstra, *A Third Pedagogical Space 5*

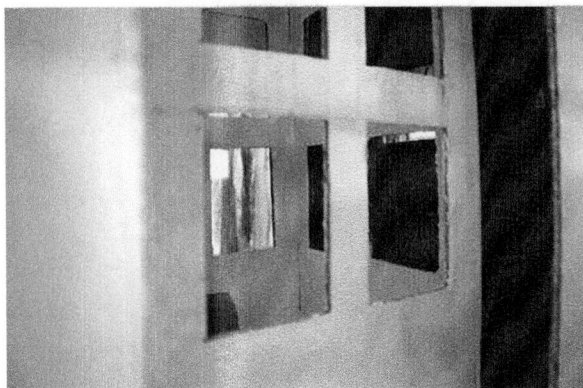

Dioramas of democratic learning spaces

Knowledge construction involves subjectivity and lived experience. Memories of image and space and identity inform my position as an insider researcher in the domain of the artist teacher and are investigated in dioramas (Figures 6.1 – 6.5). The dioramas address the conflict between tacit, embodied ideals of art educational practice and art education in schools and institutions. A spatial construction of a pedagogical landscape as an image of democratic pedagogical performance is a complex artistic medium that allows to involve different layers of knowledge (Hoekstra 2019). The impenetrability of the different zones of the diorama, which causes the effect that the space can never be fully perceived, addresses the fact that a thirdspace in education is never fixed but has to be continuously negotiated.

References

Adams, J. (2005) Room 13 and the Contemporary Practice of Artist-Learners, *Studies in Art Education: A Journal of Issues and Research in Art Education*, 47(1): 23–33.

Adams, J. and Owens, A. (2016) *Creativity and Democracy in Education*. London: Routledge.

Atkinson, D. (2011) *Art, Equality and Learning: Pedagogies Against the State*. Rotterdam: Sense Publishers.

Atkinson, D. (2017) Without criteria: Art and learning and the adventure of pedagogy, *International Journal of Art & Design Education*, 36(2): 141–152.

Aubrey, K., and Riley, A. (2016) *Understanding & Using Educational Theories*. London: Sage.

Daichendt, G. J. (2010) *Artist-Teacher: A Philosophy for Creating and Teaching*. Chicago: University of Chigaco Press.

De Backer, F., Lombaerts, K., De Mette, T., Buffel, T. and Elias, W. (2012) Creativity in artistic education: Introducing artists into primary schools, *International Journal of Art & Design Education*, 31(1), 53–66.

Dewey, J. (1916) *Democracy and Education*. New York: The Macmillan Company.

Eisner, E. (1979) *The Educational Imagination*. New York: MacMillan.

Eisner, E. (2006) The satisfactions of teaching, *Educational Leadership*, 63(6): 44–46.

Graham, M. A., and Zwirn, S. G. (2010) how being a teaching artist can influence K-12 art education, *Studies in Art Education*, 51(2): 219–232.

Haanstra, F. (2003) Kunstenaars en schoolkunst: Authentiek kunstonderwijs heeft professionals nodig [Artists and school art: Authentic art education needs professionals], *Boekman*, 15(56): 74–78.

Haanstra, F., Van Strien, E. and Wagenaar, H. (2008) Teachers' and students' perceptions of good art lessons and good art teaching, *International Journal of Education through Art*, 4(1), 45–55.

Hall, J. (2010) Making art, teaching art, learning art: Exploring the concept of the artist teacher, *International Journal of Art and Design Education*, 29(2): 103–110.

Hall, C., and Thomson, P. (2016) Creativity in teaching: What can teachers learn from artists? *Research Papers in Education*, 32(1): 106–120.

Helguera, P. (2011) *Education for Socially Engaged Practice*. New York: Jorge Pinto Books.

Hickman, R. (2010) Self portrait: An account of the artist as educator, *International Journal of Education and the Arts*, 11(2): 1–15.

Hoekstra, M. (2010) De rol van de kunstenaar in Toeval gezocht. [The role of the artist in Toeval gezocht]. *Cultuur + Educatie: Vol. 27. Max van der Kamp scriptieprijs: vier nominaties en een winner [Culture + Education: Vol. 27. Max van der Kamp thesis award: four nominees and a winner]* (pp. 8–28). Utrecht: Cultuurnetwerk Nederland.

Hoekstra, M. (2015) The problematic nature of the artist teacher concept and implications for pedagogical practice, *International Journal of Art & Design Education*, 34(3): 349–357.

Hoekstra, M. (2018) *Artist Teachers and Democratic Pedagogy; Drakakas and Thirdspace*, Doctoral thesis, University of Chester.

Hoekstra, M. (2019) A place for stupidity: Investigating democratic learning spaces in the diorama, *International Journal of Art and Design Education*, 38(3): 649–658.

hooks, b. (1989) Choosing the margin as a space of radical openness, *Framework: The Journal of Cinema and Media*, 0(36): 15–23.

hooks, b. (1994) *Teaching to Transgress: Education as the practice of freedom*. New York: Routledge.

Jacometti, R. (2011) *Het belang van de beeldende kunstpraktijk voor het docentschap in een beeldend vak [The significance of artistic practice for the professional teacher in the visual arts]*. (Master thesis). Retrieved from https://issuu.com/kunsteducatie_ahk/docs/het_belang_van_de_beeldende_kunstpr

Kalin, N. M. (2014) Art's pedagogical paradox, *Studies in Art Education*, 55(3): 190–202.

Lahman, M. K. (2008) Always othered: Ethical research with children, *Journal of Early Childhood Research*, 6(3): 281–300.

Lave, J. and Wenger, E. (1991) *Situated Learning: Legitimate peripheral participation*. Cambridge: Cambridge University.

MacDonald, A., and Moss, T. (2014) The art of practice, in N. Fitzallen et al. (Eds.) *The Future of Educational Research*. Rotterdam: Sense Publishers, 99–110.

Moss, P. (2001) The otherness of Reggio, in L. Abbott & C. Nutbrown (Eds.) *Experiences of Reggio Emilia: Implications for pre-school provision*. Buckingham: Open University Press, 125–137.

Negt, O. and Kluge, A. (1990) Selections from 'The Proletariat Public Sphere', *Social Text*, 8(3): 24–32.

Noddings, N. (2012) The Caring relation in teaching, *Oxford Review of Education*, 38(6): 771–781.

Page, T. (2012) A shared place of discovery and creativity: Practices of contemporary art and design pedagogy, *International Journal of Art & Design Education*, 31(1): 67–77.

Pringle, E. (2009) the artist-led pedagogic process in the contemporary art gallery: Developing a meaning making framework, *International Journal of Art & Design Education*, 28(2): 174–182.

Rancière, J. (2004) Who is the subject of the rights of man? *The South Atlantic Quarterly*, 103(2-3): 297–310.

Schön, D. (1991) *The Reflective Practitioner*. London: Arena.

Sholette, G. (2016) Swampwalls: Dark matter and the Lumpen Army of Art, *women & performance: A journal of feminist theory*, 26(2–3): 172–183.

Shulman, L. (2005) Signature pedagogies in the profession, *Daedalus*, 134(3): 52–59.

Soja, E. (1999) Thirdspace: Expanding the scope of the geographical imagination, in D. Massey, Allen, J. & Sarre, P. [Eds.] *Human Geography Today*, Cambridge: Blackwell, 125–137.

Thomson, P. and Hall, C. (2015) 'Everyone can imagine their own Gellert': The democratic artist and 'inclusion' in primary and nursery classrooms, *Education* 3–13, 43(4): 420–413.

Thornton, A. (2005) The artist teacher as reflective practitioner, *International Journal of Art & Design Education*, 24(2): 166–174.

Van Winkel, C., Gielen, P., & Zwaan, K. (2012) De hybride kunstenaar. De organisatie van de artistieke praktijk in het postindustriële tijdperk [The hybrid artist. The organisation of the artistic practice in the postindustrial era]. Breda: AKV/St.Joost.

Wilson, B. (2008) Research at the margins of schooling: Biographical inquiry and third-site pedagogy, *International Journal of Education through Art*, 4(2): 119–130.

Part 3

Practices

7 Art is Survival: The emergence of an artist teacher's voice

Monica Lewis

Figure 7.1 Monica Lewis (2018) *Art is Survival*, Pen on paper, 30 cm x 30 cm

> Knowledge emerges only through invention and re-invention, through the restless, impatient, continuing, hopeful inquiry human beings pursue in the world, with the world, and with each other (Freire 1970: 53).

The Bear!

I started my third and final year of my Artist Teacher Masters in crisis. For several months bad experiences in my professional life affected me to the point of making me physically ill, consequently impacting my personal life. Adding to the stress this was causing, I was expected to have a clear research project for my dissertation. I did not know where to start. I was feeling lost and deflated.

Fear and stress had paralysed me, preventing me from acting and speaking out. In this state of paralysis, I sat absentmindedly looking at an artwork I had made the previous academic year, which depicted La Ursa, a carnival character from my native region in Brazil. This character is usually played by a person in a bear costume, as part of a troupe of dancers who enslave and mistreat it. The giant beast suffers in silence, trying to escape from the chains around its waist, wanting its freedom (Emporiopernambucano.com 2022).

I was puzzled about the presence of the Bear in my thoughts. I looked for the reflective journal from my second year MA study and re-read the entry about the *Estandarte* (Figure 7.2), which is a very ornate banner used as a religious or carnivalesque ensign in Brazilian homes and festivities. When reading and reflecting I had an epiphany. It was by defamiliarising this artwork, 'making the familiar strange and the strange familiar' (Eisner 2007: 9), and using Schön's (1983) reflection-on-action that I was able to draw the parallels between the Bear and me. I understood that the name *La Ursa* suggests the Bear is female and both the Bear and I suffered in silence, being controlled, and mistreated by a 'handler' trying to escape from the chains around us, with no voice to growl, no strength left to fight. At work I was the Bear!

The situation at work was aggravating and I felt objectified as a teacher. To escape my reality, I started to use art making to channel my emotions and help me feel human again, achieving a sense of wholeness (hooks 1994: 16). With the Bear image so vivid in my mind I started to intuitively use the Bear in the small drawings I made daily on Zentangle tiles (for example, Figure 7.1), 9 x 9 cm

Figure 7.2 Monica Lewis (2018) *Estandarte de La Ursa*. Mixed media. 94 cm x 60 cm.

paper squares usually used to create miniature abstract art. Making them during the school day felt a bit rebellious, a small act of resistance, defiance.

This insight allowed me to give the Bear a new meaning, making it the visual metaphor for my research. Adams and Owens (2016: 101) see metaphors as valuable as they force the reader to translate them. In this intrinsic part of the metaphoric process, all the viewer needs to comprehend the representation is imagination and intuition. Langer (1953 cited in Feinstein 1985: 26) believes that the product of metaphorical thoughts carry truth and I had arrived at a scary realisation: the Bear was my truth. Through reflection, the metaphorical Bear facilitated a better understanding of myself and the world around me (Parsons 2010: 233), capturing both personal and cultural attributes. I began to see how my sociocultural position informed my experience and revealed who I was. Through continued reflection I discovered where I wanted to be; analysing my past guided my future (Dewey 2005: 17). Reflecting on biography and heritage revealed important nuances that allowed me to understand what was happening, confirming Wall's (2006: 9) claim that 'there is a direct and inextricable link between the personal and the cultural'. I soon realised this was the focus for my MA dissertation as the Bear and I had far too much in common, and the artwork I was producing was telling a story which was relevant to the understanding of myself.

Pedagogies of oppression

I grew up in Brazil in the last years of a military dictatorship. By then persecutions and disappearances had decreased as decades of the regime had inflicted fear and compliance on the population, but authoritarianism prevailed. The experiences of pedagogy at the Catholic school where I studied as a child reinforced the sense of controlling power structure of military domination. Knowledge generation revolved around rigid assessment through exams. Curiosity, eagerness to learn and critical thinking were seen as a threat, and heavy punishment was used to prevent it (Freire 1974). My experience at school was of silence, and to a certain extent, fear.

To shape and realise the significance of meaning I needed to find ways of expressing my experience (Dewey 2005: 14). Expressing via textual language offers several interpretations, but artistic media also has a language and, therefore, expression. Creating drawn tiles (Figure 7.3) facilitated my expression far more than using written or spoken words. They reminded me, as an artist teacher, of the need to rectify academic hierarchies which put textual narratives above visual ones. The emotional and analytical reflections gained through making art proved that text and visuals have equal value, and so I drew on both the artworks and reflective journal entries as data for my MA research. Art is a non-verbal language which has its own vocabulary and grammar and as artists we can shape our lived experiences transforming visual language through transcended configurations (Van Manen 2012: 74). My journey with the Bear represents my hope of crafting a narrative of creative advancement in the

Figure 7.3 Monica Lewis (2019) Zentangle tile, pen on paper, 9 cm x 9 cm.

face of regressive politics; a bold reinvention despite impossible odds, out of a desire for expression (Calirman 2012: 9).

Democratic platform

Having constructed a small collection of tiles I started to use Instagram (@ monicajudice) to make my work public, posting images of the tiles produced at work. My confidence was so low that it took a while to have the courage to post them, but when I finally did, I was amazed at the positive feedback. That really boosted my confidence, facilitating further reflective practice and regular dissemination of artworks. Payne (2012: 247) argues that the visual as a research method challenges old perceptions and brings new insights. Making and posting daily also gave me a sense of purpose and value, which generates knowledge and understanding about the self and life (McNiff 2010). At this stage my self-belief was low with a perceived inefficacy that was painful (Bandura 1982a: 141). Positive feedback gave a sense of direction, helping me perceive the likes and comments on my posts as a metric to success (Carr et al. 2017: 142). It helped improve my wellbeing and confirmed that knowledge and understanding can be reached through the visual (Eisner 2007; Barone and Eisner 2011: 1).

Art making empowers by providing a way to exercise choice and control where overcoming challenges results in feelings of achievement, enhanced confidence, and self-esteem (Titus and Sinacore 2013: 30; Levine 2008). With a renewed sense of self-worth and a positive self-image, I became confident to use creativity and take risks. Through developing critical consciousness by placing value on the process of making and allowing myself to become the Bear, I amplified my voice. This realisation showed how therapeutic art-making can be and how using self-actualisation to promote wellbeing enabled my voice to gain power (hooks 1994: 14). Increased self-efficacy triggered a change in attitude that resulted in me using my voice in a more purposeful way, a way I never considered would be part of my practice.

The change

Deciding to make and wear a papier maché bear mask, like the ones from my childhood, I started to enact the Bear slowly, exploring movement and silence through small performances (Figure 7.4). These generated reflection-in-action (Schön 1983) where, instinctively I reshaped my actions while I was performing. These impulsive creations gave me insight into my lived experience and made me more willing to take risks. Short videos were easy to make and post on Instagram. Inhabiting the Bear gave me the courage to let go and allow new experiences to flow naturally, with small subversive acts happening at school hidden from view. I needed help with the filming and trustworthy staff helped me in secret. The whole experience brought us together, allowing us to share collective empowerment via small acts of constructive rebellion.

This new phase indicates a shift towards a deeper understanding of who I am and where I should go next. It brought vivid memories of childhood silence, and I felt a strong urge to return to Brazil – a calling to investigate where it all began. Arriving in Brazil and revisiting the places where I felt silenced was emotional. For example, when visiting my school where I studied from six until I was 18 years old, I asked permission to visit some of my teachers who still worked there, but was refused entry. Standing on site brought me disturbing memories of feeling imprisoned as a student. Foucault (1991) compares school

Figure 7.4 Monica Lewis (2019) *Growl!* Photograph of Performance

Figure 7.5 Monica Lewis (2019) *Panopticon*. Pen on paper. 29 cm x 42 cm.

to the Panopticon design (Figure 7.5) for a prison created by Jeremy Bentham where inmates are continually under observation and controlled by their fears. During the dictatorship, arts and social sciences were removed from the curriculum in a major Brazilian education reform (1971) and supervisors were placed in each school to reinforce the new provision. I remember their presence in every corridor, making both students and teachers fearful, silencing both. Understanding Foucault's (1991) theory of how mechanisms of control and surveillance are social constructs was important in the development of strategies to deal with my incapability of speaking, helping me find ways of defying silence.

While wearing the mask I had contradictory feelings. Part of me felt free and protected, being able to perform with full anonymity; the other part felt incarcerated, unable to speak. I eventually understood that the Bear presented a visual representation of my interpretations of freedom, and my mask gave this abstract concept a concrete shape. In Brazil I wore the Bear mask everywhere. By then I had fully welcomed the Bear into my life and felt confident walking in the streets in full performance. It did not take long for the Bear to be recognised, filmed and invited to events. People always made a fuss of the Bear. The anonymity of the mask provided freedom to express myself however I wanted. As the Bear was mute, I could only communicate through mime and movement, and with music always being played I saw myself dancing all the time. The Bear had become my alter ego, separate from myself. People started filming and sharing videos of the Bear dancing in various events. Researching 'Dancing Bear' led me to the Ursari, the European Dancing Bear Act from the nineteenth century. Handlers took the act to Brazil once it was banned in parts of Europe. The act's popularity meant it quickly became part of Brazilian culture; its legacy fortified by carnival. Suddenly my narrative and heritage were connected to those of elsewhere.

Freire's pedagogy and the Bear

Paulo Freire, an educator from my hometown, is referenced worldwide for his literature on education. A few days before I arrived in Brazil in 2019, Freire's works were banned by the extreme right regime. They also wanted to remove Freire's title of 'Patron of Brazilian Education' and pass it to a military gentleman who was not connected with education but was known for torturing people who defied the 1960s military dictatorship. Jair Bolsonaro, ultra-conservative Brazilian President (2019–2022), attacked Freire as left-wing, which had no place in a country like Brazil, and also targeted minorities and undermined women. His remarks caused anger, sparking protests that the Bear participated in. In a pro-education and Freire march the Bear was a rebellious presence, a symbol of resistance (Figure 7.6). Freire (1974: 39) affirms it is important to 'intervene in order to change' the culture of silence. I saw intervention in these protests, the use of critical consciousness as an impetus for cultural emancipation, eliminating the culture of silence and allowing people the path to freedom by exercising their voices. This change allows people to become 'objects' and not mere 'subjects' of their own reality. Those pro-education protests inspired me. They made me reflect on the effect the Bear was having on people. Somehow the Bear's visual presence had an impact and it started being used as a symbol for resistance. It was funny how the Bear needed Freire's pedagogy to free itself and Freire's followers needed an image to represent their cause, a democratic exchange where both benefited.

Figure 7.6 Monica Lewis (2019) *Ursa and Freire*, Pen on paper, 30 cm x 30 cm.

Sidgwick (2010) believes artistic practices are socio-culturally informed. She affirms that artistic and culture-specific practices share a common dynamic, one that has the power to unlock a fixed understanding of the self, a self that conformed and accepted oppression. She points out oppression is often internalised by people who suffered under authoritarian regimes and refers specifically to how the repressive military regime has shaped the Brazilian people, making them feel violated and silenced. Freire (1974) believed that the knowledge acquired by learning through critical reflection on lived experience freed people by unlocking the oppressed self (Sidgwick 2010). Giving people emancipatory ways of seeing and being in the world engendered their confidence and provided tools to change the *status quo*. Thus, they freed themselves not only from the oppressors, but also from their own fearful selves. Here I draw a parallel to the transformative experience of artist teacher practices and pedagogies. Addison (2010: 159) believes creativity is a way to produce generative forces for growth and cultural renewal. He sees art as a language, a way to express people's ways of thinking and being, and the artist teacher as an agent of social and cultural transformation. This transformation gives students agency, letting them take full ownership of their meaning-making, transforming their reality and that of others.

The transformation

While wearing the mask I revealed my conflicts non-verbally, allowing me to be in possession of myself again where movement and dance freed me through expressing the ineffable. The visual becoming my voice went far beyond what any text could say (Lepecki 2016). This was particularly noticeable in the evolution of the Zentangle tiles, which began in black and white with no obvious message in them (Figure 7.3) and ended in colour with a strong message (Figure 7.7). This unintentional change was understood through reflection as the birth and development of my voice. Art in research puts a premium on evocation giving concrete form to the ineffable (Eisner 2007: 6). Evocation is what makes the work expressive creating empathy, allowing the public to experience what would otherwise be beyond their reach (Barone and Eisner 2011: 9). My narrative as the Bear allowed others to empathise and be the creators of their narrative.

Not in a million years would I have thought I could perform in public. I have always kept a low profile and the shock at the new way I was facing situations left me speechless. This time my inability to speak was quite different to being silenced. Reflecting on my education made me realise the scars of imposed silence left by the regime. I realised how much I carried fear, subservience, and self-devaluation and how that had made me believe I could not move on as I was incapable, unworthy, and weak (Ruderman 2006). Developing my art practice through the Bear gave me confidence to overcome fears and develop a voice, confirming that through learning we can change our identity and transform into our real selves.

Figure 7.7 Monica Lewis (2019) *Disobey,* Pen on paper, 9 cm x 9 cm.

Figure 7.8 Monica Lewis (2019) *Evolution*. Pen on paper. 29 cm x 42 cm.

   This transformation was not easy (Figure 7.8); to reconstruct oneself requires moving against and beyond the boundaries of what is known, to generate a change in attitude (Meyer and Land 2005: 374). As a learner, the development of critical and reflective thinking gave me the strength to continue trying to work things out, so that I could cope with changes and uncertainty. The artist teacher in me embraced pedagogies of uncertainty (Shulman 2005a; 2005b) to prepare not only myself, but also my students for life beyond paperwork and examinations, where not everything is knowable. Showing them that by being inclusive, accepting difference and exercising creativity we can adapt and create new ways to find knowledge (Addison 2010: 159).

Welcoming not knowing, embracing its complexities, and allowing intuition as a source of information facilitated the process of transformation (Lambrechts and Hindson 2016). Most importantly, engaging with self-reflection helped me accept fallibility, allowing me to generate a better understanding of the impact my sociocultural lived experiences had on my identity (hooks 1994: 47). This gave me strength to face my fears and welcome change. Dewey (2001 cited in English 2014: 100) perceives reflection and learning as simultaneously providing a medium for democracy. As an artist teacher I want to exercise dialogue and democratic pedagogies in my classroom, where teacher and student experience learning as an egalitarian process. Granville (2012) positions art practice as a pedagogical activity and artist teacher education is seen as a liberating force which enhances growth of students' agency. Artist teachers are change makers who can deconstruct inequalities by using art as a transformative power to generate knowledge and activism (Heaton and Crumpler 2017).

Another aspect of critical pedagogies important for my transformation is troublesome knowledge (Figure 7.9). This knowledge, which is difficult, causes a cognitive conflict as students compare new ideas to their prior knowledge (Perkins 1999). The knowledge I acquired in school was so ingrained that I used it without thought, impacting how I faced new challenges and exercised my voice (Meyer and Land 2005). It was through critical reflection that I was able to understand myself and welcome new knowledge, giving me the confidence to cross a threshold. Threshold concepts are a new way of seeing things, and by crossing a threshold I was able to move forward, accessing a new way of thinking. This change is transformative and irreversible, making it hard to return to the initial phase of unknowing.

Through the Bear mask I was able to express, reflect, and communicate (Levine 2008). The Bear identified the critical reflection needed for evocation,

Figure 7.9 Monica Lewis (2019) *Being troublesome.* Pen on Paper. 30 cm x 30 cm

which generated innovation and creativity (Illeris 2014). Moving beyond boundaries gave me confidence, worth and the power to understand and exercise my voice.

Understanding voice

Ribeiro's (2017) concept of *Lugar de fala* (voice) relates historically to marginalised voices, people who suffered because of oppressive powers such as colonisation or authoritarian regimes. She believes we live in a violent hierarchy which determines who can speak, inhibiting and delegitimising people's voices. Voice in this case is not a mass of words but the Foucauldian concept (Foucault, 1991) where the dominant power creates norms to control the masses and establish hierarchies between them. These dominant powers position humans as objects removing their humanity and consequently their voice, denying them the right to exist. When minorities claim their right to have a voice, they are claiming their right to exist (Ribeiro 2017), confirming Foucault's (2013: 136) comment: 'live or let die'. History shows invisibility kills and voice gives us visibility reiterating our existence.

I was able to understand the impact my lack of voice was having on me through ineffable experiences during my performances. It was through my art practice that I developed a deeper understanding of the hierarchies which dehumanised me and inhibited my voice. By understanding them and gaining strength to face them I was able to recover my humanity, developing a voice which made me visible, part of my culture and this world.

The past versus the present

A deeper understanding of the hierarchies that inhibited my voice and knowledge of Freire's (1974) pedagogy revealed parallels between the education of my childhood and the contemporary education I experience as a teacher in England. Even though my Brazilian education happened in a different social, temporal, political and economic climate (Addison 2010), both experiences contained normative rules that violate teacher and students' sense of themselves as unique. The neoliberal 'one-size-fits-all' approach from English contemporary education triggered the same silence I experienced in my childhood, dehumanising and inhibiting my agency.

This neoliberal system creates and perpetuates inequalities in society, affecting people's individualism by changing how they behave in society and who they are (Ball 2003). Its solutions for managing and monitoring the quality of schools has given education a competitive basis (Ball 2003; Addison 2010; Wild 2011) consequently reducing people to metrics (Figure 7.10). Performativity (Figure 7.11), a system that uses judgement to incentivise and control through rewards and sanctions has been detrimental to education (Ball 2003), and specifically

Figure 7.10 Monica Lewis (2019) *We are more than numbers*. Pen on paper. 42 cm x 59 cm.

Figure 7.11 Monica Lewis (2019) *Performativitea*. Pen on paper 21 cm x 29 cm

to the arts (Payne and Hall 2018). The constant observation and monitoring of school performance can affect both students and staff, making them feel insecure. This affects their behaviour, making them operate like they are following a script, leading to conformity and inhibiting innovation. Teachers struggle for control and students are limited to learning for exams and not for life. Both are dehumanised in the process (Ball 2003; Payne and Hall 2018).

Neoliberalism in my art classroom gave me as a teacher a sense of helplessness. Subsequently, I struggled with making changes that would benefit my students' agency and that helped me reclaim a culturally critical stance as a teacher, and not passively accept neoliberal reform (Mansfield 2009). In the UK, the influences of neoliberalism on art-related skills like creativity and critical thinking has transformed how we perceive art. From free personalities developing abilities vital to making transformation visible to a simple tool to be used in the labour market, art is now positioned with monetary gain as its main objective and use. The influence of these economic ratings and intentions on art education is obvious (Damerow 2023). The outcome-oriented art education we experience currently is believed by Thodos (2018) to rupture the link between creativity and skill. She argues that art education and art making are dictated by commercial and market success, replacing the democratic diversity in discourse with the power of money. This way art education in the UK today reflects the economic inequity of neoliberal times, where freedom of choice is less democratic and authoritarianism affords more power to those with money (Webb et al. 2009).

These two experiences of education silenced me. In my childhood, the dictatorship used violence explicitly to control people, while now I experience a symbolic, implicit violence as a teacher in contemporary English education. Both systems are violent, nonetheless, and in both cases Freire's (1974) dialogue is needed to stop passivity. This dialogue allows democratic transactions between teacher and learner, giving them the knowledge to understand their own reality so that they can operate social transformation – education becoming a path to social change (Gandin 2007). Lack of inclusion and dialogue can inhibit people's voice and agency; however, the presence of dialogue can be used as a means for both personal and collective liberation with criticality and creativity giving people visibility and freeing their voice (Broadhead 2018).

Activism

My trip to Brazil revealed a different side of me, as someone who embraces political activism rather than shies away from it. With self-efficacy at a high, supporting a newfound confidence, I choose to attend major events in the fight for human rights. Welcoming the different and using art to create a more humane society empowered me to make conscious choices and to actively transform my reality and work to change others' realities (Levine 2008).

Art and activism are bound together (Clement 2022). I saw my art practice slowly develop into an act of doing which was addressing political and social issues, an art form of political and social currency, addressing cultural power structures actively and directly. Clement (2022) indicates that self-expression should be a right, but it is often a privilege as not everyone can access approaches to use their voice in their chosen way. I was privileged to be in the position of using the Bear, a visual creation, as a vehicle of expression and self-representation initially for myself, but later for the oppressed and under-represented in Brazil. When the Bear was invited to different demonstrations, my presence showed the importance of the visual as a language, with its silence allowing its image to become a symbol of the voiceless and an act of resistance, confirming that the visual is a representation of society and society represents itself in the visual (Payne 2012: 246). The visual is also a way to include others by allowing other narratives to be told. By using the Bear I communicated far more meaning than I could have expected and gave audiences freedom to express their narratives in the way they desired. My belief systems reignited from this experience enhanced my self-perception of efficacy and self-regulatory capabilities for exercising self-directedness, giving my silence the status of voice and bringing my humanity back (Bandura 1982b: 754).

Freire (1974) argues that we need action and reflection (combined) on the world to change it. It was from being critically conscious that I found the knowledge and strength to engage in social transformation. Attempts to alter social systems and their practices are met with numerous obstacles and coercive threats, as well as engendering a sense of agency as collective efficacy. This collective efficacy, based on our own self-efficacy, can impact how generations shape their lives (Bandura 1982a: 145). It shows art is a path to freedom.

Liberation

The arts as a way of enriching our awareness and expanding our humanity (Eisner 2007: 11).

My liberation came in the form of art-making. It allowed me to transform my world through action and reflection, opened new paths and gave me the opportunity to make meaning through different perspectives (hooks 1994: 48). How I produced art through the Bear communicated new relevant meaning (Payne 2012: 247). I learnt the value of the process of making and how much learning derives from it. It gave me a deeper understanding of what caused my silence and strength to welcome new meanings which restored my art practice and brought transformations I needed to reinvent myself. It confirmed that art is a necessary tool to produce knowledge and humanise us to engage meaningfully in society.

The whole experience with the Bear was rewarding but was not easy. Dealing with pain and fear is a challenge and reinventing oneself is a difficult task. My journey allowed me to experience the ineffable when I noticed I was being 'heard' by simply being 'seen.' The visual allowed minorities to identify with the Bear and create their own narratives; this expanded beyond my aims and gave a voiceless people their own voices. The Bear, a character from where I originate in Northeast Brazil, shows my experiences also as a cultural journey. It allowed a forgotten carnival character to rebirth with a whole new meaning. Developing the Bear in the UK was a way of telling my story, bringing my heritage to my new reality, but also a way to allow the creation of new narratives derived from pre-existing and historic narratives (Adams and Owens 2016: 35).

As a teacher, welcoming uncertainty and using creativity and criticality to overcome my fears allowed me to share with my students that they too can be critical, creative and take risks, gaining ownership of their knowledge. Embracing uncertainty certainly paid off when educators had to face the COVID-19 pandemic, which was beyond our imaginations, with remote learning and the increase in mental illness adding significantly to the stress of modern life.

Reflection gave me the tools to question my fundamental values and beliefs imposed from home, school and church. This questioning helped me accept my identity as a strength, encouraged me to stop resisting and welcome the troublesome Bear in me, the noisy activist Bear fighting not only for the arts but for minorities' voices. The Bear as a form of artistic activism provided an opportunity to disrupt people's preconceived notions of art and protest as well as their predetermined ideas of what was being communicated, creating a chance to deconstruct fixed ideas and moral ideals by remapping cognitive patterns which facilitated transformation (Clement 2022). Who would ever think that I would have to regress, unlearn, go back to being a beast (Bear) to finally understand what it is to be human? The Bear gave me my voice, and I gave a voice to the Bear. In this exchange I claimed my life back and gave myself the right to exist.

References

Adams, J. and Owens, A. (2016) *Creativity and Democracy in Education*. London and New York: Routledge.

Addison, N. (2010) *Understanding Art Education*. London: Routledge.

Ball, S. (2003) The teacher's soul and the terrors of performativity, *Journal of Education Policy*, 18(2): 215–228.

Bandura, A. (1982a) Self-efficacy mechanism in human agency, *American Psychologist*, 37(2): 122–147.

Bandura, A. (1982b) The psychology of chance encounters and life paths, *American Psychologist*, 37(7): 747–755.

Barone, T.E and Eisner, E.W. (2011) *Arts Based Research*. SAGE Publications.

Broadhead, S. (2018) Mature students, transformation and transition, *Education + Training*, DOI: https://doi.org/10.1108/ET-02-2018-0035

Calirman, C. (2012) *Brazilian Art under Dictatorship*. Durham: Duke University Press.

Carr, C., Hayes, R. and Sumner, E. (2017) Predicting a threshold of perceived facebook post success via likes and reactions: A test of explanatory mechanisms, *Communication Research Reports*, 35(2): 141–151.

Clement, M., (2022) *The Intersection of Art and Activism – The Oxford Blue* [online] The Oxford Blue. Available at: https://theoxfordblue.co.uk/the-intersection-of-art-and-activism/#:~:text=Art%20is%20about%20being%20both,of%20a%20place%20of%20 honesty (accessed 14 November 2023).

Damerow, M. (2023) The influence of neoliberalism on arts education: "Creativity" and "critical thinking" as semantics of an educational discourse, in Jörissen, B., Unterberg, L., Klepacki, T. (eds) *Cultural Sustainability and Arts Education. Yearbook of Arts Education Research for Cultural Diversity and Sustainable Development*, vol. 2. Springer, Singapore. DOI: https://doi.org/10.1007/978-981-19-3915-0_8

Dewey, J. (2005) *Art as Experience.* New York: Berkeley Publishing Group.

Eisner, E. W. (2007) Art and knowledge, in Knowles, J. and Cole, A. (eds.). *Handbook of the Arts in Qualitative Research.* Thousand Oaks: SAGE Publications.

Emporiopernambucano.com. (2022) [online] Available at: https://www.emporiopernambucano.com/single-post/2017/01/20/A-la-ursa-o-urso-do-carnaval-Pernambucano#! (accessed 20 August 2022).

English, A. (2014) *Discontinuity in Learning.* New York: Cambridge University Press.

Feinstein, H. (1985) Art as visual metaphor, *Art Education*, 38(4): 26.

Foucault, M. (1991) *Discipline and Punish.* London: Penguin.

Foucault, M. (2013) *Archaeology of Knowledge.* Hoboken: Taylor and Francis.

Freire, P. (1970) *Pedagogy of Hope.* Penguin Books.

Freire, P. (1974) *Education for Critical Consciousness.* London: Sheed & Ward.

Gandin, L. (2007) The construction of the citizen school project as an alternative to neoliberal educational policies, *Policy Futures in Education*, 5(2): 179–193.

Granville, G. (ed.) (2012) *Art Education and Contemporary Culture: Irish Experiences, International Perspectives.* Bristol and Chicago: Intellect.

Heaton, R. & Crumpler, A. (2017) Sharing mindfulness: A moral practice for artist teachers, *International Journal for Education & the Arts*, 18(26): 1–12.

hooks, b. (1994) *Teaching to Transgress.* New York and Abingdon: Routledge.

Illeris, K. (2014) *Transformative Learning and Identity.* Routledge.

Lambrechts, W. and Hindson, J. (2016) *Research and Innovation in Education for Sustainable Development.* Austria: Environment and School Initiatives.

Lepecki, A. (2016) The non-time of lived experience: The problem of color in Hé lio Oiticica's early works, *Representations*, 136(1): 77–95.

Levine, C. (2008) *Provoking Democracy.* Oxford: John Wiley & Sons.

Mansfield, J. (2009) Creativity and the arts in the curriculum under neoliberal regimes, *Access: Contemporary Issues in Education*, 28(1): 23–36.

McNiff, S. (2010) *Art-Based Research.* London: Jessica Kingsley.

Meyer, J. and Land, R. (2005) Threshold concepts and troublesome knowledge (2): Epistemological considerations and a conceptual framework for teaching and learning, *Higher Education*, 49(3): 373–388.

Parsons, M. (2010) Interpreting art through metaphors, *International Journal of Art & Design Education*, 29(3): 228–235.

Payne, R. (2012) Seen, unseen or overlooked? How can visual perception develop through a multimodal enquiry? *International Journal of Art & Design Education*, 31(3): 245–255.

Payne, R. and Hall, E. (2018) The NSEAD Survey Report 2015-16: Political Reflections from Two Art and Design Educators, *International Journal of Art & Design Education*, 37(2): 167–176.

Perkins, D. (1999) The many faces of constructivism, *Educational Leadership*, 57(3): 6–11.

Ribeiro, D. (2017) *O que é lugar de fala?* Letramento: Justificando. Available at: https://www.sindjorce.org.br/wp-content/uploads/2019/10/RIBEIRO-D.-O-que-e-lugar-de-fala.pdf

Ruderman, E. (2006) Nurturance and self-sabotage: Psychoanalytic perspectives on women's fear of success, *International Forum of Psychoanalysis*, 15(2): 85–95.

Schön, D. (1983) *The Reflective Practitioner*. Abingdon & New York: Ashgate Publishing, Routledge.

Shulman, L. (2005a) Pedagogies of uncertainty, *Liberal Education*, 91(2): 18–25.

Shulman, L. (2005b) Signature pedagogies in the professions, *Daedalus*, 134(3): 52–59.

Sidgwick, E. (2010) Vivência: From disciplined to remade lived experience in the Brazilian avant-garde of the 1960s, *Subjectivity*, 3(2): 193–208.

Thodos, D. (2018) How neoliberal economics impacted art education, *The Independent Voice of the Visual Arts – New Art Examiner*, 32(3): 15–18.

Titus, J. and Sinacore, A. (2013) Artmaking and well-being in healthy young adult women, *The Arts in Psychotherapy*, 40(1): 29–36.

Van Manen, M. (2012) *Researching Lived Experience*. London: The Althouse Press.

Wall, S. (2006) An autoethnography on learning about autoethnography, *International Journal of Qualitative Methods*, 5(2): 146–160.

Webb, P.T., Briscoe, F.M. and Mussman, M.P. (2009) Preparing teachers for the neoliberal Panopticon, *Educational Foundations*, 23: 3–18.

Wild, C. (2011) Making creative spaces: The art and design classroom as a site of performativity, *International Journal of Art & Design Education*, 30(3): 423–432.

The demands of the artwork, complicating artist teacher practice through photography

Joanna Fursman and Melanie Woodhead

Introduction

This chapter explores the experiences of two artist educators who employ the camera and the photographic image in their artistic and education practice. The camera and its function gives the authors a unique perspective to explore the authenticity and identity of the artist educator. Our discussion focuses on how the artist teacher identity develops through this praxis. This chapter also explores how our artist educator practices are challenged and developed through the camera and photographic image making. This will be done through two projects that explore artist educator practice via photographic image-making, camera technology and their connections to the pedagogy of studying and experiencing art-making.

The chapter is structured to allow us to present individual accounts of our projects. In addition, our discussion, critical reflection and writing has led us to produce a co-authored chapter that responds to each other's practice, resulting in a combined voice interwoven through the text.

We turn first to the 2021 *Beauty and Utility* project, funded by Meadow Arts, at Avon Meadows, Worcestershire, where Melanie Woodhead explored individual artistic and co-creative photographic practices that originated during her study on the Artist Teacher Scheme at Birmingham School of Art in 2015. It was developed during MA Art and Education Practices (2016–2018) and subsequently led to current PhD study. This is followed by a Freelands Foundation commissioned film and photography project, where Joanna Fursman discusses the recent co-productive work made with students at a college of further education in the West Midlands. Using methods that have grown out of practice-based PhD research, the film explores students' experiences of being in and studying in a space of education.

Through reflecting on these projects, we argue that the camera and the process of taking and making photographic images reflect and challenge the artist teacher identity and help us to explore and examine pedagogy differently.

The writing asks, instead of defining, what if, through the actions of pedagogy, the artist teacher identity can be made more complicated, more difficult to define and more complex?

Context of practice: Melanie Woodhead

Before studying on an Artist Teacher Scheme (ATS) I had been experiencing a sense of loss (my mother, my health, my job of 10 years teaching art in further education, my identity and my artistic practice). The geography of my life had shrunk to my immediate environment, my house and garden. The garden became a source of connection and nourishment as I witnessed the daily changes that occurred there, and I could be part of a bigger rhythm that existed outside my domestic routine. I began noticing these changes with photography, using my mobile phone camera to take images. A practice that I could fit in and around my responsibilities of being a mother, this repeated act of moving between the house and garden, interior to exterior, domestic space to green, created a 'transitional' space of experiencing that the photography became a distinct part of (Winnicott 1953).

I recorded my shadow as it moved across the greenery and the garden shed, no longer viewing myself as an artist or teacher but learning from the unfolding natural processes in my garden. Uncertainty became a necessity for creativity and my mobile phone camera helped to capture fleeting moments, the images serving as reminders of what was emerging and what was lost in this fluid space of being. Photography became part of this unfolding process and not just a destination point, aiding awareness, connection and discovery. During an exhibition at the end of the ATS, a slide projector cast the images onto a bird box, highlighting the changing nature of my identity, interconnected with my environment (Figure 8.1). Photography was a method of exploring these spaces further during MA research and forming connections to the

Figure 8.1 Melanie Woodhead (2016) *Uprooted*, Slide Projection/Installation. New Art Gallery Walsall

outdoors as alternative spaces for creativity and learning. The desire to 'make with' (Haraway 2016) the environment and the co-creative possibilities of eco-photographic practices were explored during a commission by Meadow Arts and The Floodplain Meadows Partnership, to highlight the presence of Avon Meadows, a community wetland in Pershore, Worcestershire.

Context of practice: Joanna Fursman

After teaching art in secondary schools for eight years, I sought a productive and challenging way to develop my art practice through an MA Art and Education Practices. During this study, different ways of occupying spaces of education were critically explored through using digital cameras to capture images of classrooms and communal spaces in the school I worked in. This began by taking photographs as an educator interrogating the education space I worked in. It then developed into a method where I worked co-productively with the young people I taught, using the camera to capture their feelings about being in school. This investigation positioned my pedagogic and art practice into a new space, where education became a critical function of my arts-based research practice. Photographs of the MA study demonstrated my own and my students' explorations of school space with the camera (Figure 8.2).

Artist teacher identities

The role and identity of the artist educator can be experienced through a tension between the demands of art practice, pedagogy and other practical

Figure 8.2 Joanna Fursman (2012) *Not an Art Room* (Mobile). Photographic assemblage

demands, such as time and identifying spaces to make work in. Both practices pull on the identity practically, but this also questions how an art practice emerges and embeds itself alongside and because of pedagogy. Conversely, how does pedagogy appear with highly personal forms of art practice? These tensions indicate where practice and critical understanding of the artist educator has evolved through co-creating from artistic practice and pedagogy simultaneously.

Importantly, this questions how artist educator identities result in an interwoven artistic practice that can interrogate art education pedagogies. This has meant this dual role develops through two distinct demands. The first is the demands of the practice to develop through pedagogy, how this is performed through educating, who I am educating, the space, site of education and educating through art (Daichendt 2010, Thornton 2011, Hoekstra 2015). The demands of producing artwork and the demands of pedagogy pull on identity and production as an artist and practitioner. Hoekstra (2015) describes how both art and educator practices help to experience different and refreshing perspectives, but that making artwork is a reward rather than a critical reflection on the artist-educating experience. For Lucero (2016), education is approached through conceptual practices and that trying to make sense of the artist educator flattens its possibilities. For both authors, our education experience does not make sense of the artist teacher dynamic; instead it involves experiencing practice critically and messily.

The perceived duality of the artist teacher identity, and even the need to define it, becomes increasingly redundant when acknowledging that life is messy and entangled. This means moving between the spaces of certainty and uncertainty. Art education is based on learning creative skills that can be demonstrated and assessed as tangible knowledge. Artistic practice embodies tacit knowing (Candy et al. 2022) and embraces un-knowing (Paine 2022) as fundamental to creativity. This creates an aperture for ambiguity within pedagogic practice, for a critical activism as defined by Anab Jain, that removes, 'the unnecessary focus of being right and knowing everything, towards nurturing and embracing doubt. Being okay with not knowing all the answers. Being okay when others say they don't know' (Jain 2022: n.p). As artist teachers we navigate these spaces of knowledge, knowing and not knowing simultaneously with our students and participants through photographic processes and practices.

Our practices and theoretical approaches to photography and the artist teacher

Photography as transitional space

Paechter (2004: 451) identifies how language in education spaces can fix boundaries and are 'concerned with dividing up, with inclusion and exclusion, and with the drawing of boundaries'. This positions learners and educators into structured, flattened, inflexible relationships with each other and the spaces they learn in. Conversely, speaking about the wider cultural approaches to space, Massey (2005) asks that instead of something to be occupied, space might instead be a meeting-up of histories, acknowledging all the elements, relationships and people that live, work in and care for it. Linking this to the space of education, how can this acknowledging be explored through artist teacher practice?

These relationships can be affected by the mechanisms and act of taking a photograph and through the process of realising the image digitally or as photographic material. In analogue photography this would be practised through the developing and fixing process in the darkroom. In plant-based photography, a growing field of research and practice in the context of the climate emergency, the key factor in making the image visible are the ultraviolet rays from the sun triggering the photosynthetic properties of the plant-based material or emulsion. In conventional photography, as a skill to be taught, there are steps to follow that will produce an outcome. Plant-based photography challenges this as there are other factors and variables that affect its production, such as the environment, weather, season, time and materials. There is a surrendering to the process that becomes more important than the outcome in terms of learning through uncertainty. In this scenario, artist, teacher, learner, environment and plant matter are all equally significant, interdependent, co-creators in the process of not knowing, making and learning with and through each other. Images recorded on leaves or paper coated with photosensitive plant emulsion are unstable and not fixed in the sense of traditional film photography processes. They are impermanent and susceptible to exposure to light and time so that they will fade and eventually disappear. This makes the photographic surface an unstable place and the image in a state of flux.

In contrast to the traditional photographic approach of fixing an image for permanent record, the image becomes a transitional space that is subject to changing environmental factors and ultimately rendered impermanent (Figure 8.3). Originating within the field of psychoanalysis, Winnicott (cited in Johns 2005) defined transitional space as being an intermediate area, 'that space of experiencing, between the inner and outer worlds, and contributed to by both, in *which primary creativity* (illusion) exists and can develop' (Johns 2005: 1795-96). Practices and processes that allow the photographic surface to act as a transitional space of experiencing inner and outer worlds, permitting images to change and shift during the making process, have implications for the artist educator. Through this lens, the relationships between artist educator, participants, process and environment are unfolding, fluid spaces of being and learning that are not fixed and are created anew in each instance. The image and identity of the artist educator becomes variable and simultaneously responsive to internal and external agents, a transitional space of experiencing and educating from. This links the artistic identity and pedagogy performed through art education practices and spaces.

For both authors, education space is not tied to formal sites but produced in nature, gallery and other space explored and found by investigations in

Figure 8.3 Melanie Woodhead (2022) *Interleave*, Chlorophyll Print on Nasturtium Leaf

school and college. These geographies of alternative education (Kraftl 2015) are transitional spaces of learning and connection, or as Massey (2002, 293: 6) describes, 'meeting place; different stories coming together and, to one degree or another, becoming entangled'. Viewing photography as a transitional space of experiencing where the boundaries of inside and outside, me and not me, human and nonhuman become entangled, opens possibilities for learning and the reimagination of existing artist teacher narratives.

The photography walk

Beauty and Utility Project

As artist educators we engage in photowalks as creative and pedagogical practice. This opens spaces for learning outside of the studio and classroom that invites ways of thinking, creating and learning that focus less on the individual and more on the collective experience. This runs counter to most models of art education practice which centre on developing a unique creative identity. Participating in a photo walk is a shared experience of a space in real time that produces multiple viewpoints, moments of noticing and connections, to form a collective experience and response, learning with and from others and the environment. Walking as a group creates the conditions for, 'embodied, cognitive, sensual, relational, visual, communicative dimensions and possibilities' (O'Neill and Roberts 2020: 15).

In May 2021, as part of the *Beauty and Utility* project commissioned by Meadow Arts, I engaged local Year 8 High School students in a photography walk around Avon Meadows Community Wetland in Pershore, Worcestershire. The project aimed to highlight the beauty and utility of these floodplain meadows, and their important role within the community. We explored the meadows together, fuelled by the prospect of a collective experience outdoors after waves of Covid restrictions. Taking photographs on our mobile phones and digital cameras, I guided the students around the meadow, initiating a series of prompts along the route, noticing the plants and animals sharing the space, experimenting with filters, flash, and props along the way. As a speculative practice (Springgay and Truman 2018) this allowed conversations, interactions, events and encounters to unfold unexpectedly, disrupting structures, challenging expectations, and embracing the potential for failure. Some mobile phone batteries ran out of power before we had completed the walk and some props were engaged with more successfully than others, however, this encouraged collective adaptability to a changing environment. This was translated through to the following classroom-based session, when using alternative processes as agents of change. The students explored transaquatypes, which involves soaking the printed image in water which unfixes it, causing it to bleed and change in unexpected ways (Figures 8.4a and 8.4b).

Responding through the lens of an artist educator, viewing photo walks as artistic practice and not solely for the purpose of collecting visual research for

Figures 8.4a and 8.4b Melanie Woodhead (2021) *Transitional Spaces and Ages in Times of Climate Crisis #2*, Transaquatype

(a)   (b)

a project allows for disruption within a creative response. The camera records movement and moments of reflection, not as a distant observer, removed from the process, but part of it. Photo walks enable a method for reflecting and understanding how our emotions are 'interconnected with senses and perception to interpret our surroundings [...] necessary to understand the formation and reshaping of the self, our daily experience, memories and anticipated futures' (O'Neill and Roberts 2020: 25). From this position, photography is not about fixing but part of the process of unfixing, responsive to the unfolding processes we are entangled with as artist educators.

Looking for a New School Portrait, a film for Freelands Foundation

This entangling of the artist educator is explored in ongoing art practice and research called *Looking for a New School Portrait*. This work uses digital photography and co-constructive methods with students to gather images in education contexts. This has developed through practice-based MA and PhD research and seeks to explore different ways education can be depicted and represented. These practices have developed through four aspects or assemblages, and as materials of expression, which are: the intentions to take a photograph, planning and thinking how an image can look, critical discussions about the image and embodied interaction reflected through pedagogic interactions pedagogic interaction.

My film was commissioned for Freelands Foundation SHIFT series that shares the diverse approaches of artists, educators, their research, philosophies, and practices in education. The film explored my artist educator practice, produced with a series of filmed clips and still images made in a co-constructed approach with my students at a college of Further Education. Making the film defined the experience of working and thinking through projects and the different ways of approaching educating through art. Using photowalks around the college and its grounds, I extracted, decided and questioned how its space functioned and the different purposes it moved through. The photowalk method posed questions about my location, the position of my body in the space, what the environment I am in is and how I moved and interacted with it. Photowalks helped to expand my exploration, take new pathways and directions, and discover new images where the thinking about the composition and content of a photograph leads to exploring and extending the next, one decision to capture an image leads to another. The walking methodologies expanded the possibilities for the images and ideas at the same time, privileging an embodied way of knowing where 'movement connects mind, body and environment' (Springgay and Truman 2019: 4).

In photowalks, this kind of connected embodiment is experienced more profoundly via the presence and technology of the camera and directs movement and walking differently in the environment. Walking during the research detaches the photographer from normalised ways of experiencing and moves the search for photographs towards the 'precisely true to life' (Bolt 2013: 123). This locates the photograph and photographer into a unique assembled moment of making and draws upon Krauss's (1999: 25) visual theory of watching film as involving 'everything all at once' and Bolt's (2013) capture of something 'intensely present'. Through this method, everything in the education space becomes available to the camera and its screen reflects the experience back to the maker. Making film agitates the education space, creating something new in and for the space and does what O'Sullivan (2005: 65) describes as 'forcing us to thought'.

The body and pedagogy

The film explored my own experience of educating and documenting artrooms, objects, journeys around the college that are 'the affective and relational forces of art and media that generate new ways of thinking, feeling, acting, and becoming' (Hellman and Lind 2017: 219). This method was useful in helping to explore new images of education spaces intensely and purposely occupied, and re-examined the highly familiar things in that space. Images are layered, compositionally experimented, and played with. Human and more-than-human elements combine to produce different images in the education space, appearing from inside the pedagogical moment. The college space where we made the images appeared to press and demand attention in the frame of the camera lens, reflecting itself back at itself alongside the walk with the camera. This again alludes to how Krauss (1999: 25) describes the human and non-human material experience of film for viewers, 'including the audience's position caught between the source of the light behind it and the image projected before its eyes'.

This experience between humans and camera technology can be analogous to the work of pedagogy. Using the camera with this space and its contents can begin to behave like a prosthesis so that it shapes itself the needs of all kinds of bodies, while the technology shapes how these bodies move. This is also indicated by Phu, Brown and Noble (2020: 23) who use the word 'feeling' to describe embodied aspects of photography: 'The term feeling also has the advantage of underscoring tactility, to draw attention to a broader range of sensory experiences of photography, which encompass not just the optic, but also the haptic.' Pedagogy is also attached to what Benjamin (2008: 7) called the 'aura' of the photographic image. The image becomes alive to the possibilities of the pedagogic process and its feeling. Each time we made new images, it agitated this dynamic and changed visual perspectives. This has a distinct impact on the possibilities of pedagogy, how it emerges and how it is shaped.

What do the images look like and what do they do?

Using the camera quickly and effectively depicts the 'true to life-ness of situations' (Bolt 2013), and the kinds of experience confronting an educator. For the groups making photographs, the things that happen on the lens of the camera

Figure 8.5: Joanna Fursman (2022) *Looking for a new School Portrait, (Blue slice)*. Photographic still

are drawn through the technology and onto the screen. This drew a sense of the photographer and the viewer to a point where the 'image stares back' (Nancy 2005: 82). This simultaneous action brings the image and the viewer into relational confrontation with the image and the world in which it was taken.

When making the film, the camera directed interactions with the human and more-than-human; for example: the objects encountered when educating through art (Figures 8.5 and 8.6), the in-between spaces often occupied by students and used by educators to move between sessions. Taking images in this education space remade its image, it helped me to constantly reposition myself as an artist educator and helped me to see the college in different ways. Seeking an image while walking around the college space revealed important pedagogical moments, the image of the education space was sucked into the camera through its lens and appeared on its screen. In this sense, the college spoke back to me through the camera when I looked for images, this also happened in discussions about the images we chose to include in the film.

Unfixing through assemblage

The still images in the film were produced through a process of assemblage. This is linked to the surrealist and pre-war two and three-dimensional collage practice. Kurt Schwitters (1887–1948) worked in two dimensions but also with

Figure 8.6 Joanna Fursman (2022) *Looking for a new School Portrait, (Shoulders).* Photographic still

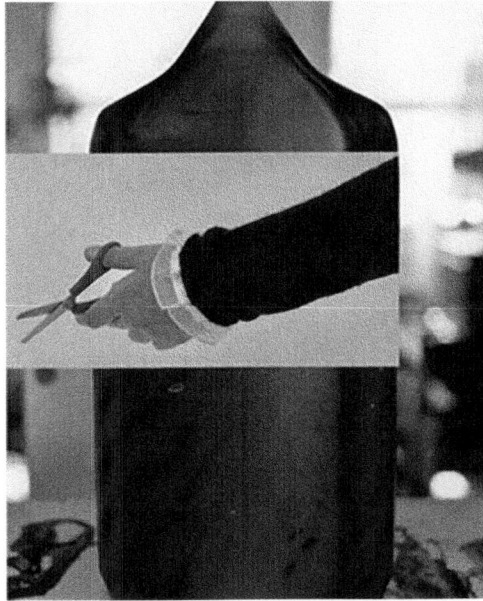

a method he termed Merz where assemblage changed human spaces (Orchard 2007). Schwitters created 'Merzbau' in the 1930s in his home and studio in Hannover, changing its rooms into multi-layered surfaces and structures that pierced and disrupted the domestic space. Assemblage is often used to combine, juxtapose and contrast meaning to make new images. Its effects prevent the eye from resting on an image composition and instead demands and pulls on the function of looking to stop the viewer making sense of what they are looking at. This visual compulsion to make sense of the space is disorientating in the images of the Hannover Merzbau, the assemblage prevents this process of 'finding the normal' or completing itself and a way of art and the human co-existing.

Similar to the experience of the artist educator, the pull into and return from pedagogy towards art practice, the assemblage of human and non-human forms in the images re-configure the visual composition and disrupt the plane of sense. The layered material of the image slowly and continuously interrupts the image space. This process of combining images clashes and weaves their meaning, diverts their visual language, and unfixes the images of the education space and my experience as the artist educator. This is important to help us know that unfixing images means unfixing pedagogy. This helps art education to continually evolve and value the ways people study and make art, and to help them shape their futures in the way that they want.

Like the description made by Krauss (1999), the body makes an assemblage in its interaction with the camera technology and the situation in which

it is producing an image. This assemblage is produced by layering of images and opens an opportunity to think about the artist educator differently. The reflexive function of the photograph and what it does when it goes into the world means pedagogical relationships can be reconfigured and recognised through the photographic process and the image. Assemblage cannot be planned, but it produces different kinds of relationships that develop through the camera technology as it guides me to look for new kinds of images to make and combine.

The spaces depicted in the film are chosen by students studying art. These are where students and educator can make the work with methods using what Lucero (2018) describes as co-constructing. This co-constructing appears explicitly in the film as the students choose and document an important space where they are educated. Images of education space and students studying art entangle, and they make new space available for discussion and negotiation to explore compositional construction.

Conclusion

This conclusion summarises how the writing process has enabled us to reflect on our practices and combined perspectives. For both authors, the artist teacher has more than two identities that can be unfixed from the art-room and involve all the possibilities of pedagogy, education space and embodied practice during making work with young people.

Knowing and not knowing

The tacit knowledge involved in exploring an education space and making images with the camera technology makes pedagogy and art practices more involved. This happens through embodied practices that involve the body where 'knowing can be embedded in, embodied with, enacted through or extended by practice through touch, feeling, know-how, intuition' (Candy et al. 2022: 197). This has distinct effect on the way the camera can direct how practice is produced, its presence in education space and in addition, how this can be approached through co-constructing practices defined by Lucero (2018).

Co-constructing

As an artist teacher, Lucero (2016: 188) employs the concept of pliability to describe what his identity as an artist might be inside an education environment and what might be at stake when the educator as artist might 'play with the parameters and materiality of that situation to tease out its potentiality (for good and for bad)'. When this approach is employed as a co-constructing method (Lucero 2016) with young people as participants who take part in the projects, they drive how images are made, might look and are presented

alongside the artist teacher. This becomes a way of recognising how the young people participating in the projects can contribute and develop ideas and what that problematises (Bremmer et al. 2021). Their approaches enrich the outcomes, demonstrate new ways of looking, examining and exploring experience that becomes detected and re-framed through the camera technology.

A camera is part of the process. Not endpoints but unfolding processes

The camera and its technology move into and out of different roles in the process of producing images. If the technology is new to students, it can be awkward and feel invasive to use. It can however become like a familiar or pedagogic prosthesis. This becoming familiar is compared by Garoian (cited in O'Donoghue 2015) to a buoy in the ocean or signpost and is a visual and haptic apparatus that extends the act of looking, combining embodiment and aesthetics. This helps to understand how the camera moves and adapts to the body and allows the education space and its image to flow through its technology, to initiate discussions and develop ideas.

Unfixing – how this affects the artist teacher

An analogue photographic image is made by exposing an image onto photographic paper, then moved through developer and finally a fix that determines the image that cannot be changed. Transaquatype methods of producing images unfix their surface, leaving them open to different kinds of possibilities, making the image look different to plans or intentions. Assemblage disrupts the image surface by mixing and combining two or more images that pull the maker and viewer out of normalised ways of looking. Embracing these speculative approaches to process, practice and pedagogy, creates space for the unexpected and what Paine describes as 'the intentional act of un-knowing' (Paine 2022: 256), encouraging creative adaptability to changing environments. The movement away from fixed intentions in the practices discussed in this chapter parallels our approach to the artist teacher identity that the authors wish to move away from defining and instead make more complicated.

Photography and why we feel it is important in the artist-educator debate

Through our research and practice as artists and educators, using photography has enabled us to combine these distinct practices to pull into question the role of the artist educator. Crucially, the convenience or available technology of the camera means it can be used to produce results and reflects the quickness and busy-ness of working in education spaces and with young people. Through our writing we have resisted a definition of the artist teacher identity and instead our projects demonstrate how this kind of practice can continuously complicate what this identity is.

References

Benjamin, W. (2008) *The Work of Art in the Age of Mechanical Reproduction*. London: Penguin.

Bolt, B. (2013), 'The athleticism of imaging: Figuring a materialist performativity', in D.

Bremmer, M.; Emiel H., and Sanne K. (2021) Teacher as Conceptual Artist. *The International Journal of Art and Design Education*, 40(1): 82–98.

Candy, L.; Edmonds, E. and Vear, C. (eds) (2022) *The Routledge International Handbook of Practice-Based Research*. London: Routledge.

Daichendt, J. (2010) *Artist Teacher: A Philosophy for Creating and Teaching*. Bristol: Intellect.

Haraway, D.J. (2016) *Staying with the Trouble: Making Kin in the Chthulucene*. North Carolina: Duke University Press.

Hellman, A. and Lind, U. (2017) Picking up speed: Rethinking visual art education as assemblages, *Studies in Art Education*, 58(3): 206–221.

Hoekstra, M. (2015) The problematic nature of the artist-teacher concept and implications for pedagogical practice, *The International Journal of Art & Design Education*, 34(3): 349–357.

Jain, A. (2022) *To doubt, to question, to say 'enough'. Reimagining Possibilities*. Available at: https://medium.com/reimagining-economic-possibilities/to-doubt-to-question-to-say-enough-1f3334d774cb (accessed 3 May 2023).

Johns, J. (2005) 'Transitional Object, Space' in de Mijolla, A., ed., *International Dictionary of Psychoanalysis*, vol. 3, Detroit, MI: Macmillan Reference USA, 1795–1796 Available at: https://link-gale-com.bcu.idm.oclc.org/apps/doc/CX3435301509/GVRL?u=uce&sid=bookmark-GVRL&xid=0d1962c9 (accessed 23 Feb 2023).

Kraftl, P. (2015) *Geographies of Alternative Education. Diverse learning spaces for children and young people*. Bristol, Chicago: Policy Press.

Krauss, A. (1999) *A Voyage on the North Sea. Art in the Age of the Post-Medium Condition*. New York: Thames and Hudson.

Lucero, J. (2016) Conceptualist as educator/educator as conceptualist, in Vella, R. *Artist-Teachers in Context*. Rotterdam: Sense, 187–196.

Lucero, J. (2018) *Teacher as Conceptual Artist*. Amsterdam, NL: Research Group Arts Education, Amsterdam University of the Arts.

Massey, D. (2002) Globalisation: What does it mean for geography? *Geography*, 87, (4): 293–296.

Massey, D. (2005) *For Space*. London: Sage.

Nancy, J-L. (2005) *The Ground of the Image*. Fordham University Press.

O'Donoghue, D. (2015) On the education of art-based researchers: What we might learn from Charles Garoian, *Qualitative Enquiry*, 21(6): 520–528.

O'Neill, M. and Roberts, B. (2020) *Walking Methods: Research on the Move*. London: Routledge.

Orchard, K. (2007) 'Kurt Schwitters: Reconstructions of the Merzbau', in Tate Papers no.8. Available at: https://www.tate.org.uk/research/tate-papers/08/kurt-schwitters-reconstructions-of-the-merzbau (accessed 1 October 2022).

O'Sullivan, S. (2005) Ten concepts following Cathy Wilkes's practice, *Afterall: A Journal of Art, Context and Enquiry*, 12(12): 64–70.

Paechter, C. (2004) Metaphors of space in educational theory and practice. *Pedagogy, Culture and Society*, 12 (3): 449–466.

Paine, G. (2022) *Un-knowing*: a strategy for forging new directions and innovative works through experiential learning, in L. Candy; E. Edmonds, and C. Vear (eds) *The Routledge International Handbook of Practice-Based Research*. London: Routledge.

Phu, T.; Brown, E-H. and Noble, A. (2020) Feeling in photography, the affective turn, and the history of emotions, in M. Durden and J. Tomey (eds) *The Routledge Companion to Photography Theory*. Abingdon: Routledge.

Springgay, S. and Truman, S.E. (2018) On the need for methods beyond procedural-ism: Speculative middles, (in)tensions, and response-ability in research, *Qualitative Inquiry* 24 (3): 203–214.

Sprinnggay, S. and Truman, S.E. (2019). Counterfuturisms and speculative temporalities: Walking research creation in school, *International Journal of qualitative studies in Education*, 32 (6): 547–559.

Thornton, A. (2011) Being an artist teacher, a liberating identity? *The International Journal of Art and Design Education*, 30(1): 31–36.

Winnicott, D. (1953) Transitional objects and transitional phenomena, *International Journal of Psychoanalysis*, 34: 89–97; and in Collected papers, through paediatrics to psychoanalysis: 229–242. London: Tavistock.

Websites

Meadow Arts (2023) *Beauty and Utility* (online). Available at: https://meadowarts.org/event/beauty-utility-2/ (accessed 24 February 2023)

Artist teacher sketchbook practice for professional learning

Emese Hall

Introduction

In the art education community, we often refer to artist teachers without offering any clear definition. It could be that we either mean an artist who teaches or a teacher who makes art. Does it matter? Daichendt (2010: 61) explains the complex relationship between the dual roles of artist and teacher, suggesting that although different interpretations of the term 'artist teacher' exist, 'when used properly, [it] is actually a philosophy for teaching. It does not presuppose an artistic lifestyle but uses the individual talents and learned skills or techniques of the artists and circumvents them into the teaching profession.' Research evidence (e.g., Hetland et al. 2013) shows that art pedagogy informed by artist practice can be both meaningful and effective for learners to exemplify diverse artistic processes in a wide range of contexts. Artist teacher learning involves the process of making to know (Buchman 2021), thus I argue that space and time for teachers' own artistic practice should be a central component of professional development.

The Department for Education (2016: 1) in England states that 'high-quality professional development requires workplaces to be steeped in rigorous scholarship, with professionals continually developing and supporting each other so that pupils benefit from the best possible teaching'. However, in England, teachers' access to professional learning opportunities in visual arts tends to be limited, largely because art is not regarded as a priority subject within statutory education (Brass and Coles 2014; Hall 2015; Payne and Hall 2018). More specialist professional development is required but this must be high quality (Cooper 2019), recognising teachers' interests and needs as well as those of their pupils. Further, artist teachers have particular needs. Importantly, Thornton (2013: 85) proposes that artist teachers require four common factors of support: 'support from other artists and the art establishment; support from other teachers and the education establishment; planned and structured practices and aims; and commitment to both practices'. Sketchbook practice can act as a bridge between these different forms of support.

This chapter focuses on artist teacher sketchbooks for professional learning. It is suggested that the best way to teach about sketchbooks is for teachers to engage with their own (Buffery 2009). Further, there is evidence that arts-based reflection enhances teachers' wellbeing (Brass and Coles 2014; McKay and Barton 2018). Here, I will share the findings from a small-scale enquiry into a regional (UK) art education community for professional learning. Informed by the successful Sketchbook Circle initiative (e.g., see Brass and Coles 2014), the 10-month programme, devised and led by a well-regarded arts organisation typically involves a group of up to 20 artists and teachers – many identifying as artist teachers, including my research participants – working side-by-side on collaborative sketchbooks, resourced by formal and informal networking events (e.g., at least termly), peer-to-peer support and skill shares. The programme involves strategic partnering, where someone less experienced will be partnered with someone more experienced, and the experienced members often lead the skill shares either in-person or online. Within this chapter, to anonymise the research participants' identity, the initiative and its host organisation will not be named, instead it will be referred to as 'the sketchbook programme'.

Research overview

The findings shared here are from a small-scale study that I conducted during the summer of 2021. The research sought to ask: *How does a CPD programme with sketchbooks at its heart enhance teachers' professional learning in relation to their self-perception as an artist teacher?* Following ethical approval from my university, to seek a purposive sample, I asked the focus arts organisation to share a research invitation with relevant contacts via email. Data are drawn from semi-structured individual interviews with two self-nominated programme participants (the total response to my research invitation) and supplementary photographs of their sketchbook content. Interviews, each approximately an hour, were conducted online and recorded via Microsoft Teams. The first interview involved a discussion about the participants' current teaching role and their experiences and perceptions of the sketchbook programme. Following this, the participants were asked to select eight images from their sketchbooks to discuss in detail in the second interview, as listed below. They emailed photographs to me in advance so I could collate these in sequence to share with them for discussion.

1 *An entry that is typical of your favourite type of making.*
2 *An entry that challenged you, but you were pleased with the outcome.*
3 *An entry that was strongly influenced by your programme partner's work.*
4 *An entry that you dislike...or even hate!*
5 *An entry that your students found especially inspiring.*

6 *An entry that you would like to use as a springboard for future work...*
7 *An entry that has strong personal meaning/s attached to it (positive or negative).*
8 *You own 'free' choice... could be a repeat of one of the categories above – or not!*

On completion of interview transcription, data analysis was inductive and involved hand-coding and constant comparison techniques (for example, Glaser 1965). In sharing visual data in this chapter, I identified two sketchbook entries from each participant which most closely connected to areas of interest in their respective narratives – presented here discursively (Squire et al. 2014). I must highlight that the images do not fully showcase the range and quality of the participants' sketchbook practice.

As the participants did not wish to select pseudonyms, I chose these: Jocelyn and Bea. Both participants are female and regarded themselves as artist teachers. At the time of interview, each had over 15 years of experience working in education, either as a teacher or in a teaching support role. They were both teaching in non-mainstream education settings and held art leadership roles. Additionally, Jocelyn was her setting's Special Educational Needs Coordinator (SENCO). Bea had a degree in textiles and Jocelyn had a degree in ceramics and glass. Both had been involved in several cycles/years of the sketchbook programme and were extremely passionate about art, art education and their students. Below I share their artist teacher 'journeys' via their sketchbooks, maximising the use of their own words for authenticity in contributing to the trustworthiness of the study (Stahl and King 2020).

Jocelyn's journey

Jocelyn explained that she had been involved in the national Sketchbook Circle as well as this regional sketchbook programme, noting: 'finding your own time to make is really important'. She thought that working regularly in the sketchbook was important and her advice to others was: 'it can just be an hour'. Although she described herself as 'quite confident', as the only art specialist in her setting, she said it was essential 'to reach out to other creative practitioners'. She added:

> We're not just teachers we're artists as well and to keep that mindset [...] that's a really important part of, I think, our personal identity [...] we all go to art school because we love art and we teach art because we love seeing other people make art and it's about hanging on to that first bit as well, about why we originally all went to art [school].

Jocelyn's enthusiasm for making was evident not least in her frequent mentions of getting messy hands: 'I just always had this real desire to make stuff and do stuff and get my hands a bit mucky [...] I still feel that [...] I want to print, make, and I want to get clay and I want to do heavy tactile things'. She said that this desire was still unresolved.

Her sketchbook programme exchanges had been mostly positive, but some experiences were less successful – for example, she described one exchange as 'amazing' 'fantastic' and 'really brilliant' and another 'didn't work out quite so well' because the partner was less engaged. She noted how she took different approaches to working in her sketchbook depending on her partner's interests and preferred approach. For her, artist teacher sketchbooks 'have a certain rhythm to them' – she mentioned there was 'a certain routine to what you do' – whereas artists' sketchbooks tended to be more diverse. Jocelyn described how her sketchbook practice had 'really changed. Oh my god, it's so different from what I first thought it would be, completely.' She went on to explain, 'When I first did it I was really nervous and really self-conscious and now I'm much more confident and open minded about it.' Further, she observed, 'It's definitely having that network of support [... it] makes you go, "Yeah, I can do this!"'

Connecting with others was a valuable aspect of the sketchbook programme for Jocelyn. She spoke warmly about the programme's face-to-face gatherings in various cultural settings, but also observed that 'even though you don't meet, there's always notes and postcards to each other and little notes inside and letters about what else you've been doing'. She thought that physical connections were 'lovely' and 'really meaningful' and preferred this connection and communication to 'social media support' and emails. However, she also noted some of the barriers to accessing in-person training, such as being unable to attend events during the school day: 'there's no capacity to take time out,' adding, 'I think it's fairly typical' and funding required 'the golden egg'.

Despite frustrations and struggles with the 'bureaucratic stuff' of teaching, Jocelyn told me she nonetheless found teaching rewarding: 'I think I care so deeply about my job because it feels like an extension of myself [...] I feel like I go and do something that is a really, really fundamental part of me.' She said her involvement in the sketchbook programme provided a 'fresh injection' and was refreshing her classroom practice. She spoke in detail about how she enjoyed sharing her sketchbooks – 'some of my best resources' – with her students: 'they'll always find something in there and they ask about it and then they want to do it as well'. She gave some examples that the students found particularly inspirational because they saw them as unusual and helped to dispel the myth that art is all about 'being good at drawing'. Her students often asked if she made art, and she had told them: 'I love seeing you make art and I love making art myself'. She wanted to make her students aware that 'there are loads of different ways to be an artist', adding 'I don't think they see being an art teacher as a proper job'. It was important to Jocelyn that art was held in high regard by her students and she wanted them to value their art lessons.

Figure 9.1 Jocelyn (2021) *An entry that your students found especially inspiring*

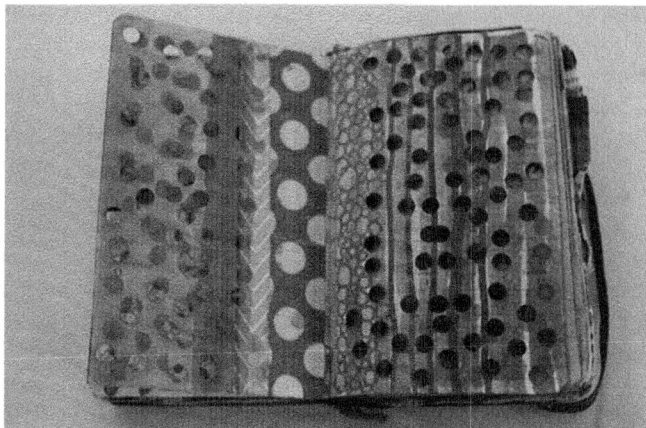

The image shown in Figure 9.1 was selected by Jocelyn as being an entry that her students found especially inspiring. This was a page about which she spoke at length, explaining its popularity: 'it's always one of the ones they're drawn to', 'they just get really excited by it.' She described how it was created by a playful approach, 'essentially vandalising a sketchbook' and producing 'something really beautiful.' She associated the holes with Barbara Hepworth's sculptures. Jocelyn said this was 'so achievable' for her students, adding 'I always endeavour to have resources that will make them go "wow!"'. She wanted to engage them joyfully.

Jocelyn's interest in special needs education was also central to her teaching identity: 'I have a great passion for it'. She commented, 'You know, I am the only art-teaching SENCO I've ever met. They generally tend to be English or maths teachers, I was told once'. She was driven to seek further training – 'you find your own CPD' – and had pursued her own action research. Relating theory to practice was of great interest to Jocelyn and reading and conferences informed her teaching. She commented: 'I know the arts grow mental health. I know the arts grow a sense of wellbeing.' She described a project she was leading locally for Key Stage 3 students, 'creating artwork as therapeutic practice'. However, she was quick to add this was not an art therapy programme, but rather a proactive intervention to help students with mental health needs who did not yet meet the threshold for formal mental health support. She believed that art making can offer fast, positive results for students. This new project – 'I had wanted to do it for so long' – involved her training other teachers to expand its reach. She described it as 'amazing' and remarked, 'I would like that provision in every school'.

Notably, Jocelyn commented, 'Wellbeing is before anything else, without a doubt'. There was a former colleague whom she sought to emulate: 'She held you and that is something I really endeavour to do because I think if people feel held, they feel safe, and they'll take risks and they'll engage in a creative process which will bring them a really great sense of wellbeing.'

Jocelyn referred to 'a very difficult time' she had experienced professionally and how the sketchbook programme has offered 'a massive boost' and had given her 'that sense of community', adding 'you're never alone'. She mentioned another programme participant who had told her something similar. Further, she spoke about the negative impact of the pandemic: 'It's felt like a year where we haven't been able to achieve, which is really frustrating and really makes you feel quite low actually…' However, she explained that she and her colleagues always looked to integrate art into their teaching wherever possible: 'it's built in everywhere'. She likened the sketchbook programme to a sewing bee from 'days of old' – 'I think it's really needed particularly as we come out of lockdown. To reconnect is really important.' Jocelyn liked that she was able to 'discover those like minds in education who don't think you're mad if you want to do things differently.'

The sketchbook entry in Figure 9.2 had a strong personal meaning for Jocelyn. She explained she had made it while on holiday in St Ives, shortly after getting a new job: 'I was really excited about the future and where it would go'. She said: 'I created those pages at a really lovely, lovely time', 'I felt really excited professionally'. Again, she noted the influence of Barbara Hepworth and the significance of the hole, and explained she had used a Cornish pasty bag, the writing on which she thought was 'fantastic'. Looking back at this entry made her feel both happy and sad as the new workplace had closed and colleagues had lost their jobs: 'it didn't end particularly well'. This was the 'very difficult time' to which Jocelyn referred in her first interview. She told me that her sketchbooks were 'really special objects, adding: 'I love them, I really love them.' She could revisit her memories via her sketchbook entries.

Figure 9.2 Jocelyn (2021) *An entry that has strong personal meaning/s attached to it (positive or negative)*

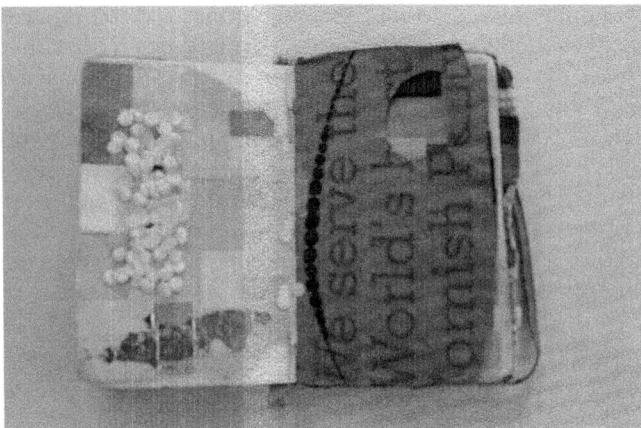

Bea's journey

For Bea, the sketchbook programme provided an opportunity to rekindle her personal art practice:

> 'it was hugely beneficial, along with the workshops as well, in my building my confidence, opening my artistic skills up again – they've been quite dormant for a very long time. And that was the beginning really, and since then, I've just remembered the person I was before I had children.'

Bea also spoke of 'focus', 'purpose' and 'identity'. Engaging in the sketchbook programme brought her happiness, 'networking connections' and 'extra friendships'. The connection to her sketchbook partners through the exchanges was a strong motivational factor for Bea:

> 'I'm a bit lost and not very good at just doing my own sketchbook. It's the swapping bit, that is the bit that appeals to me. I'm a very sociable person. I love being part of a teaching team and I think it's that connection with someone else that I really [like]. That's my incentive, the exciting bit.'

It was notable that Bea described in some detail the various approaches she took to working with different sketchbook partners, depending on her knowledge of their level of confidence. For example, she was conscious not to potentially overwhelm a partner whom she knew had less art experience than her, as she explained her typical preference was for complex, multi-layered 'fiddly' work. Interestingly, this sensitivity towards others might have been influenced by her initial feelings on participating in the sketchbook programme for the first time as she said she had been 'absolutely terrified' and 'very intimidated'. She recounted: 'it took me that whole year, that whole first cycle to just allow myself to enjoy it and not overthink it'. Now, she thought it was important to 'just enjoy the journey' and not worry whether other people liked your work or not. She felt that 'this sketchbook thing' had 'just clicked' with her, despite not working in sketchbooks since her university course.

In collaborating with some other (non-teacher) artist partners, Bea explained that she had felt challenged in a good way. For instance, one partner sparked a sense of competition and 'really pushed me to try brave new things, so it was a really nice switch'. One swap had felt 'intimidating' at first, but she then enjoyed the challenge of new provocations from her partner's entries. Bea also regarded the sketchbook as a prompt to make her observe more in her everyday life. 'I think it makes you really look when you're out and about, about things that could become a sketchbook piece.' For inspiration, she said she loved 'most things'.

The sketchbook entry in Figure 9.3 is an example of Bea's 'fiddly work'. She said she had been responding to the 'colours around me' while on holiday, saying 'I did it for ages wherever it went'. She selected this as an entry that had challenged her, but she was pleased with the outcome. Bea spent time

Figure 9.3 Bea (2021) *An entry that challenged you, but you were pleased with the outcome*

describing her art-making processes in considerable detail to me and this was an example of one of her favourite techniques, cutting into layers of fabric. This piece was made with silk offcuts which she procured from a textile designer friend. 'It might be 10 layers of different fabric' and the cutting demanded great accuracy. Bea mentioned how she'd developed the process through experimentation. She explained: 'It's very, very fiddly. I can't tell you how fiddly it is!' but she also noted that she found the process to arrive at this outcome as 'very therapeutic'.

Bea's commitment to the professional expectations of the programme was strongly evident. She mentioned that it bothered her when some people did not swap their sketchbook with their partner on the agreed timetable, which she felt was unfair. She also explained: 'I'm quite territorial about my books'. One partner had lost Bea's sketchbook and she said: 'I was really shocked how annoyed and angry I was'. For her, it was essential that the sketchbook dialogue should be maintained – she stated: 'I'm not very good at accepting excuses.' She had empathy for anyone whose partner did return the book because the programme called for reciprocity. This sense of ownership over the sketchbook was also noted by Bea when describing her students' work: 'having that thing that's theirs, it's their book'.

Bea said that the sketchbook programme was 'enriching' her teaching and offered 'a wealth of possibility'. With each partner came a new theme to explore, in addition to the sketchbook programme's meetings and workshops. Bea commented: 'I definitely magpied loads and loads and loads of ideas to use back in my classroom'. She explained: 'when you're more confident, then you're bound to relay that back in with the students that you work with, aren't you?' Bea wanted to emphasise the importance of 'not having expectations with the end product', commenting: 'it's about the journey and experimentation'.

This approach to the sketchbook process was also evident in Bea's teaching philosophy – learning through discovery. She told me that working with some 'incredibly challenging' students had taught her to 'think outside the box.' She thought that sketchbook use for these students had provided some predictability and returning to work in the sketchbook made each entry easier.

Bea spoke at length about her own current art-making and said she was 'working on a personal series of work'. The sketchbook programme, and her connections with the arts organisation more broadly, had activated her inner 'creativity expert' which 'was just very dormant before'. She had not been required to use her artistic skills in previous education posts and although she used to run adult art and craft workshops, she remarked: 'it wasn't my type of art necessarily'. In her current post, leading art in her setting, she was working towards a formal teaching qualification, which she said would be 'the icing on the cake'. However, she admitted that her studies had become somewhat 'stagnant', probably due to the day-to-day demands of her job.

In terms of relationships with other sketchbook programme participants, Bea spoke about 'a core' of inspirational people and said: 'you feel associated with them, even though you might not have had a direct swap [...] things grow and develop from a little bit of being put together'. These connections were fostered through the sketchbook programme's related events, but even without face-to-face meetings during the pandemic, Bea remarked on the emotional benefits of the sketchbook programme: 'it's really, really helped me during lockdown, and it was exhausting, and our working hours were ridiculous. But it really helped me to have that little thing of mine to focus on and feel connected with people because that's been in their house'.

In addition to her involvement in the sketchbook programme, Bea had instigated other sketchbook swaps. One group she established with her colleagues at school, another group involved friends from her university days, and she also said she was doing a sketchbook exchange with her son's girlfriend. The establishment of these additional groups highlights the positive impact of the sketchbook programme on Bea's professional practice, as an art education leader both within and outside of her workplace. In voluntarily establishing these sketchbook exchanges, Bea was keen for others to benefit from an artistic dialogue. She spoke about some colleagues 'being very brave' to participate in the sketchbook swap. In the same way she had moved beyond her initial apprehension, she wanted to support others in this move.

Figure 9.4 shows the sketchbook entry that Bea chose as something she disliked/hated. I have selected it to discuss as it connects to the insecurities that she had previously mentioned. She had attended a face-to-face sketchbook programme event 'a little while ago', saying, 'I didn't know anyone, and I just felt unworthy'. She explained that she had felt 'very nervous about doing anything' in front of people whom she regarded as well known and 'successful'. Her entry was 'over complicated' and not in her usual style as she had put 'too much pressure on myself'. She explained that: 'I can see my anxieties, my frustrations'. It was the first page of her sketchbook and she noted: 'that's always such a hard thing to do'.

Figure 9.4 Bea (2021) *An entry that you dislike...or even hate!*

Similarities, differences and key themes

There are notable similarities and differences between Jocelyn's and Bea's sketchbook programme experiences and perceptions, as well as their wider artist teacher practice. Interestingly, both were experienced artists yet still reported some feelings of inadequacy/lack of confidence. Because they knew how it felt to be uncertain about art making, they were sensitive to others' feelings and wanted to help them enjoy art. As Bayles and Orland (2021: 13) state: 'Making art can feel dangerous and revealing. Making art *is* dangerous and revealing'. For Jocelyn, fostering student confidence was a particular passion and she talked in detail about this. Although Bea also sought to encourage her students, she had a special interest in developing colleagues' and friends' sketchbook practice. Both really valued their sketchbooks as objects and reminders of past successes and frustrations – the sketchbooks served as reflective aids. It can be argued that: 'Memory, like perception, is not passive retrieval but an active and creative process that involves the imagination' (Hustvedt 2012: 95). The sketchbooks acted as portals for this process of remembering.

As previously noted, both Jocelyn and Bea were passionate about art in its widest sense. They enjoyed exploring, experimenting, and sharing their sketchbook work. Connecting with other sketchbook programme participants, whether face-to-face or via the physical exchange of sketchbooks, was seen as vitally important for their professional learning and wellbeing. The theme of wellbeing was apparent from various angles. Both Jocelyn and Bea talked about their students' wellbeing, their own wellbeing, and that of colleagues.

At the time of data collection, the negative effects of the Covid-19 pandemic could still be felt, and both mentioned how the sketchbook programme offered a feeling of being connected to distant colleagues who they could no longer meet in person. This echoes the findings of Wilson et al. (2022) about creative arts engagement supporting wellbeing during the pandemic.

Further, both artist teachers were developing their leadership responsibilities outside of their school settings – for Jocelyn, this was her outreach work with key stage 3 students (aged 11–13 years); for Bea, this involved leading workshops for the arts organisation. This finding provides evidence that art is something they are doing for the world, not just for themselves (Bayles and Orland 2012). These new ventures served to cement their professional confidence, bringing a strong sense of professional purpose and fulfilment. They both reported having plans to enhance this practice. The sketchbook programme and Jocelyn's and Bea's attitudes and aspirations provided the four factors to support artist teacher practice (Thornton 2013) – it served to strengthen their artist teacher identities and empowered them to empower others.

Conclusion

The study sought to answer the question: *How does a CPD programme with sketchbooks at its heart enhance teachers' professional learning in relation to their self-perception as an artist teacher?* Drawing on the data collected with Jocelyn and Bea, the research findings show how deeply the programme was valued and how closely connected it was to their artist teacher identities. The meanings of their sketchbook work reflected the 'messy, complex, subtle and often paradoxical ways in which creative ideas and work percolate and mingle' (Power 2018: 214). As active participants in numerous sketchbook programme cycles, they were both strong advocates for the arts organisation and its work. The creative and supportive community created by the sketchbook programme met both their personal and professional needs; it inspired them to develop as artists and also as teachers (Brass and Coles 2014; Thornton 2013). In terms of improvements, they just wanted full commitment from all participants and welcomed the opportunity for more face-to-face meetings and workshops. To summarise, the sketchbook programme greatly enhanced Jocelyn's and Bea's self-perception as an artist teacher. Involvement in the programme provided not only time and space to create art for themselves but also a crucial, validating, artist teacher support structure (Thornton 2013).

It is recognised that this research has its limitations. As a small-scale, interpretive study the findings cannot be generalised. However, overall, my findings serve to demonstrate how more regional arts organisations might fruitfully design CPD programmes with sketchbooks at their heart in order to enhance the professional learning – as well as the enjoyment, confidence and wellbeing – of artist teachers.

Acknowledgments

I offer my sincere thanks to my research participants, Jocelyn and Bea, who kindly gave their time to share their experiences with me for this study. I also thank my gatekeeper at the arts organisation for their interest in the research and assistance in communicating with potential participants.

References

Bayles, D. and Orland, T. (2021) *Art and Fear: Observations on the perils (and rewards) of artmaking.* Santa Cruz: Image Continuum Press.

Brass, E. and Coles, S.M. (2014) Artist teachers exchange: Reflections on a collaborative sketchbook project for secondary school art teachers, *International Journal of Art and Design Education,* 33(3): 365–374.

Buchman, L.M. (2021) *Make to Know: From Spaces of Uncertainty to Creative Discovery.* London: Thames and Hudson.

Buffery, J. (2009) *AccessArt Sketchbooks in Schools: Final Evaluation Report,* (online). Available at: https://www.accessart.org.uk/wp-content/uploads/2017/03/sketchbooks_in_schools_final_report.pdf (accessed 16 April 2019).

Cooper, B. (2019) *Primary Colours: The Decline of Arts Education in Primary Schools and how it can be Reversed. Fabian Policy Report* (online). Available at: https://fabians.org.uk/wp-content/uploads/2019/01/FS-Primary-Colours-Report-WEB-FINAL.pdf (accessed 24 March 2019).

Daichendt, G.J. (2010) *Artist Teacher: A philosophy for creating and teaching.* Bristol: Intellect.

The Department for Education (DfE) (2016) Standards for Teachers' Professional Development (online). Available at: https://assets.publishing.service.gov.uk/government/uploads/system/uploads/attachment_data/file/537030/160712_-_PD_standard.pdf (accessed 21 May 2021).

Glaser, B.G. (1965) The constant comparative method of qualitative analysis, *Social Problems,* 12(4): 436–445.

Hall, E. (2015, November) *Joining the dots: Professional development and evidence-based practice in visual arts education,* Paper presented at 6th International Journal of Art and Design Education Conference, Glasgow, UK.

Hetland L., Winner E., and Veenemer S. et al. (2013) *Studio Thinking 2: The real benefits of visual arts education.* New York: Teachers College Press.

Hustvedt, S. (2012) *Living, Thinking, Looking.* London: Sceptre.

McKay, L. and Barton, G. (2018) Exploring how arts-based reflection can support teachers' resilience and well-being, *Teaching and Teacher Education,* 75(2018): 356–365.

Payne, R. and Hall, E. (2018) The NSEAD Survey Report 2015–16: Political reflections from two art and design educators, *International Journal of Art and Design Education,* 37(2): 167–176.

Power, N. (2018) Re-Imagining the sketchbook as a medium of encounter, *Art, Design and Communication in Higher Education,* 17(2): 199–216.

Sketchbook Circle (n.d.) About Sketchbook Circle (online). Available at: http://www.sketchbookcircle.com/about (accessed 07 August 2022)

Squire, C., Davis, M., Esin, C., Andrews, M., et al. (2014) *What is Narrative Research?* London: Bloomsbury.

Stahl, N.A. and King, J.R. (2020) Expanding approaches for research: Understanding and using trustworthiness in qualitative research, *Journal of Developmental Education.* 44(1): 26–28.

Thornton, A. (2013) *Artist, Researcher, Teacher: A study of identity in art and design education.* Bristol: Intellect.

Wilson, C., Munn-Giddings, C., Bungay, H and Dadswell, A. (2022) Arts, cultural and creative engagement during COVID-19: Enhancing the mental wellbeing and social connectedness of university staff and students, *Nordic Journal of Arts, Culture and Health,* 14(1): 1–14.

10 Moving beyond immanence: Artist teacher networking and collaborative practice

Miranda Matthews

Introduction

Conditions for art and design practice in schools in the United Kingdom (UK) are currently notoriously difficult. There is an ongoing scarcity of subject-specific continued professional development (CPD) for teachers (Thomas 2022). Before the austerity era that started in 2010, teachers were often encouraged to go to external moderation sessions, to take a short course in a new skill, or to do a Masters qualification with support from their school (Matthews 2018). In addition, in the 2020s, everyone has had to make adjustments during and since the pandemic. The more long-term effects of the pandemic, such as learning gaps and economic adversity, are still affecting education in the UK and internationally (Moss 2022). Additional challenges have arisen for being an artist teacher, or a student of art and design, in relation to the rapid increase in costs of living, and eco-anxieties in the 'Earth crisis' of climate change (McKenzie 2020).

Art and design education is in need of adaptive, sustainable strategies. In the context of rapid policy change, artist teachers also need arguments that can act as levers in discussions where the arts are brought to the table for justification. I will argue here that the collaborative networking of artist teachers offers strategies for tackling the immanent contexts for practice. My research of *Responses to Policy in Practice* among UK artist teachers resonates with international studies of how artist teachers respond by creating fluid, collaborative practice when 'seized by a series of conflicts' (Liberman et al. 2018: 143).

The research presented in this chapter has emerged from a project I began in 2018, to investigate how art and design practitioners respond to educational policy in their practice. I set out to explore how artist teachers make adjustments in their department ethos, in resourcing practice through professional networks, and their individual and collaborative responses in practice. The research of pre-pandemic, pandemic and post-pandemic artist teacher practice informs the structure of the chapter. The research intends to offer ways of contributing theorised, practice-centred support for sustaining flourishing artist teacher networks.

Artist teachers in the UK can be seen to contribute to a contemporary 'ethical turn' in educational philosophies (Marso 2017: 7). This ethical shift encompasses equal opportunities and shared cultural capital, in supportive transactions between practitioners, students and their environments. My research indicates that artist teacher ecosystems are materially shaping intentions for art and design practice taught in schools. Contributing to this supportive ethical turn, this chapter will focus on an artist teacher group that I have connected with in research since 2018; this group is Tower Hamlets Artist Teachers – 'THAT'.

Tower Hamlets is a borough of central East London, UK, with a diverse cultural population. This borough has the highest level of child poverty in the UK, and is the second most densely populated area, with 56.1% of children below the poverty line (Action for Children 2022). Artist teachers working in government funded 'state schools' are, therefore, immersed in a context of urgency and necessity. They are contributing to students' social mobility as they assist progression to higher education and creative future careers.

THAT creates a concentrated hub of artist teacher activity. Tower Hamlets has a vibrant range of public and private galleries and museums. Many of these cultural organisations are keen to make connections with local schools. There are also galleries, museums, arts foundation and Higher Education Institutions situated more widely in London that connect with Tower Hamlets Artist Teachers (THAT 2022).

THAT is an exemplary group in my exploration of how artist teachers can move beyond the contingent conditions of their environments. Artist teachers contend with education policies that intend to condition how teaching practice happens. THAT has what Vella et al. (2020: 9) call an 'intrinsically political' approach to practice in art and design. I will discuss how this artist teacher group has moved beyond the sense of being locked in the immanence of rapid education policy changes. The mapping of this research connects with Simone de Beauvoir's feminist existentialism (Beauvoir 1948, 2001; Kruks 2012), Gilles Deleuze and Felix Guattari's (2013) post-humanist rhizomatic assemblage theory, and Patricia Hill Collins (2019) for intersectional understandings of how artist teachers take 'creative social action'.

Mapping methodology and theory in practice

When researching practice, artist educators can work with mapping processes that include an investment in lived experiences of making and doing. A comparative theoretical approach offers flexibility and multiple points of interpretation. This is sometimes called a 'multi-modal' approach to research (Kara 2020). A multi-modal theoretical approach also relates well to a creative mixed-methods research plan (Rose 2016; Kara 2020).

The methodology of this research intended to enable an immersive perspective of how artist teacher collaborations can respond to policy changes. Mixed-methods included: qualitative semi-structured online interviews with 12 artist teachers in THAT and outside this group, working in Greater London; online and in-person observations of practice and exhibitions with the informed consent of all participants; observations of group meetings; and my arts practice that maintains an affinity to the experiences of artist teachers. In some meetings I was present only as an observer, and in others I contributed information about CPD opportunities. Sam Hill, a convenor of THAT, requested the group's permission for its real name to be used, and gave permission for her real name to be included. All cultural partners and interviewed practitioners are anonymous, to protect free speech and the group's network.

Since I identified as an artist teacher when I worked in schools and colleges (2004–14), and now experience my role in higher education as an artist educator and researcher, I have an affinity to artist teachers that relates to lived experience. I would argue that arts practitioners who teach can offer social sustenance, in their spirited resistances, caring connections with students, and ways of transforming affective outlets into expressive artworks.

There are also day-to-day teaching experiences that prompt reflective artist teachers to question what is communicated as the 'right way to do things' in national or school-centred policy; I will later give some examples of this reflective pragmatism. Having an understanding of the need for a more granular response can at times assist fluid practice, when there is little centralised communication about how to proceed. In such conditions, drawing upon the adaptive strategy of an 'ethos of ambiguity' in arts practice can potentially assist artist teachers in finding the most suitable responses to their teaching experiences (Matthews 2019).

> Let us try to assume our fundamental ambiguity. It is in the knowledge of the genuine conditions of our life that we must draw our strength to live and our reason for acting (Beauvoir 1948: 8).

If strength can be gathered in responding to the 'genuine conditions' for artist teachers in schools and colleges, and for artist educators at universities, practitioners are found to sustain self-belief and collective motivation.

As often noted, there is an element of risk-taking in creativity, in that new forms of expression are always emerging, and comfort zones of practice are often challenged to make new developments. What may externally be perceived as a 'failure' or a shortfall in realising expectations, could actually be a vital experimental aspect of learning (Biesta 2013; Matthews 2020; Creely et al. 2021).

Even in the most oppressive situations, when surrounding 'facticities' appear to totally frustrate well-made plans and intentions, artist teachers try to make new projects which at once 'transcend the situation' and keep moving in the midst of that situation (Kruks 2012: 35). Artist teachers often have a passion for practice that becomes a vital aspect of their sense of self, and their sensory relations with the world. Beauvoir saw practice as moving beyond immanence in the way that the arts capture momentary experiences, for others to connect with and to interpret. In the midst of crises, artist teachers try to find ways for the 'festival' to go on, and for the arts as a 'passionate assertion of existence' (Beauvoir 1948: 137).

Practice happens in the midst of it all; this is where theoretical mapping could look to Deleuzian perspectives that encourage activism in the 'milieu' of art in education. Deleuze and Guattari (2013) support post-humanist approaches to relationships between the human, other-than-human lives and the environment. The forces that act through humanity, and beyond us, such as the more-than-human pandemic, change our ways of being with one another, in 'machinic assemblages' that bring together elements within and beyond human interventions.

Artist teacher groups, such as THAT, express and articulate the conditions that affect their existence. They could, therefore, be interpreted as forming 'Collective assemblages of enunciation' (Deleuze and Guattari 2013: 6). In this view, humans and other beings are in the midst of things. They are in the 'milieu'. By keeping a focus on being in the middle of things – in the in-between spaces (Heaton and Chan Lai Kuan 2022), artist teachers gather energy and potential to make changes. Movement beyond immanence happens in a 'line of flight', an exploration – as can happen in arts practice.

In *A Thousand Plateaus* (Deleuze and Guattari 2013), the pulse of immanence is communicated. Beauvoir related to such immanence through experiences of war, and artist teachers are currently encountering the pulse of immanence in the Earth crisis of climate change. Deleuze and Guattari (2013) encourage practitioners not to be dissuaded from collaborative practice. Vertical, hierarchical, metaphors for growth are exchanged for lateral 'transversal' being among others (p. 10). The burrow, the murmuration, the radical culture that works within and beyond the mainstream, are at the roots of 'rhizomatic' practices that have 'multiple entryways' like a map (p. 12). Artist teachers might map the histories and current actions of their radical, rhizomatic cultures, in ways that contribute to their enjoyment of teaching.

There are also 'lines of flight' as risk-taking adventures into the unknown that might be fast paced or have more resistance in their 'comparative rates of flow' (p. 2). From this perspective, the experience of a hiatus, of being 'locked in immanence' (Kruks 2012), would be a 'relative slowness' that occurs after 'acceleration and rupture' (Deleuze and Guattari 2013: 2). For example, during times of social upheaval artist teachers find themselves needing to deal with the effects of rupture, and slow communication of information to schools, in addition to accelerated demands upon their capacities.

Creative resistance to the changing conditions for arts practice happens in affective, collaborative 'micropolitics'. The daily practice of artist teachers also integrally relates to the more-than-human conditions, and 'macropolitics' (Deleuze and Guattari 2013: 249) of art and design education, within school education, and the national policies and international forces that act on schools.

The individuated practices of artist teachers, and the micro-climates of art departments, could benefit from safety in numbers in an assemblage such as THAT. Practitioners can choose pathways through the opportunities offered by membership of the group. Different choices made for individual school-based and collective ventures enable 'an ecology or resingularisation' amid the collective practice (Deleuze and Guattari 2013: 42).

Internationally, artist teachers are working in societies where participation in arts practice is still conditioned by racialised, gendered and stratified concepts that produce intersecting conditions of inclusion and exclusion. Researchers are increasingly thinking about how such social codes affect interaction and the ability to move beyond immanence, since the pandemic of the early 2020s and the Earth crisis (Harmey and Moss 2021). Patricia Hill Collins (2019) observed how the beginnings of intersectional feminism started at the roots of creative protests, in singing, making banners, staging interruptions of institutionalised racism, and making art to make change. Collins (2019: 173) calls this activism 'creative social action'. This stance can be related to the perception of artist teachers as 'socially engaged practitioners' (Vella et al. 2020: 8). Imagination of different times, and alternative ways of doing things fuels the arts activism that makes waves in the world.

THAT: A motivational assemblage for mobility in the arts

At this point it is time to bring in the voices of artist teachers, and the lived experiences of practitioners. This chapter argues that the micropolitics of inclusive practice that happen at artist teacher meetings, workshops and events, have macroscopic implications for the arts in education. With a comparative view, the energising practices of artist teacher groups such as Tower Hamlets Artist Teachers have international significance for how practitioner networks can create support structures even in times of global crisis. It could help readers to hear something about the group's history; as I said earlier, processes for mapping histories and current actions of radical, rhizomatic cultures inform understandings of their social significance. I will refer to a narrative from one of the group's founding members, Samantha Hill.

> THAT network London has evolved over time. It is based on the original idea of the borough Art Teacher network meetings, which most boroughs fund or used to fund (some boroughs employed a specific person). Twenty years ago I took part in these Tower Hamlets meetings with another colleague. The Tower Hamlets co-ordinator at that time then retired and the council decided that they would not replace the post. We tried to run it ourselves but found it difficult at that time, the internet was fairly basic back then.
>
> In 2013 three friends tried to restart a group. This is where I came along as I had been part of the original art teachers group. We decided that the network would be a space for teachers and artist teachers with the aim to engage teachers in their own practice as well as supporting departments with opportunities.

Over the last 5 years we have managed to secure funding for stages of our project, which has included school department exhibitions but also separate artist teacher exhibitions. The network is evolving slowly. It is difficult to run because we all work full-time, but it is something that I am passionate about as it creates a space for us to connect, collaborate, and share ideas.

Here the 'passion' for making a space to connect, create and collaborate in some ways transcends the pressures – the 'facticities' – of working as a full-time teacher. This movement to make art that reaches beyond expectations of what it is to *be a teacher* is a struggle that is political in its intention and materiality. In 2018 when I started going to THAT meetings, they were held at local arts venues with thirty or more attendees at the table, including art teachers, gallery and museum educators. Each person would share their news and opportunities; there was a positive energy and commitment to the proceedings. Then in 2020 the world as we knew it changed almost overnight.

There was in the first instance a hiatus as practitioners tried to assemble online learning materials for students in lockdown. Teachers hit incredibly high stress levels trying to keep hold of all of their students. Experience of arts practice became house-bound, all meetings apart from those within a household had to be online. Artist educators looked for ways to make online learning inclusive and appealing, to fill the gaps in embodiment and personal contact, the gaps in sociable interaction (Matthews 2020; Gilbert and Matthews 2021; Matthews 2021).

Tower Hamlets Artist Teachers went through the same processes. At the online meetings THAT members kept the ideas coming, they kept putting forward opportunities. There were online exhibitions of student practice, seminars and artist talks that celebrated in-between, 'liminal' practice identities (Heaton and Chan Lai Kuan 2022). The galleries and museums were as present and committed as ever. There were so many opportunities that artist teachers were having to make difficult choices from the range of opportunities presented, for the learning needs of their students.

Multiple opportunities created options for 'lines of flight' for each artist teacher, offering a mobility of online social interaction in a motivational assemblage of practitioners. Yet in their working lives teachers were struggling and stressed. Something had to keep a harmonising presence, so the artist teachers found ways of supporting each other.

Interruption in centralised information calls for transversal action

Many schools and colleges in the UK were not prepared for the emergency responses required at the start of the pandemic in 2020 (Harmey and Moss 2021; Moss 2022). Artist teachers experienced a change from rigorous external coordination to unknowing structures and processes in some schools. I spoke to members of THAT in East London, and artist teachers in North and South London, to find out about their experiences.

> The lockdown was hard because our school was not prepared with a sufficient working system for setting and tracking online work. We prepared resources which were uploaded onto the school website, but we had no idea if students were actually doing the work (Artist teacher, THAT, in email correspondence with the author, 2020).

Various online programmes were explored, with the feeling that in some cases the provision of advised online technology was 'rather too late' for the learning needs of students. There were measures put in place to adapt teaching with additional training 'keeping teachers 100% busy.' These measures did not accommodate the wellbeing or practice development of teachers.

The sense of hiatus was intensified when, in the need for physical distancing of human contact, the UK central government put more faith in a computer algorithm for assessment than in teachers' professional assessments of GCSE and A Level coursework. After an outcry, education policy had to 'climb down' from that approach, to allow teachers to grade student coursework (Naughton 2020).

Practitioners felt that they were 'kept in the dark for a long time' (artist teacher, THAT); this increased anxiety and threatened to affect teacher and student wellbeing still further (Harmey and Moss 2021). Artist teachers relied upon their rhizomatic social connections to glean up-to-date information. In more suburban or rural locations, links with regional and national networks became lifelines.

> Last minute information given. The assessment process was lengthy and time consuming in the paperwork. I am aware via social media groups that A Level art this year will be 100% coursework but have received NO information from the exam board as yet (Artist Teacher, North London 2020).

Communication about assessment was not timely or consistent for schools. Collegiate networking among teachers, unionisation and participation in online discussion forums sustained the creative energies of those who reached out to others, in the machinic assemblages of online networks that connected dispersed people and places.

> Communicating with colleagues from other schools has also been useful to gain insights into other schools' approaches to the situation, and for sharing good practice. Being involved in union discussions online along with twitter contacts from art departments/organisations from across the country/ world has also allowed for a wider perspective on the ways that creatives, educators and the arts overall have approached Covid and lockdown (Artist teacher, South London).

Action taken by artist teachers for choice in how teaching could be delivered demonstrated teacher agency in motivational assemblages of practice. In my view, an ethos of ambiguity that responded to 'genuine conditions' was created by practitioners trying to make emergency education policy instructions workable for teaching art and design.

> Most teachers move to the classroom of a group of students which also reduces movement, this is challenging for teachers to be constantly moving with limited break and lunch. The art department opted to teach in their own rooms and students move to them instead, which was allowed due to the nature of our subject and materials used (Artist teacher, THAT).

Artist teachers, exercising such choices, implemented a dissensus: reversing procedural expectations to suit the needs of the subject area (Vella et al. 2020: 9-10).

Membership of THAT enabled release of anxieties and emotions that did not have space to be processed while teachers were kept '100% busy'. 'Conversations with other schools/colleagues have been invaluable, shared frustrations have been cathartic' (Artist teacher, THAT). The transversal exploration of ideas outside the confinement of the school as institution brought comfort, and helped to nurture arts practice.

The group of teachers who convene THAT continued to make strong efforts to keep communication flowing with partnership organisations, so that supportive rhizomatic activity could be sustained through and beyond the pandemic. To keep imaginative possibilities moving, new adventurous, investigative roles for students were created between THAT and partners in Higher Education. Students in Year 11 (aged 15–16) took up the role of 'Ambassadors', exploring new terrain in what could be seen as 'lines of flight' (Deleuze and Guattari 2013) and finding new learning connections.

Collaborative online projects between Tower Hamlets Artist Teachers and Higher Education Institutions (HEIs) have kept a creative flow of interaction happening for students. Since many students in this area of London will be the first-generation of their family to go to university, strategies such as the Ambassador project are developed to empower students and to build their confidence in approaching the sometimes daunting spaces of UK HEIs. These strategies have continued beyond the pandemic and into new phases of challenge.

Artist teacher collaborations, such as those between THAT and HEIs, have enabled students and teachers to feel as though they are in the milieu of social learning spaces (Wenger-Trayner and Wenger-Trayner 2020). Resources of what Sam calls 'time and will' can be hard to guarantee for artist teachers, therefore social ways of making space for the expression of creative capacities are vitally important to partnership collaborations between schools and HEIs.

Returning to Embodied collaborative practice

Moving beyond immanence for artist teachers gathered pace from 2021, and the embodied and interpersonal began to filter back into planned events. THAT online meetings continued alongside psyche-affirming, in-person workshops for artist teachers. However the end of year exhibition was still online in 2021, with a showcase of student artwork called *Creative Disruptions* (THAT 2021; Figures 10.1 and 10.2).

Figure 10.1 Poster for *Creative Disruptions* (2021) Students of 'THAT Network' online exhibition

Figure 10.2 *Creative Disruptions* (2021) Information about the online exhibition

a THAT network London Online Exhibition

THAT NETWORK SCHOOLS' EXHIBITION

We are pleased to celebrate and showcase a selection of exceptional artwork from GCSE, A level and KS3 students, produced during an unprecedented year of blended learning.

The goal of this online exhibition is to bring together schools, students and wider communities from across the borough of Tower Hamlets to showcase their artwork, connect and take part in wonderful workshops led by our partners- universities, galleries and organisations.

Credit: Dellilah Jamal

Of course, the art pavilion, then informed us, 'Okay, you're not going to have the exhibition on site'. So there was a little bit of a panic, then thinking, 'Okay, what are we going to do? Do we attempt to do an online exhibition and then what platform do we use?' I think that took maybe between two to four weeks. Just doing research to actually work out, is it feasible? Do we have enough capacity in our small group to try and do this when we've never done it before? As long as schools have got enough time to get their own images together to email to us, then we can make this work (Sam).

Artist teachers acknowledge their initial panic when plans do not go as expected, and then they start to problem-pose, they 'keep doing' to prevent immobilisation, and research viable alternatives. There is a sense of belief in arts practice that carries practitioners through: 'We can make this work'. In addition a reversal of disruption to teaching is made in the empowerment of 'creative disruption' – again lighting upon the ethos of making suitable working conditions for students and artist teachers.

As soon as it was possible to gather socially again, THAT members were out and about, attending day long 'walk and draw' CPD workshops in Brick Lane, East London, taking school students on gallery visits, and organising away days. The arts practice of teachers in Tower Hamlets has survived by finding alternatives and gathering collective strength. In collaborative practice and 'creative social action' (Collins 2019) artist teachers and their students weathered the blasts of incoherent policy, and the blizzard of online learning, collecting digital skills that could then also support post-pandemic in-person connections.

Tower Hamlets Artist Teachers were back in-person at a venue called the Art Pavilion in 2022 for a group exhibition called *Reflect, Reconnect, Renew* (THAT 2022; Figures 10.3–10.6), with a great range of artwork from GCSE and A Level students. This show presented an essential alternative 'three R's' to the

Figure 10.3 THAT *Reflect, Reconnect, Renew* (2022) Exhibition invite front

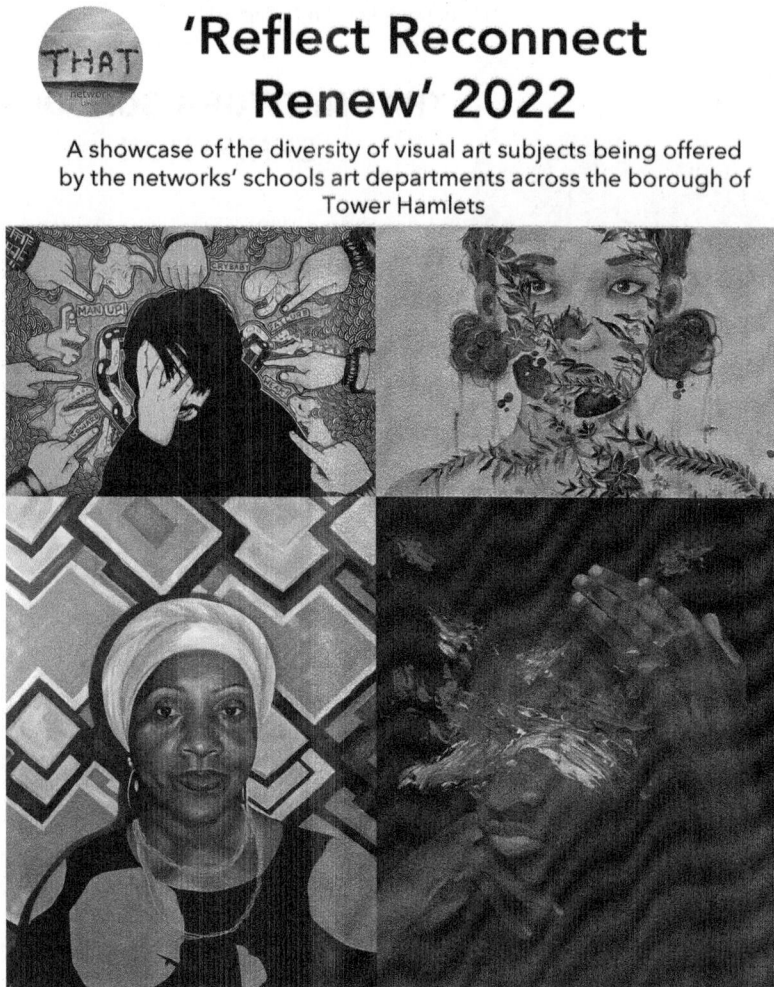

'Reflect Reconnect Renew' 2022

A showcase of the diversity of visual art subjects being offered by the networks' schools art departments across the borough of Tower Hamlets

Private View: Thursday 24th March 2022
4.30-7.30pm

The Art Pavilion, Mile End Park, Clinton Road, E3 4QY

https://thatnetworklondon.wordpress.com

thatnetworklondon@gmail.com

prevalent policy focus on 'reading, (w)riting and (a)rithmetic', for a sustainable cycle of reflective interaction and regenerative creativity in art and design education.

Skills-building workshops accompanying the annual THAT exhibition continue to be very popular: 'During the Art Pavilion event we have managed each

Figure 10.4 THAT *Reflect, Reconnect, Renew* (2022) Exhibition invite back

the Art Pavilion

The exhibition is open to the public on the following days:

Tuesday 22nd March - Wednesday 30th March
11.00am-6.00pm
Thursday 24th of March:
11.00am-3.30pm - PV: 4.30-7.30pm
&
Thursday 31st March: 11.00am-2.30pm

Participating Schools:

St Paul's Way Trust School, Central Foundation Girls' School,
Bow School, Mulberry School for Girls, Oaklands School,
Mulberry Stepney Green, Langdon Park School,
Swanlea School, Mulberry Academy Shoreditch,
Stepney All Saints School, Morpeth School,
London East Alternative Provision,
Bishop Challoner Catholic Federation of Schools

year to book out all the workshops' (Sam). In-person connections are made in celebrations of empowered practice, between teachers and students, university educators, and representatives from National Society for Education in Art and Design (NSEAD). Representatives from nationally renowned art colleges join

Figure 10.5 *Reflect, Reconnect, Renew* (2022) Private View

Figure 10.6 *Reflect, Reconnect, Renew* (2022) Private View

in the festival spirit to give prizes to the students, building confidence in realistic creative futures for young people of diverse cultural heritage. Reflecting on the ethos, collaborations and events of Tower Hamlets Artist Teachers, what could artist teachers in other areas gather from this group's active momentum that has helped practitioners to move beyond lockdown, policy hiatus and funding cuts? Where can artist teachers win out internationally with this form of approach?

There is initially a will to connect, to be kept in multiple loops, to explore locality as a vibrant materiality in-itself; these ways of working can belong to artist teachers in all areas of the UK, and internationally. Artist teacher sustainability also benefits from a clearly supportive ethos, that takes up the ethical turn in *continuing practice development* – as meaningful 'CPD' training and skills workshops.

THAT makes the ethical turn in art education apparent, in that representatives from all schools have an equal platform in the discussion. Artist teachers are therefore offering the equality essential for 'a democratic vision of education' (Hoekstra 2015: 35). Sometimes competing interests of secondary schools in the same borough appear to have been removed from the interaction of artist teachers in THAT. Schools get to exhibit their students' artwork from a platform of equality. This would also appear to be a significant transferrable point of action for artist teacher groups in all regions.

There also have to be people who see the value in their focused input to organising and materialising collective opportunities. It takes brave practitioners to carry 'a line of flight', and mobilise their creative potential beyond the immanence of day-to-day work situations, to passionately assert more durable existences (Beauvoir 1948; Deleuze and Guattari 2013). Artist teacher gatherings also energise museum and gallery education, connecting teachers and students with curatorial practice. Gatherings add shared knowledges, prioritise the creative futures of students, lighten the weight of a teacher's workload and encourage the realisation of sustainable arts practice.

References

Action for Children (2022) Where is Child Poverty Increasing in the UK? (online). Available at: https://www.actionforchildren.org.uk/blog/where-is-child-poverty-increasing-in-the-uk/ (accessed 2 October 2022).

Beauvoir, S. de. (1948) *The Ethics of Ambiguity*, 2nd ed. London: Philosophical Library.

Beauvoir, S. de. (2001) *Memoirs of a Dutiful Daughter*, 4th ed. London: Penguin Classics.

Biesta, G. (2013) *The Beautiful Risk of Education*. Boulder: Paradigm.

Collins, P. H. (2019) *Intersectionality: As critical theory*. Durham and London: Duke University Press.

Creely, E., Henderson, M., Henriksen, D., and Crawford, R. (2021) Leading change for creativity in schools: Mobilizing creative risk-taking and productive failure, *International Journal of Leadership in Education*, Ahead-of-print, 1–24.

Deleuze, G. and Guattari, F. (2013) *A Thousand Plateaus*, 3rd ed. London: Bloomsbury.

Gilbert, F. and Matthews, M. (2021) Affective digital presence: How to free online writing and drawing? *Journal of Writing in Creative Practice*, 14(2): 209–237.

Harmey, S. and Moss, G. (2021) Learning disruption or learning loss: Using evidence from unplanned closures to inform returning to school after COVID-19, *Educational Review*, DOI: 10.1080/00131911.2021.1966389

Heaton, R. and Chan Lai Kuan, S. (2022) A visual inquiry: Artist–teacher perceptions of art education provision in Singapore, *Studies in Art Education*, 63(2): 115–133.

Hoekstra, M. (2015). The problematic nature of the artist teacher concept and implications for pedagogical practice, *The International Journal of Art and Design Education*, 34(3): 349–357.

Kara, H. (2020) *Creative Research Methods: A practical guide*, 2nd ed. Bristol: Policy Press.

Kruks, S. (2012) *Simone de Beauvoir and the Politics of Ambiguity*. Oxford: Oxford University Press.

Liberman, F., Machado Moraes, M., Santalucia Maximino, V. (2018) Collaborative books: aesthetic and political dimensions of art in education, in Raphael Vella, R., Saldanha, Â., Maksimovic, M., Johnston, J. (eds.) *Art Education, Conflicts and Connections*. Viseu, Portugal: InSEA Publications, 140–158.

Marso, L.J. (2017) *Politics with Beauvoir*. Durham and London: Duke University Press.

Matthews, M. (2018) The conflicted other in policy making: Focusing on art education, *Journal for Critical Education Policy Studies*, 16(1): ISSN 1740–2743.

Matthews, M. (2019) Ethos of ambiguity: Artist teachers and the transparency exclusion paradox, *International Journal of Art and Design Education*, 38(4): 853–866.

Matthews, M. (2020) Discomfort zones editorial, *International Journal of Art and Design Education*, 39(4): 708–711.

Matthews, M. (2021) Expanding from the small screen: Arts practice for affective digital presence, *International Journal of Art and Design Education*, 40(3): 492–507.

McKenzie, B. (2020) Climate Museum UK: A contemporary response to the earth crisis, *Museum Management and Curatorship*, 35(6): 671–683.

Moss, G. (2022) Researching the prospects for change that COVID disruption has brought to high stakes testing and accountability systems, *Education Policy Analysis Archives*, 30(139), DOI: https://doi.org/10.14507/epaa.30.6320

Naughton, J. (2020) From viral conspiracies to exam fiascos, algorithms come with serious side effects, *The Guardian*, 6 September 2020 [online]. Available at: https://www.theguardian.com/technology/2020/sep/06/from-viral-conspiracies-to-exam-fiascos-algorithms-come-with-serious-side-effects (accessed 19 October 2022).

Rose, G. (2016) *Visual Methodologies: An Introduction to Researching with Visual Methodologies*, 4th ed. London: SAGE.

THAT (2021) *Creative Disruptions* (online). Available at: https://sites.google.com/view/creativedisruptions2021/home (accessed 19 October 2022).

THAT (2022) Tower Hamlets Artists Teachers Network, London (online). Available at: https://thatnetworklondon.wordpress.com/ (accessed 19 October 2022).

Thomas, J. (2022) Create aspire transform: How can creative professional development (CPD) support creative cultural learning in schools?, *The International Journal of Art and Design Education*, 41(1): 125–41.

Vella, R., Saldanha, Â., Maksimovic, M., Johnston, J. (eds.) (2020) *Art Education, Conflicts and Connections*. Viseu, Portugal: InSEA Publications. (Online). Available at: https://insea.org/wp-content/uploads/2021/08/Art-Education-Conflicts-and-Connections.pdf (accessed 1 May 2023).

Wenger-Trayner, E. and Wenger-Trayner, B. (2020) *Learning to make a difference: Value creation in social learning spaces*. Cambridge: Cambridge University Press.

Part 4

Partnerships

11 Positioning the artist teacher in Scottish education

Diarmuid McAuliffe and Sarah Yearsley

Introduction

This chapter will outline the cultural context within which artist teachers operate in Scotland. It will examine the reality of how they practise within the Scottish education system and show how multiple forms of partnership can support their work. In evaluating the cultural context for artist teachers we will see where this impacts upon how young people engage with contemporary visual art learning, both within and outwith the formal education sector in Scotland. We aim to elaborate upon the role of partnership and collaboration in facilitating the development and delivery of an art education model that truly reflects authentic artist teacher practice.

An alternative cultural context

There is much to suggest that Scotland offers an alternative, and arguably more positive, cultural context to the rest of the UK for the delivery of art education and within which artist teachers operate.

Collard (2017) describes the positive policy environment for creative learning in Scotland's schools. This is supported by ongoing partnership between Creative Scotland, the public body that supports the arts, screen and creative industries across all parts of Scotland, and Education Scotland, a Scottish Government executive agency charged with supporting quality and improvement in Scottish education, in having a clear joint framework for the development of creative learning and giving priority to its development (Creative Scotland and Education Scotland, 2022). Collard (2017) also references how this 'broad and exhilarating' concept of creative learning differs from England. Reinforcing this impression of a more favourable education policy context we see that the benefits of learning in and through the expressive arts have been enshrined in Scotland's Curriculum – *Curriculum for Excellence* (CfE) (Curriculum for Excellence, Expressive arts principles and practice) since its introduction in 2010. Again, this contrasts with the impact on the teaching of expressive arts subjects of the less favourable policy context in England, where Thomson and Maloy (2022) show its effects in accelerating the decline of the subject of art and design.

When considering the wider cultural and political landscape we see how *Scotland's Culture Strategy* (National Partnership for Culture 2022) asserts that culture and creativity is central to the future wellbeing and prosperity of Scotland. Encouragingly it states that culture in Scotland is 'valued in and of itself' and that this 'sets Scotland apart from other countries by seeking to move beyond asking the culture sector to repeatedly prove its worth' (National Partnership for Culture 2022: 1). It is unsurprising then that the cultural sector was keen to embrace the opportunities for partnership between schools, artists, teachers and young people offered by CfE (Creative Scotland visual arts sector review 2016). Worthy of more discussion is why, when the rhetoric of education policy and wider cultural policy appears to value and promote culture and art education teachers and cultural organisations have struggled to support the flourishing of creativity and its injection into the curriculum (Conacher 2018).

We should remember that the introduction of CfE unleashed a brief period of growth in aspiration, creativity and criticality in Scottish education and it was during this time that the University of the West of Scotland (UWS) launched its Artist Teacher Programme providing a framework for partnership with museums and galleries with a special focus on contemporary art. The idea that contemporary art could be used to raise contemporary issues in the classroom became central to all its work and teaching and offered a vehicle for the teaching of contemporary issues across the wider CfE curriculum. The artist teacher pedagogies promoted by UWS over this period encouraged and adopted what Denis Atkinson called 'disobedient pedagogies' (Atkinson 2018) in the hope of fostering and advancing the CfE's ambition to reset Scottish education's educational goals and pedagogical practices. More than a decade after this period of optimism, opportunity and ambition experience shows that there is still some way to go to reposition the values and agency of art in Scotland's education system.

The disconnect between rhetoric and reality

Through examining the reality of the Scottish art education system, we see a disconnect between policy rhetoric and aspiration and what the curriculum and exam system delivers. In the early days of CfE there was an aspiration to change the way art was assessed, with suggestions that it should be done locally and moderated regionally. This never came to pass and the exam system retained its centralising control until the pandemic hit. Numerous pedagogical turns and events (Granville 2012; Harris 2014; Biesta 2017; Atkinson 2018; Pirrie 2020; Heaton 2021; Humes and Priestly 2021) have emerged in the very recent past, including the now almost inevitable 'post pandemic turn' in education.

The 'pandemic assessment' arrangements for national qualifications in art and design led to the Scottish Qualifications Authority (SQA) doing what was previously considered unthinkable by allowing art and design exam work to be summatively assessed at its place of making – the art room. The SQA assessment arrangements are unique in the UK and so too are the formulaic pedagogies that often precede these assessments (McAuliffe 2014; 2018).

There is no doubt that centralising control limits student agency and constrains what is possible in the here and now (Humes and Priestley 2021). Not everything that is possible in school art can be packaged and shipped for assessment. As McAuliffe has argued elsewhere (2018) the modus operandi of the SQA is far too centralised. The assessment of art and design in one location affirms a worrying anxiety for the 'absolute' control of standards and grades rather than a flipping of the pedagogy and giving the agency and professional judgement to artist teachers as partners in learning and knowledge production. Assessment has been the driving force in determining how subjects are taught for far too long in Scottish education with scant regard for the question of pedagogy or purpose of education as reported by the recent OECD review of Scottish education (2021).

Considerable tensions in Scottish art education arise further as a result of the inequity caused by the text-based hegemony of our education system (Sousanis 2015; McAuliffe 2013; 2018). The primacy of words over images (and sounds) has deep roots in Western culture but what if all these modalities were inextricably linked, and equal partners in meaning-making? How the subject of art and design is currently examined and graded at national level rests upon this inequity causing an unnecessary tension between these different modes which should otherwise complement each other. Hernandez-Hernandez (2019: 60) draws our attention to the 'pedagogical imagination' which, he argues, 'affords us the capacity to invent, experiment and create, isolated from routines and trends'. Accordingly, the disconnect between image and text or, to put it more accurately, between image making and writing, is what lies at the heart of this concern. The 'siloed' nature of current subject teaching in Scotland has become detrimental to art learning (McAuliffe 2021). It is only when we learn to 'cross boundaries' (Giroux 1993) and work in partnership with others that we can begin to make sense of our world and engage in future work beyond the classroom (Pirrie 2020).

The subject needs to find a 'home' again (Thomson and Hall 2021) and to grow and develop in meaningful and critical ways, supported by an examinations framework that is open to the range of diverse art practices that should be considered part of a modern contemporary art and design curriculum. The current review on what will replace the Scottish Qualifications Authority (SQA), the single national accreditation and awarding body for Scotland, is being conducted by Professor Louise Hayward to come up with a system that is 'both visionary and practical' (Seith 2022). It builds upon the work of Professor Ken Muir who has already set out 12 recommendations 'that should be taken to strengthen CfE and tackle its ongoing implementation challenges as part of a structured approach to the future of CfE' (The Scottish Government 2022: 7).

These reviews will hopefully shine a light on the fractured nature of the teaching of art in Scotland and act as a catalyst for real and sustained change, bringing Scottish school art education into the twenty-first century.

Breaking from the formulaic practices of the past and present could help move the subject towards embedding a form of *Studio Thinking* (Hetland et al. 2013), a pedagogic approach delivered in schools in a number of states in the US and in the Scottish Highlands, and often seen in the approach to learning taken by galleries and visual arts organisations and the teaching artists that they work with.

Reinstating cognition: studio thinking, latency, unknowing and deep learning

The last 12 years of CfE have proven that despite the existence of a liberating set of permissions granted to teachers in the form of the policy document *Creativity 3-18* (Education Scotland 2007), the fear of failure and lack of creative infrastructure inherent in the delivery of the curriculum and assessment meant that those creative opportunities were lost or at best rarely sought. Research commissioned by Engage, the leading charity for promoting engagement and participation in the visual arts, confirmed that teachers of art and design perceive the curriculum to be restrictive and to problematically emphasise technical skills over conceptual or creative skills. This leads to a sense that governing bodies and wider society do not understand the economic and cultural potential of the subject or value its social contributions (McKinnon et al. 2022: 37–41).

Humes and Priestly (2021: 186) remind us that: 'one of the stated intentions of CfE was to encourage teachers to take more responsibility and exercise greater agency in their professional work'. The pedagogy that follows such a culture of control and reduced teacher agency is always going to be constrained with limiting scope for creativity and experimentation as evident throughout the majority of the country's secondary art departments (McAuliffe 2018). The cultural sector has recognised these constraints too in its belief that CfE offered a 'significant opportunity to engage with all young people through the visual arts, and for artists to contribute to the environment for learning' but also that 'schools often take quite a different approach to this, making it hard for artists and arts organisations to develop consistent methods of working' (Creative Scotland, *Visual Arts Sector Review* 2016: 12, 30).

As earlier mentioned, notable pedagogical practices have emerged in recent times in some regions of the United States, namely through *Studio Thinking* (Hetland et al. 2013). *Studio Thinking* embraces a range of pedagogies that mainstream art education in schools in Scotland or the wider UK have not acknowledged bar one or two exceptions. Where this *Studio Thinking* is in place it encourages what is known as *Studio Habits of Mind* (Hetland et al. 2013). These 'habits' are not unlike the dispositions engendered by Room 13, an artist teacher studio model of teaching developed in the Scottish Highlands (Gibb 2012; Adams and Owens 2016). This way of thinking and making has developed 'habits' around the concepts of 'persistence', 'reflection' and 'envisioning' to mention just a few (Hetland et al. 2013). These dispositions reflect very closely how artist teacher pedagogies are nurtured where such opportunities exist (Daichendt 2010).

Arguably, *Studio Thinking* best describes the kind of pedagogy that artist teachers model, where depth and complexity of conversations take place and where tolerance (Freire 1996), latency and difficulty (Meyer and Land 2006) are brought to the fore and allowed to become 'visible'. It is this kind of disposition that helps the preservation of ambiguity, difference and critical thinking in art-making. And these cognitive connections (Heaton 2021) make for great art and tend to result in genuine rather than formulaic artist teacher making.

We find agreement with Dias and Fernandez (2019) in their description of that latency or reflective dimension that has unfortunately been driven out of school art in Scotland. They argue,

> knowing and not knowing function as parts of the same movement of existence that does not separate singularity from plurality, real from virtual; past from future, subject from object or self from otherness (p.138).

In a similar vein, Baldacchino (2019) argues for embracing our otherness as a precondition for unlearning. That is to say, we must be prepared to 'stay the distance' for renewal to occur and unlearning to take place. He argues,

> Unlearning the certainties by which we were schooled also urges us to enter into the world of possibilities. To do so we have to embrace paradox, as we seek to unlearn what we know without presuming to relearn other certainties or find new canons on which we would secure a measurable outcome (p.xii).

Given the limitations we have discussed, it is encouraging to see that where *Studio Thinking* has been embraced by schools and arts organisations working together this can foster the creation of great art by young people. Research Scotland's 2021 report '*Face to Face Expressive Arts in Scotland during Covid-19*' shows how partnership working 'added value to the role of schools and teachers through building relationships with children and young people providing a creative output for expression and a physical and emotional space for respite and processing to happen'. This is an environment for 'exciting, high quality creative work' and *Studio Thinking* opportunities like these offer a way of allowing pupils to use whatever means they have to express themselves without having to fit in with externally imposed restrictions that are now out of step with our times.

Further examples of this kind of approach include Edinburgh Sculpture Workshop's long-term collaboration with a local primary school (McKinnon et al. 2022: 75) where children become artists and take part in 'artist-led' programmes which are 'designed to encourage experimentation and promote new ways of learning'. Also in Edinburgh, the Fruitmarket Gallery's *Making Matters* project with local primary and secondary schools aims to build a 'fluid, conversational' relationship between partners and importantly involves teacher professional development as well as workshops for pupils in the gallery and school. Teacher professional development seems pivotal here as a way of supporting artist teachers in advocating for *Studio Thinking* in their pedagogical practice. The Fruitmarket's creative learning team state that they aim to help teachers 'move beyond [...] physical and conceptual boundaries to create a collaboration that is creative, experimental, of value to teachers, and that creates memorable, fun and confidence-building experiences for pupils' (McKinnon et al. 2018).

Several alternative art school projects run by visual arts organisations and galleries further emphasise the value and benefits of *Studio Thinking* ways of working for young people (*Art Evolution Evaluation Report* 2022; McKinnon et al. 2022: 68). Rather than interpreting the existence of these alternative, informal art and design education opportunities as evidence that the formal education sector is not delivering what children and young people need, a more nuanced reading could be to see them as complementary. Where these alternative opportunities exist, and arts organisations are actively seeking to work with children and young people at risk of exclusion for example, they can be seen to be one way of tackling what the Freelands Foundation has described as 'broken pathways through art education', with specific reference to minority ethnic students (Freelands Foundation 2022).

Interdisciplinarity: reframing the partnership dialogue

The realisation that we urgently need to move away from what was earlier identified as 'silo thinking' where art speaks only to itself, is a point identified in Donaldson's review of Scottish teacher education *Teaching Scotland's Future* in 2010 and again referred to by Humes and Priestley in 2021, suggesting that this recommendation was never enacted. Evidently those who have examined Scottish education in recent times (Donaldson 2010; Biesta 2015; Humes and Priestley 2021) would agree with this move towards what Petrie has referred to as 'the desirability of the integration of knowledge into some meaningful whole' (Petrie 1992, cited in Burnard, Colucci-Gray and Sinha 2021: 114). Burnard and Colucci-Gray (2020) make a timely and compelling case for interdisciplinarity and working across boundaries in education. As teacher educators, especially now when time and content relevance seem more pressing than ever, we feel we have a moral and political responsibility (Giroux1993) to make the case for interdisciplinarity and to advance its relevance to art education.

In the opening chapter of *Why Science and Art Creativities Matter*, Pirrie (2020) posits the following explanation for why reframing the dialogue between arts and sciences is so necessary,

> Reconceptualising the interrelationship between sciences and the arts has the potential to bring us back from a different planet as it were. It is only by considering the arts and sciences from the inside rather than as reified categories that can be progressively realigned that we shall be better able to inhabit the Earth and to address the many challenges that we currently face (p.21).

In this multi-modal world (Kress and van Leeuwen 2006) where arts and sciences work together, it is foolhardy to continue to see art as an entirely separate subject rather than part of the wider set of disciplines associated with STEAM education. STEAM is STEM (Science, Technology, Engineering and Mathematics) with Arts inserted to establish STEAM (Science, Technology, Engineering, Arts and Mathematics). The STEAM movement in Scotland is in its infancy with barely a mention on the Education Scotland website (McKinnon et al. 2022).

Arguably, learning knows no boundaries and art connects everything; so where there is a desire to *see* a solution, art can help us 'see it' as it is the job of art to make things visible (Hofsess et al. 2019: 73). When set against the hard sciences (STEM) the arts feel subordinate yet when they work in true partnership with each other in equal dialogue, it is collegiate and discursive from the moment of engagement. Too often we read of the conflict inherent in the art-science binary and this divide continues to exist in most schools. The partnership discourse should start in the school staffroom where staff hangout together but increasingly, here in Scotland, we are seeing the demise of the 'common' staffroom in favour of the individual subject base. This has long term implications for the development of subject partnerships.

The intellectual space or 'oxygen' that is generated from our interactions with other disciplines should by now be considered mainstream in education. How, for example, do you begin to understand the notion of 'colour-blindness' without first understanding the concept in both arts and science? The same dynamic is true for 'game design' where art and design has a vast stake in that industry yet, despite the high levels of engagement we know students to have when involved in 'gaming', it is still not considered in Scotland as part of the art and design school curriculum. Jagodzinski (2020) argues:

> The process of designing and game thinking for non-gaming contexts as a way to engage students and solve problems is perceived as leading to more engagement by students in schools [...] gamification in education is touted as a key 21st-century approach to learning (p.17).

Scotland's visual arts and gallery sector is challenging the art/science divide. V&A Dundee – Scotland's design museum, for example offers schools tours and workshops covering themes including architecture, engineering and game design. The National Galleries of Scotland (NGS) offers a teaching resource, *The Beauty of Maths*, to inspire learning about maths, through art.

Further reinforcement of the value of interdisciplinary approaches in education comes where we see how the arts have helped get people through the serious health and wellbeing crisis provoked by the pandemic (Payne 2020). Undoubtedly, the curriculum now needs to be re-evaluated and at least some additional curricular time should be apportioned for expressive arts subjects to support the delivery of the curriculum's health and wellbeing experiences and outcomes (*Curriculum for Excellence, Health and Wellbeing*). Mental wellbeing in the Scottish Curriculum refers to: the health of the mind, the way we think, perceive, reflect on and make sense of the world (Scottish Executive 2004). During the pandemic, engaging with the arts helped children and young people 'feel calmer and more focused, express their feelings and find their voice, manage their moods and energy and providing a safe, warm space' (Research Scotland 2021: 9). Creative Scotland and Education Scotland now have an aligned outcome to improve learners' health and wellbeing through creativity and arts experiences. This will be achieved by 'promoting and facilitating creative partnerships and creative learning experiences that specifically support children & young people's health and wellbeing' (Creative Scotland and Education Scotland Creative Learning Action Plan 2022–23). As ever though we remain mindful of Gert Biesta's plea against taking art in education for granted and pointing to an emergent culture of 'instrumentalism' as in this case of the SQA where 'the potential disappearance of art from art education' (Biesta 2017: 53) is a real possibility, where art is placed in the service of other disciplines or removed altogether.

Artist teachers as curriculum developers and change agents

When Humes and Priestly (2021) advocate 'agency' in relation to Scottish Education, what is being proposed is indeed a request for radical reform of its current frameworks and anything less will fail to deliver on their aspirations to see teachers as 'curriculum developers' and 'change agents' (Humes and Priestly 2021: 176). Like 'working from home' and the adjustments we all needed to make during the pandemic, we can do the same in terms of realigning current art practices and assessment. There is an *agentive* opportunity here which if embraced could work to make teachers the 'curriculum developers and change agents' (Humes and Priestly 2021: 176) that CfE had always intended would happen but never did.

The National Galleries of Scotland (NGS) recognises the impact these *agentive opportunities* could have and has revisited its professional learning offer for teachers to counter a society-wide lack of understanding about creativity and the visual arts. With the aim to challenge and support teachers to understand what creativity is and how they can 'teach' it, NGS initiated a series of 'experiments in partnership with teachers and other creative thinkers to explore how they might support the development of resilient, creative individuals who think for themselves' (Conacher 2018: 35). In the informal learning arena, a group of freelance teaching artists in Edinburgh has secured grant funding and is working together to bridge the pedagogical gap by creating a model of peer-to-peer, non-elitist and inclusive sharing of pedagogical research by teaching artist for teaching artist – allowing them to demonstrate the creativity and power of their work (Fraser 2022).

The existence of numerous good practice examples such as these of culture in education is acknowledged in the *National Partnership for Culture Recommendations for Ministers* (2022), along with a recognition of their unequal distribution and the difficulty of sustaining and scaling up what is known to be working. Partnership working, long term commitments and changes to how culture is funded are proposed as key to embedding these ways of working.

Conclusion

Scotland is fortuitous in its outward facing administration, which values education. Education is held in high regard by Scots; they have always 'owned it', unlike other aspects of governance in the devolved arrangements at the Scottish Parliament. This, however, has not always boded well for art education as the pace of change is never quick enough. It appears that the system is not nearly responsive enough and since their inception, CfE factors, such as having a single exam board responsible for assessment in state schools and other barriers discussed here do not incentivise pace or change (McAuliffe cited in Hepburn 2020). However, despite the ongoing limitations of the education system, innovative and creative partnership models that value and nurture art education and support artist teacher practice do exist. These partnerships work best where schools, teachers, artists and the cultural sector are able to develop long term relationships based upon mutual respect and a shared aim to develop young people's learning and wellbeing in and through engagement with art.

For those wishing to develop partnership work to address these issues we can offer an emerging set of considerations:

- 'Galleries (and other arts organisations) are perceived as positive, alternative spaces for learning; and opportunities for young people to be exposed to artists and designers in the 'real world' are considered highly valuable' (McKinnon et al. 2022: 83).
- Be patient and flexible when developing partnerships.
- Value the engagement of artist teachers, listen to and work with them.
- Consider whether the activities on offer are curriculum-aligned and work collaboratively to achieve this.
- Good communication with schools is key and engagement with senior school leaders is essential.

In conclusion we propose that overcoming ongoing challenges, fostering partnership approaches and embracing the embodiment of an artist teacher mindset can combine to offer a dynamic and potent model for art education in the twenty-first century.

References

Adams, J. and Owens, A. (2016) *Creativity and Democracy in Education: Practices and politics of learning through the arts*. London: Routledge.

ART Evolution Evaluation Report (2022), *Engage Scotland* (online). Available at: https://engage.org/resources/art-evolution-supporting-youth-arts-in-the-visual-arts-in-scotland/ (accessed 28 June 2022).

Atkinson, D. (2018) *Art, Disobedience, and Ethics: The Adventure of Pedagogy*. London: Palgrave Macmillan/Springer.

Baldacchino, J. (2019) *Art as Unlearning: Towards a mannerist pedagogy*. London: Routledge.

Biesta, G. (2015) What is education for? On good education, teacher judgment, and educational professionalism, *European Journal of Education*, 50(1): 75–87.

Biesta, G. (2017) *Letting Art Teach, Art Education 'After' Joseph Beuys*. Arnhem: ArtEZ Press.

Burnard, P. and Colucci-Gray, L. (eds) (2020) Why science and art creativities matter: STEAM (re-)configurings for future-making education, in *Critical Issues in the Future of Learning and Teaching*, Volume 18. Leiden: Brill.

Burnard, P., Colucci-Gray, L. and Sinha, P. (2021) Transdisciplinarity: Letting arts and science teach together, *Curriculum Perspectives*, 41: 113–118.

Collard, P. (2017) Creative Learning Review, *Creative Scotland* (online). Available at: https://www.creativescotland.com/what-we-do/major-projects/creative-learning-and-young-people/creative-learning-review (Accessed 20 July 2022) pp. 36-40.

Conacher, L. (2018) Rethinking CPD: creating problem-solving daredevils, *Engage, the National Association for Gallery Education Publication*, 41: 33–44. Available at: https://engage.org/journals/engage-41/ (accessed 25 June 2022).

Creative Scotland and Education Scotland (2022) Creative Learning Action Plan 2022–23 A collaboration for creativity. Available at: https://www.creativescotland.com/__data/assets/pdf_file/0008/93428/EDUCATION-ACTION-PLAN-2022-23-FINAL-.pdf (accessed 20 July 2022).

Creative Scotland (2016) Visual Arts Sector Review (online). Available at: https://www.creativescotland.com/resources/our-publications/sector-reviews/visual-arts-sector-review (accessed 25 August 2022).

Daichendt, J. (2010) *Artist Teacher: A philosophy of creating and teaching*. Bristol: Intellect.

Dias, B. and Fernandez, T. (2019) Artistic event as pedagogy, in Sinner, A, Irwin, R. L and Adams, J. (eds) *Provoking the Field: International Perspectives on visual arts PhDs in education*. Bristol: Intellect.

Donaldson, G. (2010) *Teaching Scotland's Future: Report of a Review of Teacher Education in Scotland*. Edinburgh: Scottish GovernmentEducation Scotland (2007) Creativity across learning 3–18: Impact Report. Available at: https://education.gov.scot/improvement/Documents/cre39-impact-report.pdf (accessed 10 March 2021).

Education Scotland, *Curriculum for Excellence: Expressive arts principles and practice*. Available at: https://education.gov.scot/Documents/expressive-arts-pp.pdf (accessed 31 January 2023).

Education Scotland, *Curriculum for Excellence: Health and wellbeing Experiences and outcomes.* Available at: https://education.gov.scot/Documents/health-and-wellbeing-eo.pdf (accessed 31 January 2023).

Fraser, L. (2022) Bridging the Pedagogical Gap. Available at https://www.louise-k-fraser.com/copy-of-the-theory (accessed 5 June 2022).

Freelands Foundation (2022) Visualise: race and inclusion in art education, research by Runnymede Trust (online). Available at: https://freelandsfoundation.co.uk/research-and-publications/runnymede-trust. (accessed 5 June 2022).

Freire, P. (1996) *Pedagogy of the Oppressed.* London: Penguin Books.

Gibb, C. (2012) Room 13: The movement and international network, *International Journal of Art and Design Education*, 31(3): 237–244.

Giroux, H. A. (1993) *Border Crossings: Cultural workers and the politics of education.* New York: Routledge.

Granville, G. (2012) Art and design – shifting the paradigm of education reform, in Granville, G. (ed) *Art Education and Contemporary Culture: Irish experiences, international perspectives.* Bristol: Intellect

Harris, A. (2014) *The Creative Turn: Towards a new aesthetic imaginary.* London: Sense Pub.

Heaton, R. (2021) Cognition in art education, *British Educational Research Journal*, 47(5): 1323–1339.

Hernandez-Hernandez (2019) Researching the unknown through arts-based research to promote pedagogical imagination, in Sinner, A., Irwin, R. L. and Adams, J. (eds) *Provoking the Field: International perspectives on visual arts PhDs in education.* Bristol: Intellect.

Hetland, L., Winner, E and Sheridan, K. M. (2013) *Studio Thinking: Volume 2: The real benefits of visual arts* (2nd ed). New York: Teachers College Press/National Art Education Association.

Hofsess, B., Riddett, K., and Siegesmund, R. (2019) Taking Shape: Visual Appearance and Theory, in Sinner, A., Irwin, R. L. and Adams, J. (eds) (2019) *Provoking the Field: International perspectives on visual arts PhDs in education.* Bristol: Intellect, pp. 69-78.

Humes, W. and Priestley, M (2021) Curriculum Reform in Scottish Education: Discourse, Narrative and Enactment, in Priestley, M. Alvunger, D., Philippou, S. and Soini, T. (Eds) *Curriculum Making in Europe: Policy and practice within and across diverse contexts.* London: Emerald Publishing, 175–198.

jagodzinski, j. (2020) Arts education to come in the anthropocene: The cosmic artisan, in Addison, N., and Burgess, L. (eds) *Debates in Art and Design Education* (2nd ed.). London: Routledge.

Kress, G. and van Leeuwen, T. (2006) *Reading Images: The grammar of graphic design.* London: RoutledgeFalmer.

McAuliffe, D. (2013) Art and Design, in Bryce, T.G.K., Humes, W.M., Gillies, D. and Kennedy, A. (eds) *Scottish Education, Referendum* (4th ed.). Edinburgh: Edinburgh University Press.

McAuliffe, D. (2014) Mapping and forecasting the change agenda in Scottish art and design education, *Studies in Society Arts and Cultural Management*, 6: 49–54.

McAuliffe, D. (2018) Art and design, in Bryce, T.G.K., Humes, W.M., Gillies, D. and Kennedy, A. (eds) *Scottish Education* (5th ed.). Edinburgh: Edinburgh University Press.

McAuliffe, D. (2020) in Hepburn, H., 'Don't you just wish...' *Times Education Supplement Scotland* (2 October 2020).

McAuliffe, D. (2021) Using Narrative and Arts-based Methods to make visible (draw out) learning in secondary art education (Unpublished doctoral dissertation). University of the West of Scotland.

McKinnon, C., Fraser, L., Hawkins, S. (2018) Class P5A, St Mary's RC Primary School. *Engage, the National Association for Gallery Education Publication*, 41: 125–133. Available at: https://engage.org/journals/engage-41/ (accessed 25 June 2022).

McKinnon, C., Schrag, A. and Blanche, R. (2022) mapping contemporary visual art and design education in Scotland, *Engage Scotland and Queen Margaret University, Edinburgh*. Available at: https://engage.org/resources/mapping-contemporary-visual-art-and-design-education-in-scotland/

Meyer, J.H.F and Land, R (2006) *Overcoming Barriers to Student Understanding: Threshold concepts and troublesome knowledge*. London: Routledge.

National Partnership for Culture: independent report, (2022) *Scottish Government* (online). Available at https://www.gov.scot/binaries/content/documents/govscot/publications/independent-report/2022/03/independent-report-national-partnership-culture/documents/independent-report-national-partnership-culture/independent-report-national-partnership-culture/govscot%3Adocument/independent-report-national-partnership-culture.pdf (accessed 31 January 2023).

OECD (2021) *Scotland's Curriculum for Excellence: Into the Future, Implementing Education Policies*, OECD Publishing. Available at: https://doi.org/10.1787/bf624417-en. (accessed 10 March 2021).

Payne, R. (2020) The shock of the new, *International Journal of Art and Design Education*, 39(4): 724–738.

Pirrie, A. (2020) Where science ends, art begins? Critical perspectives on the development of steam in the new climatic regime, in Burnard, P. and Colucci-Gray, L. (eds) *Why Science and Art Creativities Matter – (Re-)Configuring STEAM for Future-Making Education: Critical issues in the future of learning and teaching*, volume 18. London: Brill Sense.

Research Scotland (2021) Face to face expressive arts in Scotland during Covid-19 (online). Available at: https://www.creativescotland.com/resources/professional-resources/research/research-from-the-cultural-sector/face-to-face-expressive-arts-in-covid-19 (accessed 25 August 2022).

Scottish Executive (2004) Curriculum for Excellence: Health and wellbeing experiences and outcomes. Available at: https://education.gov.scot/Documents/health-and-wellbeing-eo.pdf

Seith, E. (2022) Qualifications review lead outlines what happens next, *Times Education Supplement* (online). Available at: https://www.tes.com/magazine/news/secondary/exclusive-qualifications-review-lead-outlines-what-happens-next (accessed 23 September 2022).

Sousanis, N. (2015) *Unflattening*. Cambridge, MA: Harvard University Press.

The Scottish Government (2022) Putting Learners at the Centre: Towards a Future Vision for Scottish Education: A report by Professor Kenneth Muir University of the West of Scotland and Independent Advisor to the Scottish Government on Education Reform. Available at: https://www.gov.scot/publications/putting-learners-centre-towards-future-vision-scottish-education/pages/2/

Thomson, T. and Hall, C. (2021) 'You just feel more relaxed': An Investigation of Art Room Atmosphere. International Journal of Art and Design Education, 40(3): 599–614.

Thomson, P. and Maloy, L. (2022) The benefits of art, craft and design education in schools: A rapid evidence review, School of Education, The University of Nottingham NSEAD (online). Available at: https://www.nsead.org/files/6f85ab8587bc53ce-653702da1cc15690.pdf

12 Finding Gold... What are the alchemic conditions needed for artist teacher transformation?

Judy Thomas and Vicky Sturrs

The Baltic Centre for Contemporary Art, Gateshead and Northumbria University, Newcastle upon Tyne, MA Fine Art and Education programme began in 2003 and ran for 15 years. Supporting a wide context of art education, research and pedagogy, this jointly delivered Masters level course was established within the national Artist Teacher Scheme (ATS) and drew upon the gallery's Learning team and core group of artists, along with artist tutors at the university. Evidence demonstrates that this programme has had a dynamic legacy, inspiring and innovating practice for and with artist teachers and impacting upon thousands of young people. Internally, this course trail-blazed a new way of working for the two organisations, laying the foundation for the Baltic x Northumbria University partnership. An innovative collaboration held as a model of best practice, this United Kingdom (UK) based partnership between the gallery and university still entwines a shared commitment to supporting creative talent development, nurturing public engagement and enhancing the region's reputation for artistic excellence. The Baltic x Northumbria University Institute is a base for world-class teaching and mentorship in contemporary art practice and research, and at its core, the partnership co-delivers learning and research activity that furthers the understanding of contemporary fine art practice and engages constituents in the key debates of today.

As Assistant Professor at Northumbria University and Head of Learning and Civic Engagement at Baltic (at the time of writing), we cited ourselves within the Institute, co-leading and co-developing the MA Fine Art and Education, latterly named MA Contemporary Art and Education, for a collective five years along with further involvement, dating back to the programme's introduction. This chapter explores the value of partnership and the preciousness of community that these partnerships and distinctive spaces can offer artist teachers. Supported by alumni interviews, it unpicks how the Baltic x Northumbria

University course in particular advocated criticality, collaboration and dialogue; supporting, challenging and developing holistic, outward-facing
approaches towards engaged, creative pedagogy.

Crucially, this section champions the contemporary art gallery as a unique
environment for artist teacher decompression and presents a practical, how-to
guide to generating an alchemic framework that values transformation as the
outcome of creative professional development.

Throughout the course of its 15-year history, the Baltic x Northumbria
University MA Fine Art and Education programme supported over 210 people
to develop, mould and re-claim their artist teacher identities. Run as a two-
year, part-time programme, annual cohort sizes varied but worked especially
well when there were seven or eight students in each year group, resulting in
combined groups of 15 or 16 students. Through bi-weekly, after-school taught
sessions, five annual Saturday Schools and an introductory week-long summer school, the programme offered a curriculum that was aligned with school
calendars. With practical assessments placed at the end of August, teacher
participants were given the chance to maximise summer holidays as creative
opportunities to focus on practice.

Reflecting back, the experiences and delivery of the Saturday School sessions were a key anchor of the programme; realised through a series of full
day practical and discursive opportunities at Baltic, these remain significant.
These Saturdays were 'precious gold', facilitating breathing space and a place
for intensity, re-evaluation, experience, challenge, risk, selfishness, generosity,
sharing, thoughtfulness, play and, ultimately, transformation.

> There have been many profound impacts – the course IS practice, so some-
> times I cannot remember a 'before'. Many resources, ideas and approaches
> have gone straight into teaching practice on Monday morning after the ses-
> sions [...] I was sceptical of the full possibility of an 'artist teacher' at the
> beginning of the course, now there is simply no other way to be (learner
> feedback 2017).

The Saturday School sessions actively sought to reduce the traditionally hierarchical power relationship between students and tutors (Dewey 1938) preferring
instead to champion learning through experience (Kolb 2005) and the social
construction of knowledge together (Vygotsky 1978). As tutors, we subscribed
to the notion that we were learning too and as suggested by Shor (1992) and
Kelly (2022) understood the need to balance structure with openness to encourage empowerment.

> Having a shared experience can help bind a group together. This extends
> to those who facilitate and participate in sessions (Producers, Artists and
> Researchers), helping the whole group understand each other, relate, and
> work collaboratively (Kelly 2022: 14).

This was certainly true of our Saturdays. Through collective generosity, the sessions galvanised openness and sharing. This collaboration was crucial to the sense of community that developed within and between each cohort. There are many remembered moments where, collectively, we felt humbled by shared insights and the willingness of group members to work together, express opinions and support one another. Sharing was actively achieved through social actions and engagement as well as more subtle interactions that were often 'unconscious, unintentional, automatic or intuitive' supporting 'a collision of ideas, attitudes, and innovations' (Thomas 2014: 108–12). This encouraging exchange included collective making and creating, the sharing of academic research, demonstrations, readings, writings, performances, lesson plan suggestions, ideas for practice, supportive conversations and general comradery. Our Saturdays created spaces of supportive relationships and dynamic environments for interchange and production.

Making space

As a third place (Oldenburg 1989), the gallery environment, when done well, can be a natural leveller; an inclusive place, accessible to the general public and, in Baltic's case, free. Different from work, home and school, the gallery offers space for congregation and conversation around, and with, new ideas and new people. When considering museums and galleries as learning places, Curator and Consultant Sylvia Lahav (2005: 46) suggests these are spaces where communities of interest are established and where a plurality of 'views and voices' come together. Hosting the Saturday sessions at Baltic rather than at Northumbria University was significant because the gallery facilitates opportunities for co-constructive pedagogy and unique dialogue (Taylor 2006; Pringle 2009b; Pringle and DeWitt 2014). This setting promoted key aims of the original ATS programme:

> the richness and complexity of contemporary fine art practice and the diversity of thinking and influences which inform it can enhance teachers' subject knowledge [...] and can enable them to make positive contributions to the delivery of the curriculum (Galloway et al. 2006: 6).

During the Saturday sessions this was realised through encounters between artworks, ideas, people, experience, and individual reflection. We drew directly upon exhibition thematics and content; activities were devised to stimulate debate and exploration; we found ourselves making, discussing, investigating, intervening and performing inside and outside the gallery. This empowered immersive and experiential processes that were playful, experimental and thought-provoking. These activities challenged and united us and sparked new ways of working and thinking, which, positively, relayed back into alternative situations and our individual practices.

As public spaces, our arts organisations offer opportunities for learning and debate, safe belonging and solitude and as such are in a unique position to support individuals and communities with fast and unprecedented changes (Calouste Gulbenkian Foundation 2017). Fulfilling this civic role to its fullest requires multiple approaches for, and with, diverse publics. This is described by the Calouste Gulbenkian Foundation through a series of place-based metaphors likening arts organisations to colleges, town halls, public parks, temples and homesteads. At Baltic, our Saturday sessions held these metaphorical spaces, shifting in and out of focus across the two years for each cohort.

Away from the places where everyday pressures and demands build, our Saturdays at Baltic were hosted in a room overlooking the River Tyne, away from the immediate hustle of the gallery-space, introducing a temple-like space for decompression and reflection. Some sessions began with window-gazing activities, or breathing exercises specifically utilising the location; connected, but detached from the world outside.

Congregating in the same space each time built familiarity, comfort and, as noted by Hall and Bates (2018), a sense of belonging; the act of threshold-crossing increasingly becoming a moment of transition into a space of safety and homeliness. Our physical teaching space became 'owned' by our cohorts, a shared place of transition, transaction and transformation. However, as Botterill (2018) attests, impactful community building grows from there being a commonality that draws everyone together; an engagement in actions that encourage connection beyond merely occupying the same space.

Distinct from the classroom, we ensured that our teaching surroundings were clear and calm, encouraging communal working around shared tables spread with inspiring reading, useful resources and creative materials. We aimed to present a supportive and inspiring smorgasbord of possibilities, presenting varied journals and books, past assignments and artistic kit with which to respond to the day's programming. Debate and hospitality were equally key and came to be expected elements in our programme; weekly provocations encouraged lively, sometimes oppositional, discussion of topics that were soothed by the kinship of sharing a potluck working lunch; allegorically referencing the varied uses of a town hall.

Reflecting back, we realise that our shared practice was nurtured by its conditions; a higher education institution and an arts organisation working in collaboration, delivering within the contemporary gallery setting. Upon these foundational circumstances, we ignited the following processes. These seven components became touch points within our Saturday sessions, essential elements around which we structured our teaching and learning. Below, we outline each one, unpicking its characteristics and practical elements cited against learner feedback and established reasoning.

Figure 12.1 Thomas and Sturrs (2022) *Finding Gold... Dialogue*

Illustration © Josie Brookes 2022, Two people in playful dialogue

Finding Gold...

What is the alchemic process needed for artist teacher transformation?

Decompression

> I have really valued the focus this programme has given me. The workload was challenging to manage as a full-time teacher, however [...] the benefit of the challenging workload was that it forced me to reflect critically on my own approach to work-life-balance and working efficiency (learner feedback 2017).

Facilitating structured 'unstructured' time typically required decompression. Each Saturday would start with activities that would broker transition from daily routines, stresses and disconnection, designed to invite mindfulness, where present moment perspective could support a sense of calm and focus. For example, slow, deep breathing, meditation, reading, free-writing and, on some occasions, yoga. This enabled 'engaged relaxed attention' (Kelley and Kelley 2015: 84) supporting our ability to make fresh connections, participate and play. The fact that the Saturday School sessions were full days was important; we observed a pattern that lasted throughout the years where teachers arrived in the morning stressed out, tired and het up. The space created by the Saturdays granted permission for self-focus, requiring an acceptable selfishness and awareness to being centred within the moment. As a result, through the course of each Saturday, a noticeable process of decompression occurred.

Provocation

Inviting a sessional provocation from students was a key element in creating the deep engagement needed for development and advancement of the artist teacher identity. It brought new ideas and differing concepts to the learning space. This is supported by Mills (1998) who suggests provocation as a method to promote students' active participation and pique curiosity, positioning challenge and debate as routes to develop abstract thinking.

> The course is very humanely supported with excellent caring professional tutors [...] the eclectic nature of the Saturdays and the wide variety of stimuli are a great strength and the time to debate and exchange views is fantastic, chairing of these debates is great too (learner feedback 2016).

The inclusive nature of the programme meant the students approached their pedagogy from varying different starting points and through numerous layers of lived experience. It is suggested that collaborative learning is advanced through scenarios 'that build on socio-cognitive conflict as a trigger' (Malzahn et al. 2021: 233). Although supporting the nature of a classroom being a 'risk-taking environment', Mills (1998: 23) does caution tutors against the risk of provocation encroaching on the 'philosophic identifications' of learners. As evidenced in feedback, well-chaired debate with balanced moderation is key to avoiding this. We observed that through asking each student to prepare a provocation referencing something they were currently engaged with, for example, an artwork, article, book, or experience, diverse perspectives were permissioned and through inviting contribution respectfully, these diverse perspectives were brought into the light safely. In these instances, provocation gave a platform for individual thought to become collective and ensured that debate, and in some cases, mild discord, could ensue. These authors found merit in the TEDxRegina (2015) assertion that 'provocations instigate change that can make our community better'.

Artist-led activities

Crucial to the magic of the Baltic Saturdays were the inclusion of artist-led sessions; these involved a diversity of artists who instigated and delivered inspiring, challenging activities. Drawing upon authentic practices and processes, these instigated the exploration of ideas and materials by employing a mix of praxis, discussion, and tacit enquiry.

> The content has helped me to think more laterally and feel more audacious in my teaching approaches as well as my artistic practice. Having a teaching team which includes visiting lecturers and artists is extremely helpful and stimulating and offers an interesting variety of approaches and topics (learner feedback, 2015).

Figure 12.2 Thomas and Sturrs (2022) *Finding Gold... Artist-led activity*

Illustration © Josie Brookes 2022; Six people sit or stand around a table, happily engaged in hands-on, creative activities led by an artist.

This supports a shared belief that artists bring 'a distinctive approach and creative pedagogy' (Thomas 2014: 155). In the Saturday School sessions this drew upon contemporary thinking and references, alongside 'specialist skills' and emphasised 'art language' and 'authentic practice' (Thomas 2014: 155). These enabled us to learn together, share knowledge, and expand creative perspectives, confidence and 'artistic thinking' (Daichendt 2010: 10).

Equally, we observed that this act of doing allowed for conversation, both critical and social, to flow. This creative occupation supported students to open up more easily, forming bonds and sharing stories (Kelly 2022). This observation, alongside learner feedback, further advocates for existing literature that aligns creative practice with wellbeing (Atkinson 2021) and positive impacts on mental health (Perkins et al. 2021).

> Had I not undertaken the programme to completion I would not now be the artist/teacher/collaborator/maker that I am now, and I would also not be the person I am now [...] I am far more confident, knowledgeable and determined (learner feedback 2017).

Hospitality

Radical hospitality (Pratt 2011), which has religious, Benedictine origins, is the practice of actively seeking people who may need support and finding ways to make those who are too often marginalised and forgotten to feel welcome, comfortable and supported (Pratt 2011). Baltic talks a lot about radical hospitality and extends this definition to something that acknowledges intergenerational, intercultural and socio-economic barriers with a welcome that is generous, open and offers kinship to all. Our Saturday sessions practised this methodology. By practising radical hospitality, we were able to shape physical space that encouraged artist teachers to dwell and metaphorical places for them to be heard and understood, able to share differences and find commonality. Together, we could support and signpost.

On Saturdays, coming together to sit down and share food added to the mutual sense of care and generosity, enhancing the warm welcome we wished to foster. It enriched a sense of wellbeing, morale, trust and belonging that learner feedback tells us was highly valued. It also ensured there was space to plan, share and promote further opportunities. Signposting learners to calls for papers and publications, for example, supported their aspirations and ensured their continuity within the ecology of the sector. Organising trips and residentials, in addition to their contact time, ensured the group bonded further beyond the 'classroom' and strengthened this sense of a community of practice.

Play

> The Saturday sessions have a good mix of play, discussion, cerebral thinking and theory [...] there's a supportive and collaborative atmosphere where we can share our experiences and knowledge. [There's] plenty of fun and laughter (learner feedback 2015).

Play was an essential part of our Saturdays. When describing play, Frost (1992) characterises it as something that includes active involvement, spontaneity and exploration, suggesting work as its antithesis (Frost 1992: 14). Educational theorists Piaget (1962), Huizinga (1950 cited in Stelzer 2022), Vygotsky (1978) and Csikszentmihalyi (1975, 1990) considered freedom to be an important play requirement; the sense of freedom generated by the Saturdays was almost akin to 'stepping out of "real" life' (Frost 1992: 62) placing enjoyment, alongside trust, at their centre. Reviewing images of the sessions gives evidence of this; participants look absorbed in the activities; they are often laughing. This does not suggest these experiences were always easy. We embraced our playtime with seriousness. It is important to recognise how our constructs of play can create instability, uncertainty, tensions and discomfort; permission was, therefore, an essential requisite to embrace risk-taking and ambiguity. The impact of our play was ultimately that of transformation, enjoyment and imagination. Using the agency of play we would 'deconstruct established systems of meaning' (Muka and Edblom 2013: 16) and provoke new opportunities for encounter and dialogue.

Invited artists offered important contributions to Saturday Schools facilitating opportunities for exploration. By working collaboratively in these shared spaces of artist-led pedagogy (Pringle 2009a) and contemporary practice, every day, 'normal' boundaries no longer existed. Instead, spontaneity and imagination were encouraged via individual, collaborative and co-constructed learning. These playful interludes deliberately provoked active questioning and fluid, open-ended processes of experimentation, reflection and discovery. Observation engenders Paris' (2008) notion that play encourages an immersive, transitional state where expression, and ultimately, transformation can occur.

> Excellent inputs and strong encouragement to properly engage has led me to turbo charge my transformation as an artist teacher and to develop new skills, attitudes and approaches. I have not reached settled positions in any of the areas of study but feel empowered and encouraged to explore first and allow time for things to develop (learner feedback 2016).

When considering play as a route to recapture radical imagination, Muka and Edblom (2013: 12) suggest 'playfulness is an inherent element of the artistic process'. They propose play to have agency; helping artists 'to push boundaries and challenge norms and to insert art into a variety of narratives' (Muka and Edblom 2013: 11). Certainly, learners supported this theory, using skills, exercises, permissions and thinking gathered or unlocked throughout their Saturday sessions to further platform, and advocate for, their artist teacher identities.

During Saturday School sessions, ideas were shared, tested and evaluated through play. This approach supported game-playing, visual thinking, art creation, mental mobility, critique and knowledge creation; emphasising and embracing activities that did not seek perfection or specific endpoints, but instead, were open to interpretation and malleability. Together, we engaged in activities that required participation and quick-thinking, alongside opportunities to practise and respond intuitively. Characteristically, our activities were short and achievable; for example, games requiring playful or subversive interpretations, analysis of artworks (both serious and tongue-in-cheek), material exploration and experimentation, pick and mix activities, one-, two-, five- and ten-minute tasks, solo, partner and group responses and performative actions, to name a few. Our observations supported the assertions made by Thomas (2014) and demonstrated that these intentionally playful interludes allowed learners to 'unstick':

> Play indicates movement or a shift; no play indicates solidity, rigidity or a block. Playing implies fluidity, release or moments of potential, where movement represents a state of transformation or change (Thomas 2014: 149).

When designing an approach to support artist teacher transformation, play proved to be a powerful element. This understanding of play and its transformative nature endures at Baltic through a long-held, concerted effort to develop playful experience with, by, and for constituents from birth to adulthood. It is also a key strand of all current programming. Play-led exhibitions including *The Playground Project* (2016), Pippa Hale's (2019) *Play Rebellion* and Albert Potrony's (2021) *Equal Play* continue to weave the power of play into Baltic's everyday pedagogy.

Dialogue

In the text *Keywords,* Raymond Williams (1976: 6) considers 'vocabulary' as something shared with others 'to discuss many of the central processes of our common life'. Our commonality as artist teachers brought us together in a space of creative pedagogy and this enabled us to engage in a critical and creative vocabulary, enriched and infused by contemporary art and subject specific awareness. This dynamically nurtured 'artistic thinking' (Daichendt 2010: 10) and innovative practice.

Dialogue is an essential requirement for any creative and pedagogic practice but to make meaningful dialogic connections, space is needed to recognise and value experience. The Saturday School sessions carved out capacity for thinking, and created supportive spaces for connection and expression, offering invaluable moments for self-dialogue. These occasions created time to *'be'*, alongside time for dialogue with others. Verbal discussion was part of this, additionally, there was a dialogue generated through shared engagement and actions. By giving ourselves wider permission to be critically engaged, we explored dialogues of experimentation and making, through a vocabulary of gesture and being. The result of this became new knowledge and conversation that fed practice beyond the sessions.

> The course makes you think about teaching very differently [...] I am now better able to unpack, substantiate and evaluate best working practice whilst teaching – which in turn strengthens, focuses and reinforces this for myself (learner feedback 2015).

Reflection

When describing the research-led practice employed across learning programmes at Tate galleries in the UK, Pringle and DeWitt (2014) describe 'a model of enquiry', with an emphasis on 'questioning, exploration and reflection' which leads to 'the construction of new knowledge and understanding' (2014: para. 7). As a contemporary within the field of gallery learning, Baltic engages with a similar enquiry model. Analysis and reflection was, therefore, central to the Saturday School experience and was evidenced as a strength for learners:

> The full impact on my practice as an educator is just starting to happen. I have made many connections from Saturday content to my own artwork through items that were featured in the sessions, not least starting to write poetically. I am now starting to challenge the compartmentalising of my activities – education – art – job – life etc. (learner feedback 2016).

Making time to reflect is vital. However, for most artist teachers, possibly educators in general, making time for reflection can be challenging. Constant rushing between tasks and continuous demands is a common experience that can leave little, or no, opportunity to take stock. It is only when there is a definite halt to activities that critical, reflective absorption can take place. This requires self-permission which, regrettably, can get overlooked within daily practices. Prioritising reflection is key, not only to improve practice but to prove impact. We posit that carving out time to reflect not only makes us better facilitators, educators and teachers but makes better learners, collaborators, and artists. We consider reflection to be essential.

Graham and Shier (2010 cited in Grant and Kinman 2012) referenced the positive impact of reflection and noted a correlation between the successful utilisation of reflective practice and improved happiness. Through our Saturday School sessions, we noted that creating space for reflection and the express permission to engage in personal and peer analysis, evaluation and reflective exchange, promoted positive feelings of personal growth, reinvigoration and renewal. In turn, in agreement with Graham and Shier (2010), this impacted positively and significantly on personal wellbeing, not only for learners but equally for us as session leaders too.

Conclusion

It is the experience of these authors that artist teacher transformation occurs when teaching content is intentionally designed to permit breathing space, to provide challenge, support playful experimentation and to nurture thoughtfulness. Holding generosity as a core belief, we argue that tutors aiming to support learners through their artist teacher transformation should co-construct learning environments *alongside* their learners, developing a shared experience that builds and bolsters the notion of community.

Enquiry, artist-led pedagogy and playfulness should be at the heart of this experience. We assert that the gallery environment provides this like no other. Encountering artworks, interventions and exhibitions, whether directly scheduled or indirectly through independent activity, promotes different and diverse ways of thinking about the world that are practically applicable to the artist teacher identity. Made possible, in this instance, through partnership, we maintain that the gallery's unique position, as a space outside of our 'traditional' learning lives (i.e. not school, home or work), affords it an enigmatic quality; a place where the not-yet-known has the freedom to occur. For these authors, the gallery environment is a space where the individual becomes collective and through regular, routine engagement, the collective's shared experience offers ownership; a familiar springboard from which learners can both leap ambitiously and, perhaps most importantly, return safely.

Across their professional practice, we have prospected within these conditions forging the following 'golden' model of activity:

Decompression

Full days of contact time allow learners the opportunity to immerse themselves in their artist teacher pedagogy; to have space away from the everyday to pursue their own development with permission to think expansively. Scheduling designated time to actively decompress at the start of each session enables learners to engage without the daily stresses of normality.

Provocation

Sessional, learner-led provocations encourage active participation and ensure that individual interests, lived experiences and varied perspectives are brought to the fore. Learner-led opportunities further underline learners as co-collaborators, promote community of practice and engender safe debate among peers.

Artist-led activities

Sessions should include artist-led interactions. Artists bring authentic experiences and specialist skills. Artists who facilitate workshops as part of their practice offer comparable blueprints for artist teachers to learn from and signpost to. Their interventions offer the community opportunities to converse critically while being physically occupied creatively.

Hospitality

Practising radical hospitality builds kinship. Scheduling time to share food and eat together as part of the day fosters moments that further social connection. Tutors should consider mindfully collecting and signposting new opportunities beyond contact time in order to demonstrate investment outside of academic achievement. This encourages artist teachers to find their wider place within the sector.

Play

The power of play, and its ability to transform, should never be under-estimated. An adult learning *through* play is absorbed; immersed in imagination. Tutors should design fun learning experiences that encourage discovery and new encounters. They should observe laughter and, in doing so, acknowledge that it is in these moments of ease and natural fluidity that individuals are free to realise potential.

Dialogue

Within sessional agendas, there should always be time and space allotted to discussion. Conversation with like-minded colleagues, where participants share the same vocabulary and similar frames of reference, ensures learners have the opportunity to critically engage with concepts and approaches.

Reflection

Reflection and reflective exchange is so often overlooked in a busy life. Like decompression, tutors should ensure that designated space is provided, alongside conversational or individual prompts, to give permission for individual and collective reflection. This time should be used to consider the day's learning and experiences, but also their wider applications to pedagogy and 'prepare the ground' for further and future thinking and doing.

As a conclusion to this chapter, we present a visual representation of Finding Gold....

Figure 12.3 Thomas and Sturrs (2022) *Finding Gold... Model of Activity*

Illustration © Josie Brookes: 18 people are engaged in seven different pursuits; decompression, provocation, artist-led activity, hospitality, play, dialogue and reflection. Their thoughts, ideas and experiences are represented by looping and swirling lines leading to a central nucleus; 'the gold' of collective, and shared, transformative practice.

References

Atkinson, S. (2021) Art Spaces, in G. Andrews, V. Crooks, J. Pearce and J. Messina (eds.) *COVID-19 and Similar Futures: Pandemic geographies*. Springer: Cham, 299–304.

Botterill, K. (2018) Rethinking "community" relationally: Polish communities in Scotland before and after Brexit, *Transactions of the Institute of British Geographers*, 43(4): 540–554.

Calouste Gulbenkian Foundation (2017) Rethinking Relationships: Inquiry into the Civic Role of Arts Organisations. Phase 1 Report (online). Available at: https://gulbenkian.pt/uk-branch/publications/rethinking-relationships/ (accessed on 22 August 2022).

Csikszentmihalyi, M., and Bennett, S. (1971) an exploratory model of play, *American Anthropologist*, 73 (1): 45–58.

Csikszentmihalyi, M. (1990) Flow: The psychology of optimal experience, *Journal of Leisure Research*, 24(1): 93–94.

Daichendt, G. (2010) *Artist Teacher: A philosophy for creating and teaching*, Bristol: Intellect Books.

Dewey, J. (1938) *Experience and Education*. New York: Macmillan.

Frost, J. (1992) *Play and Playscapes*. New York: Delmar Publishers Inc.

Galloway, S., Stanley, J. and Strand, S. (2006) *ARTIST TEACHER SCHEME EVALUATION 2005-2006*, Corsham: National Society for Education in Art and Design.

Graham, J. and Shier, M. (2010) The social work profession and subjective well-being: The impact of a profession on overall subjective well-being, *British Journal of Social Work*, 40(5):1553–1572, cited in Grant, L. and Kinman, G. (2012) Enhancing wellbeing in social work students: Building resilience in the next generation, *Social Work Education*, 31(5): 605–621.

Hall, E. and Bates, B. (2019) Hatescape? A relational geography of disability hate crime, exclusion and belonging in the city, *Geoforum*, 101:100–110.

Kelley, D. and Kelley, T. (2015) *Creative Confidence: Unleashing the creative potential within us all*. London: Harper Collins.

Kelly, J. (2022) *20 Babies: Research Report May 2022*, Baltic Centre for Contemporary Art and Newcastle University (online). Available at http://balticplus.uk/20-babies-research-report-c35536/ (accessed on 31 August 2022).

Kolb, A. and Kolb, D. (2005) Learning styles and learning spaces: Enhancing experiential learning in higher education, *Academy of Management Learning & Education*, 4(2): 193–212.

Lahav, S. (2005) A Special Place, A Learning Space@ Museums in the 21st Century in Museums and Galleries as Learning Places, *engage extra*. London: engage.

Malzahn, N., Aprin, F., Hoppe, H. U., Eimler, S. C., and Moder, S. (2021) Measures of Disagreement in Learning Groups as a Basis for Identifying and Discussing Controversial Judgements, in Hmelo-Silver, C. E., De Wever, B., and Oshima, J. (Eds.), *Proceedings of the 14th International Conference on Computer-Supported Collaborative Learning - CSCL 2021* (pp. 233-236), Bochum, Germany: International Society of the Learning Sciences (online). Available at https://repository.isls.org/bitstream/1/7325/1/233-236.pdf (accessed on 31 August 2022).

Mills, J. (1998) Better teaching through provocation, *College Teaching*, 46(1): 21–25.

Muka, E. and Edblom, S. (2013) *Play! Recapturing the Radical Imagination*. Stockholm: Art and Theory.

Oldenburg, R. (1989) *The Great Good Place: Cafes, coffee shops, community centres, beauty parlours, general stores, bars, hangouts, and how they get you through the day*. New York: Paragon House.

Paris, A. (2008) *Standing at Water's Edge: Moving past fear, blocks, and pitfalls to discover the power of creative immersion.* California: New World Library.

Perkins, R., Mason-Bertrand, A., Tymoszuk, U., Spiro, N., Gee, K. and Willamon, A. (2021) Arts Engagement supports social connectedness in adulthood: Findings from the HEartS Survey, *BMC Public Health*, 21(1208): 1–15.

Piaget, J. (1962) *Play, Dreams and Imitation in Childhood.* London: Taylor & Francis Group.

Pratt, L. C. (2011) *Radical Hospitality: Benedict's Way of Love.* Paraclete Press.

Pringle, E. (2009a) The artist-led pedagogic process in the contemporary art gallery: Developing a meaning making framework, *International Journal of Art and Design Education*, 28: 174–182.

Pringle, E. (2009b) *The Artist as Educator: Examining Relationships between Art Practice and Pedagogy in the Gallery Context* (online). Available at https://www.tate.org.uk/research/publications/tate-papers/11/artist-as-educator-examining-relationships-between-art-practice-and-pedagogy-in-gallery-context (accessed on 23 August 2022).

Pringle, E. and DeWitt, J. (2014) *Perceptions, Processes and Practices around Learning in an Art Gallery* (online). Available at: https://www.tate.org.uk/research/tate-papers/11/artist-as-educator-examining-relationships-between-art-practice-and-pedagogy-in-gallery-context (accessed on 23 August 2022).

Shor, I. (1992) *Empowering Education: Critical teaching for social change.* Chicago: University Chicago Press.

Stelzer, J. (2022) The seriousness of play: Johan Huizinga's *Homo Ludens* and the demise of the play-element, *International Journal of Play*, DOI: 10.1080/21594937.2022.2135537

Taylor, B. (2006) En-quire: Learning through action research, *engage Journal*, 18: 12.

TEDxRegina. (2015) *Provoke (Something Good)* (online). Available at: https://www.ted.com/tedx/events/13260 (accessed on17 August 2022).

Thomas, J. (2014) *Why Make a Case for the Artist Facilitator?* Newcastle upon Tyne: Northumbria University. Available at: https://ethos.bl.uk/OrderDetails.do?uin=uk.bl.ethos.639862 (accessed 17 August 2022). pp.108 -112.

Vygotsky, L. S. (1978) *Mind in Society.* Cambridge: Harvard University Press.

Williams, R. (1976) *Keywords: A vocabulary of culture and society.* London: Fontana Press, Harper Collins.

Meeting in the Middle: Documenting change in collaboration

Tamar MacLellan and Philippa Wood

Introduction

The aim of this chapter is for us to share something of the shifts in partnership that were enabled having taken a collective decision to explore new ways of working. As artist teachers, our professional roles first overlapped when working at Lincoln College of Art and Design in 1994 within the disciplines of Textiles (Tamar) and Graphic Design (Philippa). Twelve years later we began to work collaboratively as part of a collective called the *Caseroom Press* to produce limited edition artists' books drawing upon our individual areas of practice (http://www.the-case.co.uk). While we shared an interest in exploiting traditional making processes within a contemporary context, it was the completion of individual postgraduate study that became a key turning point for our collective practice. We moved from a sporadic working pattern to a more formalised system of collaboration utilising a WordPress blog to enable analysis and documentation of our practice. It was at this point at the end of 2015 that we began the original *Meeting in the Middle* project (Figure 13.1) following a chance discovery of the 88-mile Jurassic Way linking our individual hometowns of Banbury and Stamford respectively.

Having produced work in partnership since 2006, we recognised a division of labour had become established drawing heavily upon our individual areas of expertise and were both interested in adopting alternative approaches to making aligned to standpoints presented by Ravetz et al. (2013). We agreed to embrace ideas shared by Bolton (2010) and take a more open-ended approach to projects moving away from safe understood structures to allow room for development of practice and scope for effective learning. We agreed to document progress on a WordPress blog as a collective space to share individual, intellectual, and emotional responses (https://meetinginthemiddleblog.wordpress.com).

Figure 13.1 documents a section of *Meeting in the Middle* which was published in August 2016 as a limited edition of eight concertina books constructed from 36 individual postcards representing each of the settlements along the Jurassic Way. Having concluded this project where we embraced alternative ways of working, we reflected on the change in our practice. Individual visits

Figure 13.1 Tamar MacLellan and Philippa Wood (2016) *Meeting in the Middle*

to each settlement along the route had informed ideas and led to a reading around social history which had in turn been shared and common areas of interest emerged, correlating with theories of collectivitiy presented by Wenger (1998). Recognising opportunities to develop alternative approaches to making by working outside of our existing experience (De Wachter 2017), subsequent projects have continued to build upon this central commitment around adjustment in ways of working.

This chapter offers a sequential account of these changes through the realisation of four collaborative projects produced from 2021 onwards. Informed by standpoints presented by Billing (2007), this chapter offers an account of this change. We draw upon pivotal blog posts and images of work, alongside an overview and conclusion of each project, to document the new ways of working that we adopted, shifts in practice, and ultimately change in collaboration.

Project 1: Herbarium

In 2020 we produced two limited edition artists' books in response to the COVID-19 government-imposed rules introduced within the first and second United Kingdom (UK) national lockdowns (http://www.the-case.co.uk/168.html; http://www.the-case.co.uk/stopstart.html). Enforced restrictions throughout this period of homeworking around limitations in scale and choice of materials available had afforded opportunities to do things differently. First, outcomes had been developed individually, shared digitally and visually each week via the blog and a FaceTime conversation, and then cut-up, embellished and re-interpreted in partnership on making days (Figure 13.8). Outcomes echoed ideas presented by Lave (2009) around situated learning and activity, which afforded change in our collective practice.

Figures 13.2 and 13.3 Tamar MacLellan and Philippa Wood (2020) *The Herbarium*

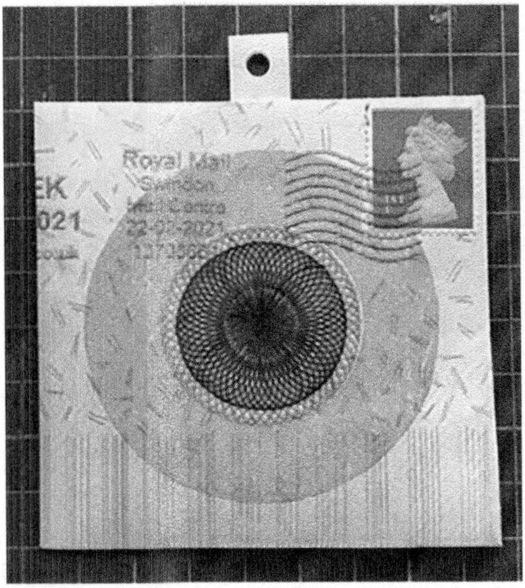

13.2

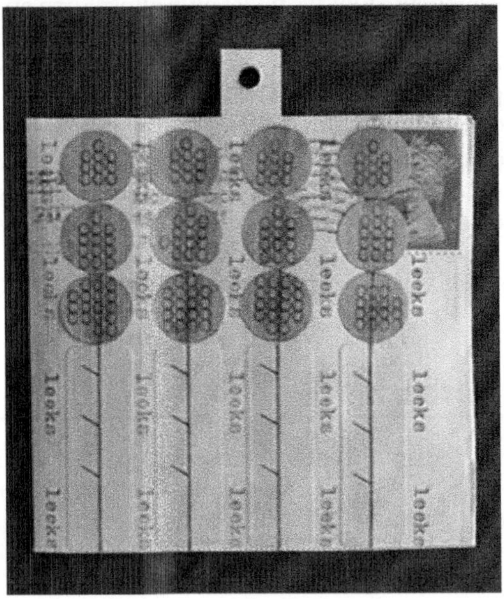

13.3

As the UK government published their roadmap out of lockdown in 2021, we agreed to pause production of our book arts projects and trial elements of these collective activity-led ways of working with responses to the annual *World Book Night* event organized by University of West England, Bristol (https:// cfpr.uwe.ac.uk/world-book-night-2021-the-herbarium/; Figures 13.2 and 13.3).

Within the first research undertaken around the 2021 *World Book Night* theme *The Herbarium,* the phrase companion planting emerged as salient. This notion of pairing plants for their mutual benefit resonated with us – both in terms of aligning to standpoints presented by Ravetz et al. (2013) around reciprocal enhancement of practice when working in partnership - and in offering a new sequential approach to the production of imagery.

Our weekly FaceTime discussion, established during lockdown, enabled clarification of first ideas about which plants to select, and the scale of working and timings to be collectively agreed. We determined to produce an individual response on the outside of a C6 envelope and post this to each other to add to, so that a pair of companion plants would be partnered together in some way within a single outcome. Selecting to work on the outside of the envelope extended an approach to making previously trialled in 2020 around opportunities for unplanned marks to be added throughout the postal journey of the envelope, which we were interested to further explore (http://www.the-case.co.uk/stopstart.html).

The action of adding to each other's work to create a shared image in response to a given outcome offered a new approach to making which built upon working methodologies employed within our precursory collaborative lock-down project *Stop/Start* (http://www.the-case.co.uk/stopstart.html). These included the opportunity to extend visual practice through a return to the use of an abstract approach to art making and employing the envelope as a substrate. Embracing a new subject matter offered some alternative ways of working, including an adjustment in colour palette; we recognised an ease in making throughout this project, enabled in response to the short timescale and a familiarity around adding to each other's work.

Project 2: Good Companions

Interested in continuing to make use of subject matter explored within *The Herbarium* in some way, from June 2021 we began to discuss gardens and gardening within our weekly FaceTime conversations. Recognising the potential for this theme to offer a positive approach to image making around growth and new beginnings; we shared stories about favourite plants and most-used garden implements. Common areas of interest emerged through this process which align to ideas presented by Billing (2007) and Wenger (1998) around collectivitiy, accumulation and long-collaboration.

We agreed to allocate time to discuss these further during a subsequent making day, and working alongside each other during this event afforded time for ideas to be reflected upon and explored through discussion, visual interpretation and further reading around the theme. We agreed to begin by producing a book work about companion planting. Returning to the shared way of working employed within *The Herbarium* offered an opportunity to extend individual ideas and produce a collective response. As conversations continued, we made further decisions around the imagery, scale, and book schedule to align to our next pre-planned making day in five weeks' time. We recognised that this detailed planning enabled via dialogue both aligned to standpoints presented by De Wachter (2017) around the division of labour within collaboration and offered something of a return to earlier ways of working.

Research undertaken in preparation for the 2021 *World Book Night* response provided a starting point and offered information about how each plant benefited the other. These characteristics were made use of within the development of individual images, as seen in Figures 13.4 and 13.5. The agreed book structure informed a systematic approach to the ordering of images and determined a sequence of weekly making tasks for each of us. This resulted in an edition of eight illustrations co-produced each week throughout June 2021, with imagery representing one plant posted to each other to add to its companion in some way.

While a previously employed way of working was returned to in the production of the inside pages, discussions around the front cover were explored, which offered the potential to consider other ideas and notions around our own companionship. A FaceTime meeting afforded time to discuss these further, and with a nod to the simplified visual language employed throughout this book, we selected colour, pattern, and text to represent our friendship. Using the same font as an inside page and mixing a colour to match a cabinet owned by both of us, we set and printed the title text and planned the concept for an additional wrap-around cover. This referenced the number of years we have known each other aligned to the gardens we have each owned.

A pre-arranged making day in August 2021 offered an opportunity to work side-by-side with the aim of completing this book. Our experience of realising projects in collaboration has informed a systematic way of working and while we adopt specific roles in the production process, a continuous dialogue affords clarification around each aspect of the book (De Wachter 2017). This offers opportunities for issues arising to be contested, discussed and solved in partnership.

A return to the theme of companion planting, following *The Herbarium* submission, enabled an ease in the production of *Good Companions*. Co-produced layered images were made which adopted something of the visual practices first employed within book-works produced within the UK national lockdown period (http://www.the-case.co.uk/168.html; http://www.the-case.co.uk/stop-start.html). These included the use of an abstracted form of visual language (Figures 13.6 and 13.7), which was co-developed throughout weekly FaceTime meetings. This afforded time for individual ideas to be visually shared and next steps collectively agreed. The value we place on this visual form of idea development aligns with positive standpoints presented around collective activity by Billing (2007), De Wachter (2017), and Wenger (1998), and is a partnership practice we would advocate to others.

The finished book uses a series of coded categories to accompany each illustration as shown on the left-hand side of each of the pages within Figures 13.6 and 13.7. Playing with the space afforded to text and image, and exploring alternative presentation formats, offered something of a new way of working

Figures 13.4 and 13.5 Tamar MacLellan and Philippa Wood (2021) *Good Companions*

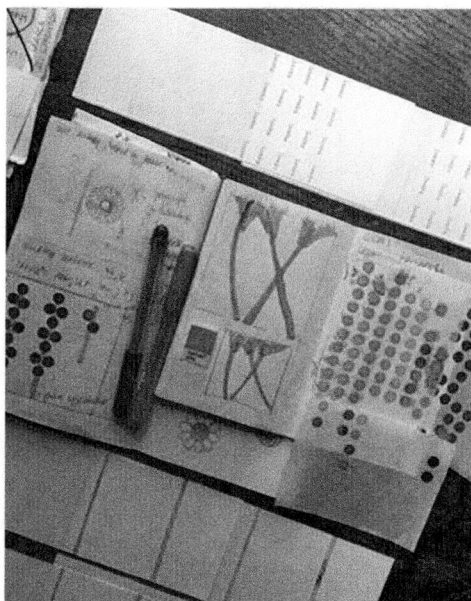

13.4

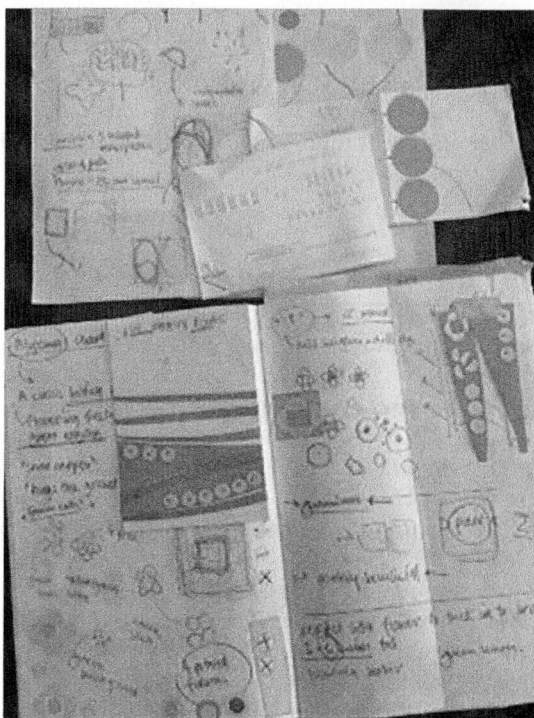

13.5

Figures 13.6 and 13.7 Tamar MacLellan and Philippa Wood (2021) *Good Companions*

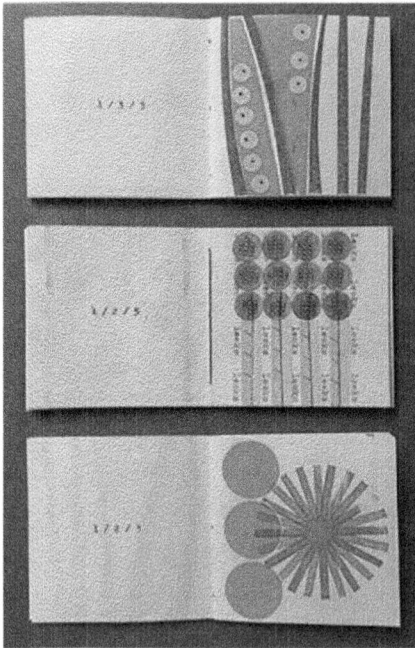
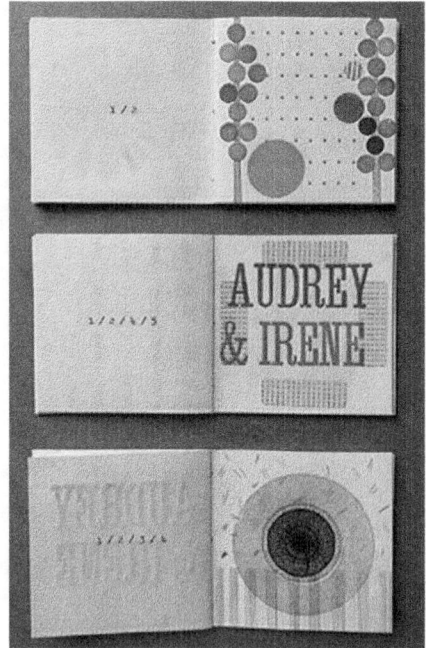

13.6

13.7

within the intimate nature of a book form which suits our nature (Prince 2008). This small and decorative format is an approach that we have returned to within subsequent projects.

Project 3: Common Ground

Towards the end of September 2021, we began to discuss ideas for a new collaborative project. Having enjoyed the approach to process and production adopted for *Good Companions* we decided to continue making in this way through further exploration of our respective gardens. Initial discussions within weekly FaceTime meetings highlighted a shared interest around maintaining an interchange of both ideas and work. With no pre-conceived outcome, or timescale for completion, reading around the theme and sharing found phrases became the starting point to inform ideas. A first visual response was a production of an individual memory-drawing of our respective back gardens within an A5 piece of paper. This was shared at the subsequent FaceTime meeting and ideas around maps, grids and location evolved further by folding the drawing into quarters, both horizontally and vertically. We recognised that this process had unconsciously produced the format of a one-sheet book and considered making use of this in some way within the design of the book structure.

Echoing something of the abstracted visual language employed within *Good Companions*, we identified key components within each garden and began to plot their positions within our respective garden grids. Trees offered a shared starting point within this process, and by selecting only those that appeared in the same position within our corresponding grids we agreed to explore the potential of these through text and image. Ideas exploring colour, collage and text listing garden actions emerged from this process and we continued to discuss combining sections of our gardens together in some way. The found phrase 'round and round the garden' resonated with both of us, offering us an approach to garden documentation and an opportunity for individual interpretation in response to being right and left-handed respectively. Subsequent FaceTime conversations explored this notion further, with suggestions about image placement restricted to the left- or right-hand side of book pages considered. A new approach to research and idea generation began to emerge and visual first ideas were posted to each other with further thoughts exchanged via text and email in addition to weekly FaceTime conversations.

As the project evolved, research around thematic mapping led to the identification of common actions undertaken in both gardens; the same grid reference and first visual interpretations of our gardens were considered here. Further investigation into the cardinal direction of our gardens had revealed that they faced in the opposite direction to each other, which offered a visual way of working that informed the book format. These were trialled and agreed. Having experimented with a series of ideas over eight weeks, the stories of our back gardens began to emerge and we determined to draw upon the rule-led approach to art making employed by Cage (1968) and Philips (1992) to start to develop visual responses. We began this process by developing a number of rules to determine the visual appearance of common activities undertaken in our gardens and agreed to work sequentially on each page, making a first individual visual response, posting this and inviting the other to add their response in return.

Continuing to take a rule-led approach to making, we returned to our initial memory drawings and identified two pages which had nothing in common. We agreed to embrace the distinct difference of these, returning to our individual areas of expertise within textiles and typography. The imagery produced embraced specific characteristics of each process, offering an opportunity to extend our practice which we returned to within the next stages of the project.

Having explored words that were common to us both and developed a range of visual responses to communicate each action, further examination of research revealed a series of activities which only took place in one garden. By placing these individual actions onto a flat plan, we were able to allocate a single page for each so they would appear just once within the book. Ways to differentiate between these and the first shared actions were discussed and we determined to produce a nine-word short story for each, which offered an alternative solution. It also referenced the shared quantity of actions we planned to respond to. First iterations of the short stories were exchanged, with a shared approach to making agreed.

Final analysis of the list of actions generated at the start of the project highlighted six words that had not been used in any form within the book pages. By reviewing the flat plan and the pages allocated for the key and title pages, we identified that these unused words could be assigned to two pages within the book. Further discussion around these, informed by a process of cataloguing, led to one action being selected which we would each respond to. With a nod to the direction of our individual gardens, this action was added to the book to reflect the number of times it was mentioned in each location of our individual gardens.

In continuing to make visual responses informed by research and data collected, one page on each garden began to emerge as an anomaly. With no clear alignment to any of the previously identified themes, we made use of our weekly FaceTime meetings to talk through alternative visual approaches for this page. Returning to the grid reference and our original garden drawings, we exchanged ideas noting thoughts around objects, surface and colour. The use of an object of significance from the specific location resonated with both of us and we explored ideas around how best to represent these. Returning to an approach to mark-making used within a previous project, we determined to transfer a black and white section of the object to the page. Further details around significance of scales of working and techniques employed were shared as final images were developed.

A face-to-face meeting in Birmingham was an opportunity to exchange individually completed sections, enabling the next layer of imagery to be added. Free flowing discussions around the project enabled next steps to be identified, discussed and collectively agreed in preparation for the making day. A newly established part of our collaborative process, the making day, as illustrated in Figure 13.8, enabled independently produced elements to be assembled in the

Figure 13.8 *Common Ground* (2022) A collaborative making day

Figure 13.9 Tamar MacLellan and Philippa Wood (2022) *Common Ground*

finalisation of *Common Ground* (Figure 13.9). Working alongside each other, tasks were divided equally, and decisions discussed and trialled before being confirmed. The number of pages produced for Common Ground resulted in this particular making-day involving a variety of processes, materials, and techniques in order for all final stages of the book production to be realised.

Common Ground continued to explore the theme of the garden. An evolving process of written and visual research included the production of individual memory drawings of our back gardens, which became the basis for this project. Commonality was examined through a process of cataloguing and an agreed systematic approach to making emerged in response to sequentially analysing data. This is illustrated within the series of eight double page spreads shown in Figure 13.9. With no preconceived idea of the final outcome, the book

Figure 13.10 Tamar MacLellan and Philippa Wood (2022) *Common Ground*

developed gradually as we established new ways of working over the four-month making period. Ongoing conversation and organisation played a pivotal role in the realisation of this project as ideas emerged over time. Cataloguing and systems-led art making underpinned each stage of this project, including the front covers depicted in Figure 13.10.

Project 4: Plot

Following on from an approach to making developed throughout the process of realising *Common Ground*, we discussed the possibility of producing a second iteration specifically for a book fair. With a limited timescale, a decision was formed which offered the opportunity to make use of outcomes produced individually, within textiles and typography respectively, to lead a new way of working. With a nod to the garden memory drawings produced at the start of *Common Ground*, we determined to produce a new book work which would represent each of the four cardinal points within our collective gardens. The geographic location of each garden offered a system to divide the project in half and we individually produced two images informed by our own gardens, which were responded to by the other. In this way, a collective response to each cardinal point was produced across each double page spread (Figure 13.11). Blog posts written at the time include commentary around changing ideas in

Figure 13.11 Tamar MacLellan and Philippa Wood (2022) *Plot*

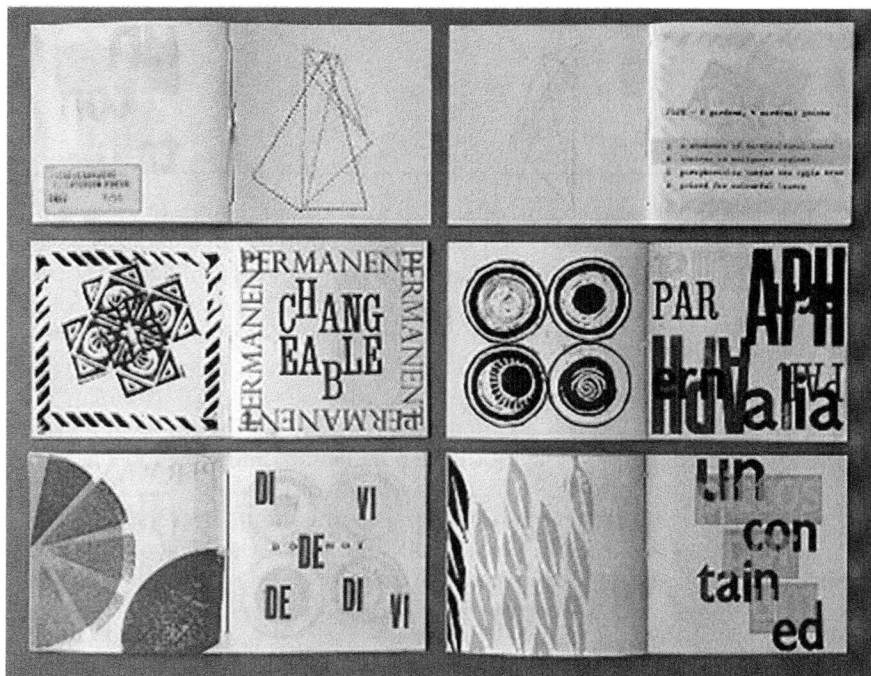

response to the work of the other, and acknowledge this as a shift in the development of individual and collective practice.

The lead up to the Bristol Artists' Book Event (https://cfpr.uwe.ac.uk/23-24-april-2022-bristol-artists-book-event-babe/) afforded time to conclude *Plot* by bringing pages made individually together for the first time. As we collated and prepared to bind, we talked through approaches to making we had employed and a mistake in the key was noted and corrected. This highlighted challenges around working with the book's imposition and at a distance from each other. Reflecting on this, we noted that the act of correcting did not impair but rather enhanced the meaning within the key.

Plot became a limited-edition twelve-page book produced within a short timescale for a specific book fair event. Based on an idea within *Common Ground*, the book was an opportunity to return to individual areas of expertise and create work independently, albeit through discussion and collective agreement of ideas. On reflection, we note that this approach to making employed elements of our initial collaborative practice first established some sixteen years previously. The opportunity to make a response informed by the work of the other had extended this approach and had been both thought-provoking and challenging. A new approach to making was trialled with the co-production of the front cover, which aims to represent the process of making within a layered diagram representing where we make in our individual home studios.

This observes similarities and differences in practice as lines connect, overlap, and separate, and perhaps suggests a new way of working to document future collaborations.

Conclusion

Writing this chapter has been a collaboration with multiple drafts started by one, and added to by the other, in a similar approach to the embellishment of our collective arts practice. Returning to projects and re-reading blog posts written throughout the time of making has afforded something of an objective examination around change in collaboration. Conclusively, significant themes have emerged in response to the unique dynamic of each collaboration (Drucker 2021) in addition to how, when, and why we work in partnership. The process of making aligns with standpoints presented by Billing (2007) and De Wachter (2017) around long-collaboration partnership and most closely to our shared backgrounds in design. The commonalities observed situate both our own education and the education of others around value afforded to conversational exchanges when developing ideas. Styles of working encouraged with student groups, problem solving, multiple iterations and research-led enquiry, are also employed within our practice, and align to ideas around practice explored by Ravetz et al. (2013). An ease in making is enabled in response to our long-term friendship, which affords an open and direct dialogue at the start of each project. Ideas are formed through mutual agreement and inclusion of each other's opinions (De Wachter 2017). While compromise is inevitable, we agree that there is more to be gained through collaborative practice. Over time strategies have evolved to support the systematic completion of our projects in sections, which allow outcomes to be produced independently, sequentially and in combination on making days. Our shared WordPress blog has become pivotal and has continued to be a space to share ideas and support the realisation of projects. We note the shared value placed on a self-led practice and the opportunity making books offers to determine how the story is told and how it is received (Prince 2008).

The open-endedness of approach is joyous, and we share a playful approach and a deep mutual appreciation of each other's sensibility (Drucker 2021). In this way research is shared, feedback generously given, and solutions found collectively, providing continued motivation and encouragement to inspire and enable new ways of working. Increasingly, we both worry less about the outcome and enjoy the surprise of finding out more (Billing 2007; De Wachter 2017; Drucker 2021), representing the benefits of employing a collective approach to making. Ways of working employed within the four projects highlight a cyclical approach, which has evolved unintentionally through our partnership. As a result, we have reached a balanced approach to making collaboratively and each recognise an increase in confidence using text and imagery in response to data collectively collected and catalogued.

References

Billing, J. (2007) *Taking the Matter into Common Hands: On contemporary art and collaborative practices*. New York: Black Dog Publishing.

Bolton, G. (2010) *Reflective Practice – Writing and professional development*. London: Sage Publications.

Cage, J. (1968) *A Year from Monday: New lectures and writings*. London: Calder and Boyars.

De Wachter, E. (2017) *Co-Art: Artists on creative collaboration*. London: Phaidon Press.

Drucker, J. (2021) *Transformative Texts and Images: Susan Bee interviewed by Johanna Drucker* (online). Available at: https://bombmagazine.org/articles/transformative-texts-and-images-susan-bee-interviewed/ (accessed 11 May 2023).

Lave, J. (2009). The Practice of Learning, in Illeris, K. (Ed.) *Contemporary Theories of Learning*. Abingdon: Routledge, 200–208.

Philips, T. (1992) *Works and Texts*. London: Thames and Hudson.

Prince, M. (2008) Women and Books: Contemporary artists share their thoughts, *The Bonefolder*, 4(2): 3–10.

Ravetz, A., Kettle, A. and Felcey, H. (2013) *Collaboration Through Craft*. London: Bloomsbury.

Wenger, W. (1998) *Communities of Practice: Learning, meaning, and identity*. New York: Cambridge University Press.

Index

Page numbers in italics are figures.